D0207512

THE
CANADA-UNITED STATES
RELATIONSHIP

THE
CANADA-UNITED STATES
RELATIONSHIP

The Politics of Energy
and
Environmental Coordination

JONATHAN LEMCO
EDITOR

 PRAEGER

Westport, Connecticut
London

Library of Congress Cataloging-in-Publication Data

The Canada-United States relationship : the politics of energy and
  environmental coordination / edited by Jonathan Lemco.
        p.   cm.
    Includes bibliographical references and index.
    ISBN 0-275-94239-2 (alk. paper)
    1. Energy policy—Canada.   2. Energy policy—United States.
  3. Environmental policy—Canada.   4. Environmental policy—United
  States.   5. Canada. Treaties, etc. United States, 1988 Jan. 2.
  6. Canada—Foreign economic relations—United States.   7. United
  States—Foreign economic relations—Canada.   I. Lemco, Jonathan.
  HD9502.C32C3777   1992
  337.71073—dc20   91-34774

British Library Cataloguing in Publication Data is available.

Library of Congress Catalog Card Number: 91-34774
ISBN: 0-275-94239-2

First published in 1992

Praeger Publishers, 88 Post Road West, Westport, CT 06881
An imprint of Greenwood Publishing Group, Inc.

Printed in the United States of America

The paper used in this book complies with the
Permanent Paper Standard issued by the National
Information Standards Organization (Z39.48-1984).

10 9 8 7 6 5 4 3 2 1

Contents

Illustrations

TABLES

FIGURE

Acknowledgments

I would like to thank Martha Lee Benz, Kim Broadhurst, Krista Kordt, Vivian Noble, Laura Subrin, Jean Wellman, and especially Kelly McClenahan for their careful reading and editing of these chapters. My colleagues at the National Planning Association gave freely of their time and wisdom. The Ford Foundation and the Donner Foundation were most generous in supporting the earlier publication of some of the papers in this volume. I would also like to thank my family for their love and support.

THE
CANADA-UNITED STATES
RELATIONSHIP

Chapter 1

Energy and Environment Concerns in the Binational Relationship

Jonathan Lemco

Until recently, U.S. political and economic leaders and the general public devoted scant attention to the problems associated with environmental pollution. The natural resources available to North Americans seemed infinite, and advocates of environmental conservation proved unable to convince policymakers that major efforts were needed to avoid eventual devastation to air, water, and land. No consensus existed about the causes of environmental pollution, and the enormous costs of cleanup militated against concerted action. Perhaps former President Reagan reflected the attitude of many political leaders when first he questioned whether a serious problem even existed and then blamed trees for causing acid rain.

Environmental concerns have never been at the forefront of the American political agenda. Not only are countermeasures to preserve the environment costly, but many feel they interfere with the more immediate priorities of extracting and exploiting energy resources. For it is water, nuclear power, coal, oil, and gas that fuel American industry, which in turn has propelled the United States into the first rank of world industrial powers. Environmental damage has been the byproduct of this remarkable growth.

Only now are most Americans beginning to appreciate the high costs of industrial development; most Canadians have recognized them for some time. As early as the 1970s, Canadian polls revealed widespread understanding of the implications of acid rain, and demands have been nearly unanimous for the Canadian government to use any leverage to convince American leaders to stop polluting an environment that recognizes no national boundaries. Officials in some Canadian provincial parks have adopted the practice of putting *Stop Acid Rain* bumper stickers on tourists cars. The Canadian media have taken up the themes of environmental degradation and what our big brother down south is doing to Canada now. Frequently, the case has been overstated and the accusations misplaced, for Canadian industry and government have been no less guilty at times. Furthermore, such Yankee-bashing has been convenient for English-Canadian nationalists with their own political agendas to pursue. Nevertheless, the United States has probably been responsible for more of the environmental damage, and Canadians have been passionately aware of this. Polls in the 1980s and during the free-trade debate showed that the binational issue of most concern to Canadians was environmental pollution, particularly acid rain.

Thus, as a result of intense public pressure, throughout the 1980s a majority of Canada's Parliament supported bilateral action to clean up the environment. However, federal and provincial environment and energy policies have not been consensual. Indeed, the two levels of government have often been at odds over issues such as the limits to energy extraction, the taxes to be paid, the degree of environmental pollution to be permitted, and so on. By no means do Canadian officials speak with one voice on these issues. The absence of a systematic, consistent, and comprehensive Canadian policy program has confused American leaders and thwarted effective binational cooperation.

Clearly, energy and environment issues pose complex and difficult challenges. Nevertheless, certain generalizations can be made.

1. Business and labor can play a more active role in overcoming environmental degradation and in promoting education about the problem.

2. Action in any one sector of the economy is not sufficient to solve our environmental problems. Rather, consultation and cooperation across all relevant sectors, including management, labor, and public service, are necessary. Indeed, some of the evidence suggests that economic interests and opportunities are strengthened as energy use is made more efficient and environmental degradation is lessened. This is particularly clear in regard to the effort to curtail activities that contribute to global warming.

3. Strategies to clean up the environment can have other positive effects. For example, efforts to site hazardous wastes in an environmentally responsible manner have proved also to have positive economic benefits for the communities involved.

4. It is likely that consumption patterns in both countries will have to change. Conserving energy for economic reasons, and more

particularly to combat environmental pollution, will become more necessary than it is at present.

5. Policymakers in both Canada and the United States will find their energy and environmental decisions to be increasingly dependent on the strategy pursued in the other country. Thus, policy coordination between the two countries will be necessary for their mutual benefit.

A GLOBAL CONCERN

Energy and environmental policies in the United States and Canada necessarily have an impact on and are influenced by the policies of other countries. In fact, increased global awareness has made environmental issues a priority in both domestic and international arenas. It has been stated that what defense has been to the world's leaders for the past forty years, the environment will be for the next forty.[1] As Irving Mintzer stresses in this volume, global warming is caused by the negative by-products of industrial development, with origins in many countries.

In 1987, the World Bank began to view the environment more seriously, and the United Nations World Commission on Environment and Development, the Brundtland Commission, published a report that outlined the steps necessary to achieve sustainable economic growth.[2]

The report paid particular attention to strategies for resolving some of the planet's environmental problems by creating a complementary energy system. These strategies are particularly pertinent because calls for economic growth and conservation have often been viewed as contradictory, forcing difficult trade-offs in the energy/environment relationship. Further, at a 1989 World Energy Conference in Montreal, over half the speakers focused on environmental problems arising from energy use, including global warming, acid rain, nuclear accidents, hazardous waste, and urban smog.[3]

The health and success of nations are often measured by their levels of economic growth. Yet, national income accounts make no calculation of the value of natural resources or environmental conditions. A country that dug up all its coal, burnt down all its forests, killed off all its wildlife, filled its air with smoke and its rivers with dirt would appear from its national accounts to have gotten richer in terms of GNP per person.[4]

A recent example is the *Exxon Valdez* oil spill in Alaska. In terms of standard economic measures, the money spent cleaning up Alaska will be recorded as an increase in U.S. national income, and the environmental losses may go unmeasured. Thus, the question remains: how can one value a nonsubstitutable natural resource? It is unlikely that any system of national accounts could capture the economic cost of depletion or destruction of our natural resources. However, some record should be devised to capture their depreciation value as is done for assets made by people.[5]

Such concerns will drive policymakers and will have far-reaching implications for business and labor in the coming decade. Whether the policies chosen will be regulation that imposes costs on industry, incentives that leave compliance voluntary, or some mix remains to be seen. Some argue that regulation of sulfur dioxide (SO_2) emissions, for example, would inspire efficient plants to clean up even more than they would have, given additional regulations requiring that inefficient plants either pay to pollute or close down.[6]

The Organization for Economic Cooperation and Development has published a review of eighty five different economic schemes that have been devised to penalize polluters. One promising but often overlooked scheme focuses on the potential role of finance ministers. These senior officials could insist that other ministers consider the environmental impact of their budgets. For example, agriculture ministers should question the effects of farm subsidies on pesticide use and soil erosion; transportation ministers should look at tax relief schemes for motorists; and energy ministers should examine how energy is priced, focusing especially on hidden coal subsidies.[7] If finance ministers replace regulations with duties, they can both raise revenue and improve the quality of life for the general population.

However, policy decisions are not made in disregard of political concerns. American voters bred on cheap energy and led by a president who once had promised not to raise taxes would not welcome higher prices for fossil fuels. This issue is high on domestic agendas, as evidenced by the ten relevant comprehensive bills that have been under consideration in the U.S. Congress and most important, the 1990 passage of the clean air legislation.

The Clean Air Act will cut the typical new car's pollution to 2 percent of that emitted by 1970 models. It will also extend auto emission controls to trucks. Acid rain is expected to be cut in half, and industrial toxic air emissions will be reduced by three-quarters.

Canadians responded positively to the U.S. legislation. This was followed in early 1991 by a binational accord cutting acid rain by 50 percent by the year 2000 which will support the U.S. legislation. The agreement also includes a dispute resolution mechanism to deal with future transboundary air pollution problems between the two countries, a joint research and monitoring program for transboundary air pollutants, and a joint U.S.-Canada panel to oversee implementation of the agreement.

THE CONTINENTAL PERSPECTIVE

The United States and Canada share an atmospheric environment and an energy market. The important concerns stemming from this continental perspective are the focus of this volume.

Problems and Potential

To a significant degree, acid rain, polluted water, and the newly created deserts are a result of mismanagement of the continental environment and its resources by officials on both sides of the border. However, the fault does not rest exclusively with policymakers or policy implementors. The energy/environment problem is inherently thorny and, where interests diverge and even compete, solutions in which everyone gains and no one loses are rare. In addition, both estimating and equitably distributing the costs and benefits of a particular policy are formidable undertakings. Thus, ameliorating conflict is politically difficult, and differences usually can be resolved only on an ad hoc basis.

Not only is resolution of binational differences over energy and environmental issues hampered by many competing interests with intense preferences, it is also handicapped by differences of perception. The United States is a superpower fairly secure in its identity and purpose. Americans often entertain the illusion that environmental concerns respect national boundaries. In contrast, Canadians are far less secure about their sense of national identity and are affected directly or indirectly by every American action. Canadians insist upon national solutions to energy-related problems and the need for continentwide responsibility for environmental protection. Sigler and Doran note that the United States seeks to share resources but to divide the environment; Canada attempts to preserve a division of resources while stressing the shared burden of protecting the environment.[8] These different perceptions further impede resolution because various levels of government and private individuals and firms have differing responsibilities, and because resources are regulated differently from level to level.

Still, there is cause for optimism. In a real sense the North American energy resource base is not finite. When depletable resources become scarce, the normal reaction is to switch to renewable resources. This is clearly happening, for example, in the limited transition to various forms of solar energy or gasoline that has already begun. Furthermore, at current consumption rates, vast amounts of certain finite resources are left. Concern should be focused on the rising cost of extracting these resources rather than on the threat of exhausting them. The limits on our uses of resources are determined not by their scarcity in the earth's crust but by what we have to sacrifice to extract and process them. We may not be willing to pay the price required to extract some of the lower-grade sources.

The Market Solution

Some have argued that the free market system should be allowed to respond swiftly and automatically to the increasing scarcity of accessible resources. They maintain that demand would be reduced and substitution encouraged. As long as property rights are well defined, the market system provides incentives for consumers and producers to respond to scarcity in a variety of useful ways.

However, the evidence suggests that the private market does not always automatically choose a dynamically efficient or sustainable path for the future. The market will tend to over-exploit common property resources such as air and water, substantially lowering the net benefits for future generations. Uncontrolled markets often will produce too much pollution and underprice commodities that contribute to pollution when produced or consumed. Firms that unilaterally attempt to control their pollution run the risk of pricing themselves out of the market.

As a result, government intervention is needed both to protect the environment and to ensure that firms that neglect environmental damage in their operating decisions do not thereby gain a competitive edge. Government action must be carefully scrutinized, however. For example, acid rain effects were worsened by a U.S. policy structure that focused on local rather than regional pollution problems. The requirement of scrubbers for all new coal-fired electrical generating stations was enacted for purely political reasons and raised the cost of compliance unnecessarily.

Because certain U.S. government regulations are very stringent, some polluters have been able to receive delays for compliance. From the polluters point of view, it has frequently been wiser to spend resources to change the regulations than to comply with them. With sounder and less-stringent regulations, firms would have had no legal grounds for delaying compliance.

On balance, simple prescriptions such as "leave it to the market" or "more government intervention" are ineffective by themselves. In both the United States and Canada, the relationship between government and the private sector must be complementary to promote efficient, fair energy and environmental policies.

In this volume Lynton Caldwell notes that in recent years, transboundary conflict between the United States and Canada on environmental issues has grown, especially in the Great Lakes region. North American demand for growth, so keen in past decades, has involved degradation of the natural environment, sometimes at both countries' expense. By examining a number of controversial cases of this resource-energy conflict, in the critical areas of energy production, mining, and agriculture, Caldwell seeks to identify factors common to all that may serve as a basis for a general set of energy and environmental policies.

Caldwell notes that energy policy is inseparable from policies concerning economic development, population growth, and the use of natural resources, and that inconsistency among these policies, given the politics in each country, is inevitable. However, with the combined pressure of scientists, concerned citizens, and environmental groups, whose interests are the same on both sides of the border, and an acceptance of a certain amount of inconsistency in policy, a de facto North American policy for the environment may be achievable. Such understandings have, in fact, already been negotiated on the regional level, and appear to be a trend on the international level. It may be that with increased public comprehension of environmental issues and an increased ability to anticipate events on the part of political leadership, a consensus of values in this area will be shared across political boundaries.

Eric Uslaner outlines the differences in the federal structures of the United States and Canada, particularly with regard to energy policies. Uslaner notes a critical difference: Americans have a strong sense of national identity which Canadians lack. This, in part, explains why Americans place greater confidence in their federal government in formulating policies attractive to the whole country.

In the United States, energy regulation traditionally was a state responsibility until the 1970s, when responsibility shifted to the federal government. While states readily accept federal policies that will bring benefits to their constituents, some states, particularly Alaska, have felt threatened by federal control over energy policies and have even threatened secession. Yet, as energy policy regulation became increasingly dominated by the federal government, conflicts between Washington and the states were replaced by conflicts between regions and between various energy sectors, thus creating many cross-cutting cleavages in the U.S. energy debate. By the mid-1970s, conflicts between Washington and the states were replaced by regional debates.

In Canada, the conflicts over energy policies reflect a more comprehensive battle between "province-builders" and "nation-builders." Conservatives argue that energy resources belong to particular provinces (such as Alberta), whereas the Liberal governments maintain that these resources belong to Canada as a whole. Following the 1980 election, the Liberals created the National Energy Program, establishing federal dominance over energy policy. The ensuing debate was clearly between the liberals and the conservatives, the energy consumers and the producers. There were no cross-cutting cleavages as noted in the United States. When the conservatives won the 1984 election, they repealed the NEP as expected.

Uslaner suggests that the reasons for the different problems confronted by the United States and Canada are not due to structural problems but rather to cultural differences. Canada's main problem is that it lacks a strong sense of national identity. Thus, Canadians are quite suspicious of federal authority over policies such as energy. While some U.S. states have not always supported federal power and have discussed secession, they have not done so as seriously as have Canadian provinces such as Quebec. Uslaner notes that although both Canada and the U.S. have encountered serious debates over energy policy, the strong sense of national identity felt by Americans allows the federal system to better deal with these problems. Any attempts to solve debates (such as this one over energy policy) through structural reforms would only exacerbate the problem. Their problems are not rooted in a faulty institutional design.

Rodney Schmidt investigates the role that Canadian and U.S. governments should play in energy and environmental policy making. Schmidt argues that in today's policy arena, these two policy objectives are increasingly overlapping. He outlines four reasons why government involvement in this policy arena is necessary. First, energy is of importance to national security. Second, the government is the landlord of natural resources and is responsible to capture resource revenue that should, in turn, be appropriated to the benefit of the general public. Third, the government plays an important role in gathering information regarding the efficient exploration, development, and conservation of these resources. Finally, the government has a responsibility to monitor energy policies to ensure the preservation of the ecosystem.

The government has two major fiscal tools it can use to achieve these objectives: the right to levy taxes and the right to regulate prices. Using these tools the government can simultaneously achieve energy, security, and environmental objectives. Government tax policies should focus only upon the expropriation of a fair share of economic rent in order to minimize uncertainty. Concerning price regulation, there are significant advantages and disadvantages to setting domestic prices either above or below world prices. Thus, another mechanism, stockpiling, can be used in order to ensure energy security.

In addition to energy security, the other major issue that governments must face is environmental protection. This problem is one of market failure: the marginal private and social costs are not the same. Externalities are imposed on third parties. Emphasis on externalities limits the scope of hydrocarbon-producing activity. At the same time such restrictive policies may not be as attractive when economic growth potentials are considered. Some industries may be allowed to violate certain policies if they promise a high level of economic development. Schmidt suggests that different policies can be tested using the "nth-best" approach to determine their ultimate effects on energy security and the environment.

John Carroll argues that free trade between the United States and Canada has negative repercussions for the environment. In addition to their traditional clashes on political and economic issues, which reflect moves toward and against further integration, Canada and the United States have been engaged for the past decade in a vociferous debate on acid rain. In the end, that debate has put Canada in the role of a nation "sinned against" by the United States. Yet, within a global environment, both nations are sinners. Consuming energy and natural resources at a rate many times greater than that of the rest of the world, the United States and Canada are responsible for far more than their share of global depletion. That depletion, it is argued, will be accelerated by free trade between the two. Free trade fosters greater consumption and hence industrial production. It also tends to subordinate environmental concerns to economic concerns within the framework of the bilateral relationship.

Thus, despite the rhetoric heard on both sides, action on environmental issues has been and will continue to be halting at best.

Policies aimed at alleviating current and future environmental problems will have to address three key areas. They must 1) work to reduce the imbalance of resource consumption between the U.S.-Canadian bloc and the rest of the world; 2) ensure equitable consumption of resources among nations; and 3) aim to rectify the imbalance between humanity and the planetary ecosystem. Such policies demand not only a change in North American values but also the political will to effect such a change.

Mary Ann E. Steger and her colleagues ask whether the political culture within which environmental groups operate determines how they pursue their agendas. They compare the behavior of environmental groups in the state of Michigan and the province of Ontario and assess how their access to governmental decision-making bodies and their tactics are affected by the differing United States and Canadian political systems. Functioning within an open, competitive system in which power is quite fragmented, groups in Michigan were found, for example, to interact more with all types of government officials, to lobby more aggressively, and to file more lawsuits. The centralization of power characteristic of the Ontario political system has led to noticeably different behavior on the part of Ontario's environmental groups. Pursuing a quieter strategy geared to elite accommodation, these groups were found to have fewer contacts with legislative officials and midlevel bureaucrats than did their U.S. counterparts, for example; they also lobbied less. Thus, even though groups in both countries share a number of characteristics in areas such as organizational resources, their methods of achieving goals differ as a result of the respective political systems within which they operate.

Gilles Paquet argues that neither the United States nor Canada appears ready to take a strong stand on energy of environmental issues. Current economic woes, ignorance of the real cost of initiatives, and uncertainty about the public's willingness to pay for those initiatives are part of the reason for such foot-dragging, as is the fact that the short-term view so characteristic of corporations and politicians is at odds with the long-term nature of energy/environment issues. What this has resulted in, for both nations, is a de facto policy that relies on market mechanisms to achieve energy/environment goals. Yet there are several issues that economics and the market approach cannot handle, including that of sustainable development, which assumes a resiliency in the system that will prevent irreversible damage.

It is proposed that a social learning approach to energy/environment issues could help to counter the effects of the "invisible foot," a symbol of the negative-welfare effects that the market mechanism creates. Such social learning would stress the concepts of collective property, individual accountability, and providing for future generations. An organization such as a Joint North American Task Force on Environmental and Energy Resources, which would provide a forum to discuss these continental issues, could promote such a crucial new viewpoint.

Colin Isaacs discusses the extent to which business can promote environmental awareness. He considers the recent history of ties between business, labor, and environmental awareness, and notes strategies for changing one's behavior to become more conscious of environmental issues.

Irving Mintzer writes that with the attention of U.S. politicians, their counterparts overseas, and international organizations focused on preserving the environment, energy companies will face a variety of challenges in the coming decade. Chief among them may be how to mitigate the effects of global warming, which, in tandem with increases in population, ozone depletion, and tropospheric air pollution, stands to create problems (such as rises in sea levels and changes in distribution of rainfall) that will affect agriculture and energy use. The demand for more energy-efficient technologies and the use of alternative energy sources such as natural gas and nuclear power will lead to new government policies to encourage the use of these technologies. Such policies may focus on energy efficiency standards, tax incentives, or pollution reduction requirements, and they may lead to new business opportunities for forward-looking firms that will develop such technologies. The challenge for oil and gas companies in particular will be to maintain profitability while moving to change their traditional modus operandi. These companies will also, in the 1990s, have to court public opinion by demonstrating their commitment to protecting the environment, possibly through initiating new projects to develop low-emission technologies, expanding research on the environmental effects of alternative fuels, and the like.

Richard Stroup argues that policies devised to deal with environmental pollution may have unintended effects that can do more harm than good. The basic problem is a dearth of information: how can one fairly assess the costs that polluters impose on other parties? "No regrets" policies, which anticipate the possibility of environmental damage, do not necessarily increase social health and safety—additional safety devices on nuclear reactors, for example, may increase danger due to the new complexities they introduce. Thus a resilient society, which can respond quickly to problems posed, may be better able to cope with such problems than can an anticipatory one. Further, the witch hunt for potential risks can result in accusations and law suits leveled at what may be innocent parties, as well as needless expense.

A regime based on property rights may offer a better way to control pollution than can government regulation. Owners of any assets have an incentive to maximize the value of those assets, which means that they would be unlikely to pollute and hence lower the value of, say, land holdings. A property rights regime, which uses simple economics to make owners accountable for their actions, encourages responsiveness to others' wishes, good stewardship, and the prevention of damage to others. The intervention of government, which sometimes has no such incentives, can create havoc, as was evident in the infamous Love Canal case. The use of the property rights system backed by liability law should be the focus for any governmental action in environmental policy.

The ecological dangers that face our continent and the world ultimately demand comprehensive policy and behavior changes of national, continental, and global scope by governments, businesses, and private citizens. The chapters in this volume approach this theme from a variety of perspectives. Some offer policy suggestions to government and business while others concentrate on the more technical aspects of alternative behavior patterns. However, in different ways, they all address vital binational energy and environment issues.

NOTES

1. "The First Green Summit," *The Economist* (July 15, 1989), p.13.
2. Charles Caccia, M.P., "Balance of Bankruptcy for the Environment" *Policy Options* (September 1988), p. 35.
3. Craig McInnes, "Environmental Conference Told of Energy-Related Woes," *The Globe and Mail* (September 19, 1989).
4. "Growth Can be Green," *The Economist* (August 26, 1989), p. 12.
5. "Getting Physical," *The Economist* (August 26, 1989), p. 53. While there have been often-discussed and unofficial efforts to measure net national welfare, it remains that GNP figures do not incorporate the

lost value of environmental resources. For a discussion, see William Nordhaus and James Tobin, "Is Growth Obsolete?" in *Fiftieth Anniversary Colloquium V* (New York: National Bureau of Economic Research, 1972).

6. "Growth Can be Green," p. 12.

7. "Money from Greenery," *The Economist* (October 21, 1989), pp. 16-17.

8. John Sigler and Charles Doran, "Twenty Years After: Change and Continuity in United States-Canada Relations," in *Canada and the United States: Enduring Friendships, Persistent Stress*, eds. Sigler and Doran (Englewood Cliffs, NJ: Prentice-Hall, 1985), pp. 231-247.

Chapter 2

Transboundary Conflicts: Resources and Environment

Lynton K. Caldwell

The topography and hydrology bisected by the political boundary dividing Canada and the United States makes binational environmental policy problems inevitable. Many of these problems are handled without dissention, but some are causes of conflict. From the Lake of the Woods to Puget Sound, and from the Gulf of Alaska to the Beaufort Sea, the international boundary is ruler-straight. Geophysical and bioregional features are bisected politically, with little regard for ecosystemic relationships. For resolving the problems growing out of the transboundary flow of rivers, the machinery of the International Joint Commission has proved generally effective. For the Great Lakes, however, where there is joint custody over a very large hydrological ecosystem, it is not evident that existing arrangements for basinwide management are adequate to the need.

The International Joint Commission (IJC) provides transboundary oversight, research, and fact-finding for the two governments, but its function respecting the Great Lakes-St. Lawrence ecosystem differs significantly from its more limited role in issues arising across the straight-edge boundaries dividing states from provinces in the North American northwest.[1]

The eastern boundary divides the Great Lakes-Upper St. Lawrence basin, but the two national governments under the 1978 Water Quality Agreement are committed, in principle, to treat this region as a basinwide ecosystem and have authorized several transboundary institutional arrangements for conflict avoidance or resolution and for fact finding and research pertaining to the status and health of the lakes. In addition to the IJC and its Great Lakes Regional Office in Windsor,

Ontario, these include the Great Lakes Fisheries Commission and the (U.S.) Great Lakes Commission. A number of unofficial nongovernmental organizations are now concerned with the future of the Great Lakes basin and are increasingly interacting with the IJC on matters of environmental policy.

Environmental conflicts in the West have largely been caused by the use and abuse of transboundary rivers, notably the Red, Roseau, Poplar, Milk, Flathead, Columbia, and Skagit. The possible damming of the Yukon has also been a potential source of binational conflict. Transboundary rivers have also been problematic in the east (e.g., the Richelieu and St. Croix), but fewer in number. In additional to problems of water, air pollution has been an issue since the Trail Smelter Case in 1928 and has become a matter for negotiation between state and provincial governments in default of action by the Canadian and U.S. federal governments.

RISING LEVELS OF CONFLICT

In comparison with recent years, there formerly was less occasion for transboundary environmental conflicts. The Boundary Waters Treaty of 1909 committed the respective parties to preventing the pollution of transboundary waters and flows found to be damaging to health and property. Regarding the Great Lakes, binational concerns were chiefly associated initially with navigation and water levels. Fisheries were also a topic of concern, resulting in the formation of the Great Lakes Fisheries Commission in 1955. Beyond the Great Lakes, periodic flooding became a binational issue along the Roseau and Richelieu rivers, but the controversies related more to economics than to ecology. Flooding has also been a source of conflict resulting from hydroenergy development. Planned impoundments behind high level dams on the Yukon, Skagit, Columbia, and St. John rivers have been opposed in Canada where permanent inundation of forest and farm land would occur. Pollution of water courses has been an issue in several cases involving energy production (e.g., Cabin Creek and Poplar river) and from industrial activities (e.g., pulp and paper on the St. Croix River, where dams for water power have also been involved).[2]

Most transboundary resource-environment conflicts are directly or indirectly attributable to energy demand. Dam construction for electric power sometimes joined to flood control has led directly to both environmental and economic binational disputes. These and other energy-related projects have been generated by commitments in both countries to economic growth and development. Since 1950, "growth," which is seldom defined and less frequently examined, has become a kind of universal civic religion, nowhere more revered than in Canada and the United States. North American governments have promoted growth and development since the mid-19th century, at first through assistance to railroad construction and mining, later through highway construction and aviation. But 20th-century technology and population increases have raised levels of development to unprecedented heights and demands for inordinate quantities of water and energy have led to corresponding impacts on the quality of the human environment.

Economic development preceded the emergence of the environmental movement and was a major factor in its advent. In both countries, a major strategy for promoting economic growth was through the exploitation of those natural resources that were most conducive to energy production. Energy is the indispensable driving force behind nearly all material development. Direct and indirect effects of its generation and use tend to degrade the natural environment and affect the urban environment in contradictory ways, making it both more and less livable. Public attitudes have been, and remain, divided in response to explosive resource development. Many people have been gratified by its cornucopian flow of jobs, profits, and convenience. Others have thought the asserted "price of progress" to be unnecessarily high, and that the qualities of life and the environment were being impaired for short-term benefits, which would be followed by long-term or permanent deprivations.

Because many large development projects were under way before the emergence of organized environmental efforts, the environmental movement in both Canada and the United States necessarily assumed an opposition character. Its posture has been almost inevitably negative, opposing projects that are long planned, politically approved, and often under construction. Two related features of the environmental movement in North America have affected the course of conflict. First has been the organized and popular character of the movement, and second has been binational collaboration among nongovernmental organizations on many environmental issues. A striking example of this development was the appearance of more than 400 Canadian and American environmental activists at the 1989 Biennial Review of the Great Lakes Water Quality Agreement held in Hamilton, Ontario, by the IJC.[3]

Complicated political situations have often taken shape in different resource-environment conflicts. In some cases, citizens of both countries have joined forces to obstruct or prevent development schemes endorsed by one or the other national government. States or provinces have found themselves in contradictory relationships with federal authorities of one or the other country, and at odds with certain of their constituents who have formed binational nongovernmental environmental coalitions. Public authorities also feel pressure from economically and politically powerful development interests with influence at high levels of government. Into this matrix of relationships, scientific information and theory have been interjected. Science, with some differences among its practitioners over details, has become the strongest weapon in the armory of the environmentalists. It has been frequently used to reinforce and justify ethical and value positions which, hardly more than three decades ago, had little empirical support. Today it is possible to measure the residues of pesticides in the milk of human mothers living in the Great Lakes basin. This is not the kind of finding that elected officials can easily pass off.

An additional complicating element in resource-environment conflicts has been the mobilization of native peoples in both countries. Native people have seldom been able to avoid their forced relocation to make way for development projects, such as the Garrison Dam and the James Bay development, or to obtain abatement of deadly pollution, as on the St. Lawrence River at Massena, New York. Their predicament has elicited sympathy and support from the larger environmental movement. For example, the displacement of the Cree Indians and the massive environmental destruction which would follow from further development of the James Bay hydropower project has aroused opposition in the United States. A project based wholly within Canada has become a transboundary issue because of projected transmission of electric energy across the international border -- energy tainted by environmental destruction and disregard of traditional human rights and values. Environmental groups and persons sympathetic to the plight of the Cree Indians have sought with some success to persuade American public utilities to decline to buy James Bay energy.[4]

In the sections that follow, three selective aspects of the resource-environment conflict will be considered, including (1) energy, (2) mining, and (3) agriculture. All three are interrelated in that energy is crucial to both mining and agriculture. Of course, energy is sought for other purposes: powering cities, manufacturing, transportation, heating, cooling, and lighting. But the actual generation and uses of energy in mining and agriculture are geographically localized, however extended their ultimate effects may be. When these localized effects are experienced in areas transcending artificial jurisdictional boundaries and result in adverse consequences for environmental and economic values, conflicts are almost certain to arise.

There are other transboundary environmental conflicts in which the effects of energy production or utilization are at issue. Principal among them is acid precipitation. A major binational source of conflict, acid rain is very widespread, and is associated with other problems of atmospheric deposition (e.g., PCBs), notably contributing to the contamination of the Great Lakes. Acid rain has now become a nearly global issues and because its incidence occurs separately on both sides of the Canadian-United States boundary and cannot be tied to any specific single source, it will not receive detailed discussion here.

Issues of water levels, diversions, and flooding have been sources of controversy, especially in the Great Lakes basin. Energy has sometimes been a factor in these water policy issues and has been a factor of controversy in the cases of the Garrison Diversion, James Bay and the Roseau, Richelieu, St. Croix, Poplar, Columbus, and Skagit rivers.

Complexity and interrelatedness characterize nearly all environmental conflicts. In analyzing the causes of conflict, neat segregation of topics or even cross-referencing of issues risk failing the test of "ground truth" (e.g., the actual reality on the scene of action). The evolutionary configuration of natural phenomena is seldom the preferred ordering of modern technological society. Humans have achieved a growing but inevitably limited control over natural forces and play out an urge to rearrange nature. Through the manipulation of natural forces, mankind can apply energy to make water run uphill. But there are environmental and economic costs of harnessing nature to work against nature. These various costs are ultimately borne by human society, which characteristically seeks to allocate or evade them through the instrument of government. We will now see how this is done in specific situations where binational Canadian-American collaboration is needed to achieve intended outcomes.

PURSUIT OF ENERGY

All life and activity involve energy exchange, but in modern industrial society, energy has acquired a special meaning which narrows its practical definition. The energy of primary concern in the modern world is generally that which conveys the power to move machinery. This energy may be transmitted from generators over long distances through electric power lines or by electronic radiation. Its sources are largely nonrenewable fuels, chiefly coal, oil, and natural gas. Water power and atomic reaction are less prevalent sources; wind power, geothermal and direct solar energy remain as minor sources.

With the extraordinary growth of population and technology since 1950, the demand for energy has more than correspondingly increased. This is because the people and organizations that determine energy needs have envisioned an ever-expanding economy and have sought guaranteed sources for future expansion of energy generation, hence the pursuit of energy sources by governments and private corporate enterprise.

Because the predominant sources of energy today are unevenly distributed and locally concentrated, transmission of energy has become a major industrial activity. Involving large-scale transnational material and economic transactions, energy has also become a major factor in Canadian-American economic and environmental interrelationships. Canada has been an important source of electrical energy, and the United States a major consumer. The direct environmental impacts of this transboundary relationships have been felt primarily in Canada, but indirect environmental effects (e.g., water and air pollution) have been felt in the United States.

In Canada, the indirect impacts of energy development have frequently emanated from hydroelectric dam projects in the United States, which have resulted in impoundments backing into Canada and permanently flooding Canadian territory. Some proposals to dam the Yukon River in Alaska could have had this effect. But impounding the Yukon, projected in the great Rampart Dam, would also have destroyed large areas of wildlife habitat in the United States—especially wetlands important to migratory waterfowl. Nongovernmental environmental groups mobilized to fight Rampart, and the project failed to materialize.[5] Other development projects on the Yukon have since been proposed on the Canadian side of the border. These projects involve generation of hydropower and water diversion (especially in relation to mining and minerals processing) and could adversely affect water quality, distribution, and fisheries in Alaska.[6]

Possibly worse, from the broader perspective of energy and environment, was the North American Water and Power Alliance (NAWAPA), which proposed to channel Canadian water throughout extended regions of the United States (chiefly in the water-hungry Southwest).[7] First proposed in 1964, NAWAPA would today confront a public more knowledgeable in energy and environmental affairs. Nonetheless, this superproject doubtless has proponents biding time until the western states have exhausted or ruined their oversubscribed water resources. It is not difficult to predict political sentiment in California if and when the state runs out of water.

Too much rather than too little water has given rise to transboundary environment-energy controversies. Consider the consequence of an effort by the Seattle City Light Company to accommodate the growth of customers by increasing available hydropower by raising the level of the Ross Dam on the Skagit River in the state of Washington. Although the project would have provided more electricity for urban growth, it aroused opposition because it would have flooded recreational forest land in British Columbia that was valued by environmentalists on either side of the international border.[8] Extended negotiations involved Seattle City Light, the province of British Columbia, the two federal governments, and the IJC. Resolution of the issue was undertaken primarily at the local level, and a compromise was influenced by collaboration among organized nongovernmental groups. The Skagit-High Ross Dam controversy illustrates the consequences of unforeseen change in public attitudes and values. During the 1940s and 1950s, environmental impacts did not enter into negotiations between Seattle City Light and the province of British Columbia. But during the 1960s, changing public opinion injected environmental consequences into the debate over compensation to British Columbia if the dam were raised and to Seattle if it were not.

No general conclusion as to policies or to institutional arrangements is deducible from the Skagit-High Ross controversy. But the case is a clear example of the collision since the 1960s between upsurging economic growth and growing environmental concerns. Legal arrangements for protecting Seattle's access to energy would probably not have led to serious controversy if Seattle had experienced only modest growth, or if an environmental movement had not emerged. And, as often happens, political "practicality" and unique circumstances precluded the establishment of policies and institutions to meet unforeseen contingencies. Nevertheless, the case suggests the advantage of forecasting possible futures and evaluating alternative scenarios for coping with them. The question of how far great cities may justifiably reach to obtain the power and water needed to sustain their desire for unlimited growth becomes doubly difficult to address where the reach crosses international boundaries.

The Columbia River Treaty is a similar but simpler case involving negotiations between the two federal governments. Former IJC commissioner Maxwell Cohen observed that the "agreement negotiated between 1959-60 and 1963-64 did not express a developed environmental viewpoint because that was not a significant political and psychic factor at that time."[9] The treaty was negotiated solely for power development and flood control, and made no provision whatsoever for the environmental priorities and protective measures that arose during the 1970s.

Environmental effects are both more and less localized when the pursuit of energy extends to fossil fuels, notably coal and petroleum. The mining of coal may damage local streams through acidic drainage and the discharge of coal refuse screenings in the form of culm. Air quality may be impaired through dust raised by surface mining and by the burning of coal, especially coal of high sulfur content. Burning coal for energy may emit pollutants over a very extended area, and oil spills may occur hundreds of miles from oil fields.

Two transboundary controversies have arisen over coal mining in Canada that would send residual discharge into the United States. One of these, the Cabin Creek conflict, has resulted from a proposal in the early 1970s to open a coal mine on a tributary of the Flathead River in British Columbia.[10] The proposal was backed by the province and opposed by the United States. American policy was to designate the U.S. side of the boundary as a wild-river wilderness area adjacent to the Glacier and Waterton Lakes national parks. Giving wilderness status downstream on the Flathead River in the United States would complicate and more likely preclude Canadian development of coal deposits upstream in Canada if Canada accepted an obligation to prevent the pollution of the water flowing from the mine site. Again, as in the dam cases, environmentalists on both sides of the international boundary made a common cause, as did U.S. and Canadian public officials responsible for national parks and environmental protection.

A second controversy relating to the pursuit of energy through coal mining occurred between the state of Montana and the province of Saskatchewan over electric power development on the Poplar River.[11] In 1975, the Saskatchewan Power Corporation was licensed to build a coal-fired generating plant within six miles of the international border. In addition to possible water and air pollution issues made more probable by surface-mined coal in the vicinity, an issue of water diversion arose because operations of the power plant required more water than was obtainable from the East Fork of Poplar River, upon which the plant was located. Ultimately an apportionment scheme was worked out by the IJC, but the problem of air and water quality remains only partially resolved. In the Poplar River case, as in that of Cabin Creek, the benefits of energy development occur on one side of the border and the costs on the other. In such situations, John Carroll notes the advantage of involvement of the two federal governments in the balancing and allocating of benefits and costs.[12] Where the costs of a project fall on one side of the border and the benefits are enjoyed by the other, regional authorities may feel little compulsion to compromise. The federal governments have greater latitude for trade-offs.

Another controversy similar in principle but differing in detail centered on the coal-fired power plant at Atikokan, Ontario, adjacent to the Quetico-Superior Boundary Waters binational wilderness area. To be constructed by Ontario Hydro in successive enlargements, the plant was intended to stimulate economic growth in Western Ontario. Opposition arose both in the state of Minnesota and among some Canadian guides and outfitters, whose livelihood depended upon outdoor recreationists in the Quetico-Superior wilderness. It was feared that fallout from an immense coal-fired plant would impair the wilderness character of the region. Opinion in the local community was divided, and even beyond the region some Canadians as well as Americans opposed the project and its planned expansion. However, failure of the plant to generate economic activity commensurate with the energy produced, coupled with Canadian sensitivity to the acid rain issue, persuaded Ontario Hydro to abandon plans for subsequent enlargement of the plant.[13]

Differing local circumstances have thus led to differing scenarios in conflict resolution over the generation and distribution of energy. That remoteness of an energy-related environmental impact does not necessarily lessen its intensity has been demonstrated by public reaction to the immense oil spill by the tanker *Exxon Valdez* in Prince William Sound, Alaska, in March 1988. Although this catastrophe did not affect Canadian waters, it aroused Canadian apprehension regarding oil tanker traffic in Puget Sound and the Inland Passage of British Columbia. Similarly, transmission of electric energy over long distances may extend the range of transboundary relationships and controversies over hundreds of miles. The controversial hydropower project on Canada's James Bay is a case in point to the extent that energy generated there is sold in the United States contrary to the wishes of American environmental groups.

The Arctic Ocean is another relatively remote area in which drilling for oil and exploiting mineral deposits have aroused multinational concern over the environmental consequences of pollution in a fragile environment. In April 1990, representatives from eight nations with territories bordering the Arctic Ocean met at Yellowknife, in the Canadian Northwest Territories, following an earlier initiative by the government of Finland.[14] The possibility of a treaty to protect the Arctic environment has been under consideration. Positions of the parties to the conjectured treaty are not clear and may change with events and negotiation procedures. Both Canada and the United States are in pursuit of energy in the Arctic. How they may approach a multinational treaty is not yet apparent, although the United States' position at the moment appears to be cautious and reserved.

MINING THE EARTH

Mining, in this context, is extraction from the earth of minerals (inorganic substances useful to man). There are various mining technologies, all of which require energy. Some, such as surface and subsurface mining of coal, and drilling for natural gas and oil, produce materials that can be converted into energy suitable for industrial purposes, particularly for internal combustion engines. Mining also yields metals and other materials (e.g., stone) useful in manufacturing and building. Energy is required not only for the actual process of mining, but also for transforming raw materials into commodities. Metals, in particular, must undergo smelting and often other treatment before they can be made into finished goods.

The processes of mining, especially for massive quantities of such energy-producing materials as coal and oil, has unavoidable adverse environmental impacts. Nearly all mining uses water, often diverting it from other uses, and almost always impairing its quality. These effects were at issue in the transboundary conflicts over coal development on Cabin Creek and Poplar River. But mining, as noted above, is an early stage in a longer process of material conversion in which energy is required. The smelting of metallic ores not only consumes energy, but may cause environmental damage greater than that resulting directly from the mining process itself. Smelting operations have, on at least two occasions, been objects of transboundary international contention between Canada and the United States.

The more notorious of these was the controversy over damage to agriculture in the state of Washington from a zinc smelter at Trail, British Columbia. The controversy was referenced to the IJC in 1928 and marked its first involvement in the issue of air quality. The facts regarding damage and its causes were ascertained early in the investigation, but because of diplomatic maneuvering involving a joint Canadian-American economic agreement, 15 years elapsed before a binational arbitral tribunal awarded damages to the Washington farmers (or their heirs) who had sustained injury. The Trail Smelter Arbitration was an ad hoc arrangement outside IJC jurisdiction, and provided no more than a possible precedent for future conflict resolution.[15]

Emissions from the smelter of the International Nickel Company (INCO) at Sudbury, Ontario, have been sources of sulfur dioxide and other acidic depositions harmful to agriculture and forestry in Canada. In the United States, the effect of the INCO smelter was more political than ecological, although environmental damage allegedly occurred. INCO's massive contribution to air pollution provided the government of the United States with an excuse to delay or diminish efforts to reduce sulfur dioxide emissions from American plants, notably in the Ohio Valley. The INCO (and nearby Falconbridge) emissions have been reduced, but the misuse of energy in the smelting process was an irritant handicapping Canadian-American cooperation to abate atmospheric acidic deposition. Enactment of new and expanded clean air legislation in the United States in November 1990 may significantly reduce this source of binational conflict.

The probability of conflict relating to mining and its environmental impacts, however, is increasing by the continuing demand for materials needed for economic growth and development, and by greatly increased prices for certain metals, especially gold. The market for materials is international, and its pressure now pushes mineral development into once remote and hitherto unspoiled natural areas. For example, a proposal to develop the Windy-Craggy copper mine in northwest British Columbia has caused anxiety on both sides of the international border. The case is similar to Cabin Creek in that wilderness areas and primeval national park are potentially threatened.[16]

The Windy-Craggy mine site in northwest British Columbia is believed to be the largest undeveloped copper reserve in North America. Situated near the confluence of the Alsek and Tatshenskini rivers, mine and highway development at Windy-Craggy could severely impair water quality in the Alsek River and downstream in the Glacier Bay National Park and Preserve (which is also a United Nations Biosphere Reverse). A 70-mile haul road between the mine and the Pacific port of Haines, Alaska, would open the region to other mine sites now being prospected. A number of Canadian and American governmental and nongovernmental groups are opposing the application of Geddes Resources, Ltd. of Toronto for a license to open the mine and construct the access road. The life expectancy of the mine has been estimated to be between 40 and 50 years, but its environmental impacts could be continuing and irreversible.

Fundamental to this and other resource issues, especially involving minerals, are the questions of rights of ownership and rights to develop. Also involved are questions concerning the applicability of the respective laws of two countries when the policies of one may preclude the use of natural resources situated in another. In such a circumstance, conflict between national and international law may be expected. In neither country today have policy priorities been established to resolve conflicts of the kind represented by Cabin Creek or Windy-Craggy. The policy process thus involves maneuvering among interests and values to find a politically acceptable solution. A question answered in Canada and the United States is whether there is a moral right to develop mineral deposits, however rich, merely because they are there.

IRRIGATED AGRICULTURE

Few people today associate energy with agriculture and agriculture with environmental degradation. Nevertheless, agriculture provides a source of energy indispensable to people everywhere—namely food—and for the large and populous societies of the modern world, there is no alternative. Modern agriculture, moreover, consumes vast quantities of energy, directly in the form of petroleum as fuel, and indirectly in the energy costs of producing farm equipment, herbicides, pesticides, and artificial fertilizers. Agriculture, through green plants, also captures solar energy which through photosynthesis becomes available for a variety of human uses, including such sources of energy as ethanol and methanol.

The extension of agriculture into semi-arid regions has been facilitated through the development of irrigation systems, but almost invariably at high and accumulating energy, economic, and environmental costs. Irrigated agriculture requires energy to deliver the necessary quantities of water to the places where it is wanted. It also ultimately requires that energy be used to overcome the salinization and waterlogging of soils (which has often threatened irrigated agriculture in arid and semi-arid regions). When the water needed flows across international boundaries or even across national subdivisions, political problems of allocation, distribution, and water quality may arise. These aspects of the resource-environment controversy have been at issue between Canada and the United States, as in the Canadian diversion of Poplar River waters by the Saskatchewan Power Corporation. The quality, quantity, and distribution of water from the St. Mary and Milk rivers have also been in controversy between Montana, Alberta, and Saskatchewan. In this particular case, apportionment of the river waters (which originate in the United States, flow into Canada, and return to the United States) was addressed in the Boundary Waters Treaty of 1909 (Article VI). Ecological considerations were not even imagined in 1909, but are certain to be introduced in any negotiations toward future developments dependent upon water resources.

The major conflict between Canada and the United States over irrigated agriculture and its residual effects arose over the Garrison Diversion project in North Dakota. The proposal to divert Missouri River water impounded by the Garrison Dam into the Souris River and by canal and tributary streams for purposes of irrigation and supplementary municipal use has a long history, at least since 1957. A subsidiary environmental effect of the project as planned originally would be discharge of Missouri River water from irrigated land northward into the Hudson Bay drainage system in Canada, which includes lakes Manitoba and Winnipeg.[17]

The project was developed at a time when the adverse environmental effects of return flows from irrigated agriculture were not generally understood. Thus the project was well along before its environmental consequences were discovered and Canadian public opinion was aroused. What was perceived as a local issue in the United States became a major national grievance in Canada.

Unequivocal support for the Garrison Diversion characterized the political leadership and press of North Dakota. There was opposition to the project chiefly among environmental groups outside the state, but the dominant attitude in local business, banking, and government was that completion of the entire 250,000-acre project by the United States government represented repayment of a "debt" owed to North Dakota for agricultural land submerged by the building of the Garrison Dam. (Much of this land, however, belonged to Native Americans, who were denied any benefits from the Garrison project.)

Authorization and funding of the project depended upon the U.S. Congress, which traditionally has voted huge sums for public works (the so-called "pork barrel"), often over the objections of the president and the General Accounting Office. But even a profligate Congress does establish cost-benefit criteria, ostensibly to rule out the least economically justifiable projects, but in fact to put a class of economic rationality over the distribution of political favors. Estimates of benefits, however, can sometimes be adjusted to justify estimated costs, preferably by enlarging the scope of a project. Beyond the borders of North Dakota and the offices of the U.S. Water and Power Resources Service (WPRS), Garrison appeared, at best, marginal. And so, seeking to boost the ratio of benefits to costs, the former Bureau of Reclamation (now WPRS) enlarged the project's coverage. In doing so, however, it also extended the project's environmental impact into Canada, with unanticipated political consequences.

Added to the original irrigation project was municipal water supply and low flow augmentation for American cities in the Red River Valley, which separates North Dakota from Minnesota. But nature has directed the flow of the Red River northward into Canada. And the Souris River, which would have provided the other major outflow of the project, loops into North Dakota from Canada and back into Canada, where its waters ultimately reach the Assiniboine River and Lake Manitoba. Thus the Garrison Diversion project would have discharged large quantities of diversion water into Canada—water which not only would have been degraded in quality from agricultural and municipal use (carrying residues of salts, pesticides, and fertilizers) but, unless preventive measures intervened, would have also carried Missouri River biota into the Lake Manitoba-Lake Winnepeg-Hudson Bay drainage systems.

During the 1950s and early 1960s, when the actual planning of the project began, environmental considerations were largely ignored. Although the Boundary Waters Treaty had been in effect for half a century, no difficulty with Canada over the project appeared to have been foreseen. By the binational environmental standards of the 1950s, the lowered quality of the diversion waters was not perceived to be pollution, under the terms of the treaty, "to the injury of health and property." By the 1970s, however, environmental quality had become an issue in both Canada and the United States. The promoters of the Garrison Diversion unexpectedly found themselves on the defensive. Their political ambitions and economic interests were suddenly threatened by forces external to North Dakota. Environmentalists from outside the state were not only perceived as interfering in North Dakota affairs by lobbying against the Garrison Diversion unit in Congress, but were suspected of stirring up opposition to the project in Canada. And as the Garrison project moved closer to realization, concern over its possible effects grew in the province of Manitoba and extended to the federal authorities in Ottawa.

In addition, reduction in North Dakota wetlands as a consequence of Garrison Diversion raised questions regarding United States obligations under the migratory bird treaty. Reduction of breeding areas in North Dakota would disrupt migratory behavior of waterfowl and adversely affect hunting and tourism in Manitoba. Although the U.S. Fish and Wildlife Service proposed mitigation areas to be purchased as replacement for wetlands destroyed by Garrison, the landowners whose acres would have been taken for mitigation were opposed to the proposal. Moreover, the governor of North Dakota, angered at the delay of the project and what he perceived as covert opposition by the Fish and Wildlife Service, refused state approval of land purchases by the service beyond that required for mitigation. Thus the United States risked double violation of international treaty obligations. The governor's action was subsequently overruled by the Federal District Court in North Dakota, but opposition to the acquisition of land for wildlife habitat continued to be widespread through the state.

On their side, the Garrison promoters had the support of congressional delegations from other states in which water projects were threatened by the growing influence of economic and environmental analysis. And whereas President Richard Nixon had asserted the right to impound funds voted by the Congress for uneconomical projects, the Congress, reacting against the "imperial" presidency, enacted legislation to prevent President Carter from withholding authorized appropriations. In 1978, the Senate passed a resolution requiring the president to spend all funds appropriated for Garrison and requiring the U.S. Department of the Interior to construct the project as Congress authorized. But when the Congress was unable to override President Carter's veto of the energy and public works appropriation bill of 1979, a compromise was reached under which work on Garrison could proceed, provided that no part of it would affect Canadian waters. The case against Garrison, economic and environmental, had been building during the preceding five years, and provided a rational basis for the Carter veto.

The political maneuverings leading to this compromise had been long drawn out and frustrating to all parties concerned. If the Garrison Diversion were found in fact to contravene the Boundary Waters Treaty, and if redesign or reduction of the project were required, serious questions regarding its economic feasibility would arise. Although this possibility was recognized, the official position of the U.S. Department of State was that the Garrison Diversion would not degrade Canadian waters within the terms of the treaty, i.e., involving injury to health and property. Bilateral negotiations continued into 1975 until it became evident that no agreement by this route would be forthcoming. When studies of the U.S. Environmental Protection Agency confirmed Canadian misgivings regarding Garrison's environmental impact, the Department of State abandoned its official position of no significant degradation. However, it reached no final conclusion as to whether the Garrison Diversion would violate Canadian rights under the Boundary Waters Treaty. Faced with this stalemate, the two governments agreed to refer the issue to the International Joint Commission for resolution.

In October 1975, the IJC established the International Garrison Study Board, which proceeded to work chiefly through six technical committees. In 1977, the board reported to the IJC, which itself held public hearings in North Dakota and Manitoba both before and after the board reports. On August 12, 1977, the IJC issued its findings and recommended:

> That . . . those portions of the Garrison Diversion Unit which could affect water flowing into Canada not be built at this time . . . .That, if and when the governments of Canada and the United States agree that methods have been proven that will eliminate the risks of biota transfer, or if the question of biota transfer is agreed to be no longer a matter of concern, then the construction of that portion of the Garrison Diversion Unit which would affect waters flowing into Canada may be undertaken (subject to certain conditions) . . .

In February 1979, the U.S. Department of the Interior issued its *Special Report on Reevaluation and Modification of the Garrison Diversion Unit*, which recommended a reduced project of 96,000 acres that would avoid all direct discharge of diversion waters into Canada. Except for some remaining risk of biota transfer, the Canadians expressed satisfaction with the revised plan. There was less satisfaction among some Americans. North Dakota proponents of Garrison were unhappy with anything less than the original project. Many environmentalists hoped for the termination of the entire project. Meanwhile, the modified Garrison Diversion unit has been constructed.

IMPLICATIONS FOR POLICY

Do the cases just considered have any common factors that might help form at least part of a basis for a general set of energy and environmental policies? In nearly every case, developments to advance economic growth preceded and induced opposition on behalf of environmental values. Economic growth requires energy, and the dominant sources of energy today cannot be developed without some damage to the natural environment. Thus, in Canada and the United States, national commitment to indefinite economic growth and widespread desire for environmental quality are chronically in collision. Public policies may be devised to reduce the causes and occasions for conflict, but cannot wholly eliminate them. Factors common to these cases appear to have greater long-term significance for Canadian-American relationships than the specific issues in dispute. Could a binational agreement on principles governing developments affecting the environment reduce the likelihood of future transboundary conflicts?

The emergence of each of these environmental controversies may be in part attributed to the advancement of scientific knowledge and the refinement of measurement capabilities. These are relatively new factors and will continue to influence public policies. Our ability to detect and quantify pollutants in air, water, and soil has grown greatly in recent decades. Our predictive capability in ecology and our understanding of biogeochemical flows and cycles have grown to a point at which political decisionmakers must take account of scientific information pertinent to the environmental impacts of their proposals. Environmental assessment procedures are now established in the federal governments of Canada and the United States, and in many states and provinces. Regard for scientific evidence is required as a practical matter to protect the credibility of any proposal, public or private, that can be shown to have a significant effect upon the environment.

The close professional association of Canadian and American scientists almost ensures that whatever differences there may be in scientific opinion in environmental controversies, they are not likely to occur exclusively along national lines. Instead, differences among scientists and engineers are more often attributable to disciplinary or technical orientation. But when scientific evidence is firm and unequivocal, Canadian and American authorities cannot easily ignore it, although they may still discount it in their decisions. Science may provide a common empirical foundation for a North American environmental policy in the long run. At present it is at least a factor in public decisions affecting the environment, and may tip the balance of decision in closely contested cases. A common denominator for energy policy seems less probable. The driving forces behind energy decisions are mainly technoeconomic, emphasizing need, and are not often supported by scientific or ethical arguments.

The emergence of a universalized environmental science, represented by a transboundary collegial network of scientists, is paralleled by the advent of cooperative relationships among citizen-organized environmental action groups. These groups exchange information, develop joint strategies, and importune their respective governments on issues of common concern. Experience has shown, however, that it is often easier to obtain symbolic declarations of environmental policy and intent than to obtain effective implementation. To mobilize opinion in support of an environmental policy or law requires the sustained and watchful monitoring of legislative, technocratic, and bureaucratic behavior to see that principles are realized in practice and subversion of policies exposed.

The probability of conflict will probably persist as long as the push for indiscriminate growth continues. Population increases and the urge for improved economic status drive present growth and development policies. Yet an expanding economy will assuredly press upon a finite environment. Directly or indirectly, ever-increasing energy demands will threaten the protected status of national parks, pristine lakes and rivers, wilderness areas, and bioreserves. Protected areas are secure only as long as pressure for their development can be contained. This means that energy policy is inseparable from policies regarding economic development, population growth, and the utilization of natural resources. The segmentation of these policies in the political process may be politically convenient, but contributes to policy contradiction and conflict. Inconsistency in policy may be the inevitable consequence of inconsistent perceptions and values in society. The political decision makers will often reflect a divided and ambivalent state of public opinion.

The obstacles to implementation of international environmental agreements are apparent, but there is reason to believe that those pertaining to Canada and the United States can be overcome. In many cases, environmental issues between the two countries are also domestic issues within each country, where organized pressures on governments urge cooperative protective action. For example, acid rain affects the northeastern United States as well as eastern Canada and is a popular concern in both countries. Opponents of the High-Ross Dam and the Garrison Diversion were from both sides of the international borders. Offended parties in each country have usually had allies in the other. And both governments are presumed to adhere to Principle 21 of the Declaration of the United Nations Conference on the Human Environment, which affirms that:

> States have, in accordance with the charter of the United
> Nations and the principles of international law, responsibility to

ensure that activities within their jurisdiction or control do not cause damage to the environment of other States or of areas beyond the national jurisdiction.

It is possible that the international character of some of the major environmental problems in North America may speed rather than retard their resolution. The same may well be true of the countries of the European Community. An international obligation to overcome national causes of environmental damage strengthens the hand of domestic advocates of environmental quality. In the United States, if an obligation is confirmed by treaty, a more powerful instrument of policy is available than would be likely under statutory law.

Under the Constitution of the United States, a ratified international treaty has precedence over most other laws, subordinate only to the provisions of the Constitution itself. As in the case of the migratory bird treaty of 1916, the United States was able to obtain, through a treaty with Great Britain, authority for environmental protection that it probably could not have obtained through statute. Thus, if the Clean Air Act of 1990 proved to be insufficient to resolve the acid rain problem, it is conceivable (although improbable) that two-thirds of the Senate might ratify a treaty so worded that it would, in effect, give the United States government the power to see that the job was done without requiring senators to vote on legislation directly affecting their own states.

If one does not demand more consistency in international policy than is customary in many domestic policies, it would be realistic to anticipate the possibility of a de facto North American policy for the environment. We have suggested that this possibility has increased with the growing presence of environmental protection organizations, both voluntary and professional, with membership and leadership on both sides of the international border. At the official level, the International Joint Commission is now firmly identified as an instrument of international policy, with parameters laid down for the time being by the two federal governments.

A comparatively recent development has been transboundary agreements at the subnational level, between states and provinces. These negotiated understandings (called paradiplomacy by some political scientists) have been undertaken without objection from the respective federal authorities. As of 1989, at least seven such paradiplomatic environmental agreements had been consummated: New York-Quebec (1982), New York-Ontario (1983), Minnesota-Ontario (1983), Michigan-

Ontario (1985), Wisconsin-Quebec (1985), and Washington State-British Columbia (1985).[18] Their purpose has been to advance the abatement of acid rain and to research its causes and control methods. (New York and Quebec, however, concluded a more comprehensive environmental agreement in 1986.)

Such paradiplomacy is at least in part a consequence of the failure of the federal governments (especially the United States) to deal effectively with the acid rain problem. But it also moves policy initiatives to regional levels, among the states and provinces of the Great Lakes basin respecting Great Lakes water quality and diversion issues. These regional arrangements may presage other regional agreements in the future. The institutional structure within which public policies are made appears to be pulling away from large central governments toward more regional initiatives on the one hand and toward international commitments on the other. This, at least, is suggested by developments in North America, the European Community, Yugoslavia, and the Soviet Union.

The national governments may be persuaded to move beyond essentially protective measures to a more positive set of policies (e.g., to anticipatory and restorative action). Remedial Action Plans for Areas of Concern in the Great Lakes could lead to coordinated federal-state-provincial-local cooperation. Elements of a binational policy would include the uses and quality of international lakes and rivers, especially the Great Lakes-St. Lawrence system, the protection of coastal lands and waters (including management of watershed and development activities), and the issues of migratory wildlife, air quality, and reconstruction of degraded ecosystems and urbanized areas. In none of these areas can either country obtain adequate environmental protection without the cooperation of the other. And although there are in each country economic and political interests that disagree on environmental versus other priorities, a substantial body of organized public opinion exists in both Canada and the United States that accords high priority to common environmental quality values. Institutional means to accomplish joint purposes have been developed (e.g., transboundary agreements and commissions). They could be extended and strengthened if experience indicates that the interests of both countries would thereby be advanced.

Whether a North American policy on energy and environment, if feasible, can include Mexico is very uncertain. Profound historical differences separate Mexico from the two northern federal republics. Nevertheless, a series of North American seminars (the first, in Banff on energy policy, May 14-16, 1980) was initiated by the Institute of Public

Administration of Canada, the American Society of Public Administration, and the Instituto Nacional de Administración Publica of Mexico. Whether the present growth of bilingualism in the United States will ultimately reduce cultural differences with Spanish-speaking countries in a manner that would facilitate cooperative relationships with Mexico is uncertain.

A realistic summation would thus appear to be that the obstacles to transborder cooperation are, at least in the short run, substantial for some environmental issues, but that the force of practical circumstances tends toward joint efforts in the long run. A common set of environmental policies appears gradually to be emerging for the European Community and Scandinavia. A comparable trend is evident in North America where, although the urgency may not be as great, the requisites for effective cooperation are simpler and public pressures for cooperative action are growing. These trends have been interpreted as indicating a shift in Western society toward a new social paradigm, in which quality-of-life and environmental values are accorded relatively high priority and are increasingly assumed to be the responsibilities of government.[19] To the extent that this may be true, environmental issues may be expected to be less often points of controversy between the United States and Canada and more often occasions for common North American policies. But cleavages of opinion and priority continue to persist among some groups of Canadians and Americans, chiefly in relation to economic growth and development.

LIMITS OF PRESCRIPTIVE ADVICE

In the course of human events, policies are more often shaped by, and after the facts of, a case than before the event. Forethought and wisdom have rarely characterized the actions of governments. Policy making is more often an adaptation to the changing conditions of political life than creative anticipation of emerging issues. It is possible that current fashions in policy analysis, with heavy reliance upon statistical methods and quantifiable data, mislead decision makers as often as they reveal the truly critical situations taking shape around them. Current research strategies tend to apply predetermined methodologies to investigations, thus risking failure to identify data critical to the issue that are not accessible to the chosen methods of research. It is particularly difficult to apply techniques of measurement to conflicts in which feelings are intense and the facts do not readily yield obvious solutions. Many environmental issues such as those described here are of this type.

The examples of transboundary conflicts that have been considered, and others that might have been added, reveal a variety of local circumstances that give a unique character to each dispute. Their histories seem to suggest that none of these controversies could be or have been resolved solely at local or national levels. Involvement of local people and governments was generally indispensable in resolving the problems encountered. But concerns of wider publics, both popular and corporate, were often factors in the issue in the first instance. The transboundary character of the issues brought in agencies of the national governments, states, and provinces. Thus multilevel complexity is to be expected in the process of environment-energy conflict resolution.

There is no uniformity in this process; its components and procedures vary with circumstances. The basis for conflict resolution must be found in general principles governing decisions regarding energy and environment to which all parties adhere. A North American charter or convention for the environment could set the parameters within which particular negotiations could take place. A background would thus be provided against which advice to policymakers could be given with a much greater prospect of receptivity than advice in a largely unstructured setting. Scandinavia has already institutionalized a multinational environmental consensus, and the European Community appears to be moving toward agreement on basic environmental policies.

Once a political decision is made to develop a binational environmental policy, the key to resolution of transboundary conflicts over energy and environment is anticipatory research and planning. In the cases here described, the likelihood of conflict could have been foreseen had the relevant factors been identified and considered. In some cases, however, foresight was limited by popular attitudes and perspectives that were to change in the course of the project, thus giving rise to opposition not anticipated by the development planners of the 1940s, 1950s, and early 1960s. The attitudinal and value changes that are now identified as "environmentalism" were generally unforseen or discounted by most economists, planners, and politicians. Max Nicholson, the British conservationist and scholar, has described the environmental movement as a "revolution," an opinion shared by sociologist Robert Nisbet and others.[20] Attitudes and preferences among the general public appear to be more receptive to comprehensive environmental quality policy than those of the political leadership. This deficiency in official perceptivity is not uncommon in the history of government and has been notably evident in failure to foresee the paradoxical reaction of the public to unlimited growth. In describing official opacity to the changing societal context for policy making, the opening lines of Alexis de Tocqueville's history of the French revolution are particularly apt: " ... never were there events more important, longer in ripening, more fully prepared, or less foreseen."[21] Official prescience is even more than customarily lacking when, as in the environmental movement, a significant shift in popular values occurs between the planning of development projects, such as described here, and subsequent efforts to implement them when their environmental impacts become known.

Is our present mode of incremental policymaking the best possible given the unpredictable real-life circumstances? Will circumstances a few decades hence complicate, divide, or reverse attitudes and values? This could happen if energy sources diminish and demand does not. It also seems probable that the full effects of the environmental revolution have not yet been felt. Whatever the turn of events, we are better equipped today to anticipate more of them than ever before. Whether our capabilities will be used with optimality and objectivity is uncertain. Institutionalized curbs to self-serving ambition are needed in both Canada and the United States. Devices such as environmental impact analysis and technological assessment have at least incrementally led to sounder policies. But news media coverage of issues, as yet, contributes little to rational public understanding.

Opening the decision process to public scrutiny helps, although this openness is as yet somewhat restrained in Canada, where an aura of the British Official Secrets Act may still be detected, and in the United States, where certain matters of foreign policy and military planning are closely held. Nevertheless, in the long run, policy differences between Canada and the United States over issues of energy and environment will diminish to the extent that consensus in values is shared across political boundaries. The trend in this direction can be strengthened by energy-environment reconnaissance of emerging problems and anticipatory planning for their resolution. Perfect prescience is not to be expected, but given adequate resources of personnel and funding, substantial improvements over past policy making are possible. It is more important to emphasize once more, however, that the effectiveness of the best-conceived policies will depend on public acceptance and comprehension. To disregard this reality—as often happens among "policy experts"—is to engage in political games and to fall into the delusion that they are really shaping the significant movements of history.

NOTES

1. For comprehensive accounts of the role of the I.J.C. in transboundary disputes see John E. Carroll, *Environmental Diplomacy: An Examination and a Prospective of Canadian - U.S. Transboundary Environmental Relations* (Ann Arbor, Michigan: University of Michigan Press, 1983), (extensive annotations); also Robert Spencer, John Kirton and Kim Richard Nossal, eds., *The International Joint Commission - Seventy Years On* (Toronto: University of Toronto. Centre for International Studies, 1981). On the Great Lakes see Lynton K. Caldwell, ed., *Perspectives on Ecosystem Management for the Great Lakes* (Albany, New York: State of New York University Press, 1988). Theodora E. Colborn et al, *Great Lakes, Great Legacy?* (Washington, D.C. and Ottawa: Conservation Foundation: Institute for Research on Public Policy, 1990).

2. *Water Resources of the St. Croix River Basin*: Maine-New Brunswick. Report on Preliminary Investigations to the International Joint Commission (under the Reference of 10 June 1955 by the St. Croix River Engineering Board—Supplementary Report on Pollution Survey, 1959, and subsequent progress reports to the IJC.)

3. *Fifth Biennial Report on Great Lakes Quality - Part I* (Washington, D.C. and Ottawa: International Joint Commission, February 1990).

4. "In Canada, an Environmental Disaster Looms", *New York Times* (14 July 1990), editorial page.

5. "Rampart Canyon Dam", *New York Times* (1 September 1964): 34, also *Times Index* (1965-1966) and (25 June 1967) and (6 July 1967): 2. See also *National Parks Magazine* 41 (August 1967): 20, and *Izaak Walton Magazine* (May 1966): 12-13.

6. Carroll, *Environmental Diplomacy* Chapter 8, "Wilderness and Development: Alaska - Yukon Issues": 168-171.

7. "NAWAPA: A Continental Water System - Symposium", *Bulletin of the Atomic Scientists* 23 (September 1967): 8-27 and R.S. Lewis, "NAWAPA: Water for the Year 2000", *Ibid.*, 21 (May 1965): 9-11.

8. For a detailed account see Jackie Krolopp Kirn and Marion E. Marts, "The Skagit-High Ross Controversy: Negotiation and Settlement", *Natural Resources Journal* U.S. - Canada Transboundary Resource Issues (Spring 1986): 261-289. Also David G. LeMarquand, "The Skagit Valley in Canada and the High Ross Dam", *International Rivers: The Politics of Cooperation* Chapter 5 (Vancouver: University

of British Columbia, Westwater Research Centre, 1977): 79-94; and *Environmental and Ecological Consequences in Canada of Raising Ross Lake in the Skagit Valley to Elevation 1725* (International Joint Commission of Canada and the United States, 1971).

9. Maxwell Cohen, "Transboundary Environmental Attitudes and Policy—Some Canadian Perspectives". Paper prepared for Harvard Center for International Affairs (September 1980): 25; John V. Krutilla, *The Columbia River Treaty: The Economics of International River Basin Development* (Baltimore: Johns Hopkins Press, 1967); David G. LeMarquand, "The Columbia River Treaty", *International Rivers: The Politics of Cooperation* Chapter 4, (Vancouver: The University of British Columbia, Westwater Research Centre 1977): 53-78; and Neil A. Swainson, *Conflict Over the Columbia: The Canadian Background to an Historic Treaty* (Montreal: McGill-Queens' University Press, 1979).

10. Carroll, *Environmental Diplomacy* Chapter 8, "Wilderness and Development: Cabin Creek": 163-168.

11. International Poplar River Water Quality Study Main Report International Poplar River Quality Board of the International Joint Commission, 1979. See also Carroll, *Environmental Diplomacy* Chapter 9, "Prairie Water Issues: Poplar River": 182-190.

12. Carroll, *Environmental Diplomacy* Chapter 12, "Formalizing Environmental Relations": 277-309.

13. *Ibid.*, Chapter 12, "Air Quality at the Border: Atikokan": 216-223; and United States Environmental Protection Agency, *Impacts of Airborne Pollutants on Wilderness Areas Along the Minnesota-Ontario Border*, Gary E. Glass and Orie L. Loucks, eds., (Duluth, Minnesota: Environmental Research Laboratory, May 1980).

14. "Eight Arctic Countries Agree to Ministerial Meeting on Environment", Canadian Secretary of State for External Affairs Press Release, April 23, 1990.

15. D. H. Dinwoode, "The Politics of International Pollution Control: The Trail Smelter Case", *International Journal* 27 (Spring 1972): 219-35.

16. Eric Halle, "Undermining a Mountain", *Sierra* 75, no. 4 (July-August 1990): 55-56.

17. Nancy J. Doemel, *The Garrison Diversion Unit: Science, Technology, Politics, and Values* Bloomington: Indiana University, Advanced Studies in Science, Technology and Public Policy, 198; Lynton K. Caldwell, "Garrison Diversion: Constraints on Conflict Resolution", *Natural Resources Journal* 24 (1984): 839-63 and Charlotte K. Goldberg, "The Garrison Diversion Project: New Solutions for

Transboundary Disputes", *Manitoba Law Journal* 11, no. 2 (1981): 177-89.

   18. Nancy Paige Smith, "Transboundary Relations and Acid Rain: New York's Memorandum of Understanding with Quebec and Ontario" *Journal of Borderlands Studies* 5, no. 1 (Spring 1990): 111-133 and "Paradiplomacy Between the U.S. States and Canadian Provinces: The Case of Acid Rain Memoranda of Understanding" *Ibid.*, 3, no. 1 (Spring 1988): 13-38.

   19. See Ronald Inglehart, *Cultural Shift in Advanced Industrial Society* (Princeton, New Jersey: Princeton University Press).

   20. Max Nicholson, *The Environmental Revolution* (London: Hodder & Stoughton and New York: McGraw-Hill), and *The New Environmental Age* (Cambridge: Cambridge University Press, 1987) Robert Nisbet, *Prejudice: A Philosophical Dictionary* (Cambridge, Massachusetts: Harvard University Press, 1982).

   21. Alexis de Tocqueville, *On the State of Society in France Before the Revolution in 1789; and on the Causes Which Led to That Event.* Translated by Henry Reeve (London: John Murray, 1856).

Chapter 3

Energy Policy and Federalism in the United States and Canada

Eric M. Uslaner

Sniderman *et al.* remarked over a decade ago, "Americans look back on their civil war, Canadians look forward to theirs (1974, p. 268)." The United States has a national motto, *E pluribus unum*, one out of many. In contrast to the American idea of a melting pot, Canadians view their society as a mosaic or in the words of former Prime Minister (and now Minister of External Affairs) Joe Clark, a "community of communities." Americans have national heros, ranging from the "yeoman farmer" (Hofstadter 1955) to other rugged individualists such as Horatio Alger and Babe Ruth.

There are few distinctly Canadian institutions or myths (Malcolm 1981). Canadian provinces, unlike American states, can and do impose tariffs on each other. Most Canadians identify more with their home province than with the country (Clarke *et al.* 1984, p. 41); indeed, Canadians rarely refer to their country as a nation, instead choosing the term "confederation." In 1980 and again a decade later Canada faced the prospect of Quebec secession, leading to the possible dismantling of the country. Protest parties in the West have espoused varying degrees of separatism and have occasionally gained substantial support. In contrast, the dilemma of the United States is not opting out, but wanting in: should Puerto Rico and the District of Columbia become states?

On few issues is the problem of federalism so acute in Canada as energy.[1] The federal and provincial governments have battled since confederation over control of natural resources. Constitutional disputes over energy have played major roles in election campaigns and, indeed, in the question of whether Canada has a future as a country. While there are some important conflicts between the national government and the states on energy in the United States, federalism plays a distinctly secondary role in energy politics. Policy making is largely concentrated in Washington. The states are bit players on this issue, rarely challenging the legitimacy of the federal government. Energy reflects larger battles in each society.

Energy and the environment interact differently in the two countries. In the United States the two issues are strongly intertwined. Energy consumption produces pollution. Abatement measures require major shifts in energy policy. Coal must be scrubbed, nuclear plants must be highly regulated or even shut down, and the government places moratoriums on offshore oil drilling. Environmentalists are key players in energy politics and energy producers and consumers take active roles on environmental issues.

The two issues are largely distinct in Canada. The environment does *not* play a considerable role in energy policy making. There is overwhelming public support for environmental regulation in both countries. Even in Alberta, Canada's premier energy-producing province, there is widespread support for environmental controls even if they limit energy production (Jackson 1980). Yet the politics of the issue are more confrontational in the United States than in Canada. Canadian environmental activists are well organized only in Ontario (Vogel 1986, Doran 1984, p. 205). Many Canadians see environmental problems as foreign policy concerns—acid rain coming from the United States (Lanouette 1982). As such, it is not an issue of federal-provincial conflict. Energy, on the other hand, is all about jurisdictional issues.

What is the source of these conflicts? Why is federalism so critical to Canadian (energy) politics and why does it play such a lesser role in the United States? Students of Canadian politics offer two different and not altogether consistent accounts of why federalism dominates the country's politics.[2] One stresses institutional design, the other historical and cultural forces. Institutionalists argue that Canada inherited a Westminster system of government from Great Britain, a parliamentary regime in which legislative and executive power are merged. Yet, it also had a much more diverse population than the mother country. Indeed, Francophones in Quebec constituted one of the two "founding peoples," in need of special protections. The British North America (BNA) Act of 1867, Canada's initial constitution, thus established a regime that mixed parliamentary supremacy with provincial rights. On energy, for example, the BNA Act reserved all lands, mines, minerals, and royalties within a province's borders to provincial control. On the other hand, the act also permits the federal government to regulate international and interprovincial trade and to control any provincial works that it "declares" to be "for the general advantage of Canada" or "of two or more of the provinces." Ottawa has used this power to secure control of the atomic energy industry (Toner and Bregha 1981, p. 4).

In contrast, the U.S. Constitution is rather vague on where the division of power lies between Washington and the states. There are few rights specifically allocated to the states in the Constitution. The Tenth Amendment states equivocally: "The powers not delegated to the United States by the Constitution, nor prohibited to it by the States, are reserved to the States respectively, or to the people." The Thirteenth through Fifteenth Amendments, adopted after the Civil War, specifically restricted states rights with respect to slavery and civil rights. The courts have later expanded the scope of these amendments rather broadly to enhance federal power at the states' expense. States' rights were also embedded in an equal second chamber of the federal legislature, the Senate. Until the 20th century senators were selected by state legislatures. By late century the distinctions between the Senate and the House of Representatives had largely faded into history.

Where the U.S. Constitution was vague, the BNA was specific. Where the BNA granted conflicting claims, the U.S. Constitution was silent. In the United States this permitted ultimate federal dominance over the states, for the latter had no specific statutory guarantees. In Canada the battle for supremacy has raged on because there is no straightforward institutional solution. The instruments of governing exacerbate the conflict in Canada and soothe it in the United States. Westminster systems at both the federal and provincial levels make for ready assaults on minority interests (Cairns 1968). Majority governments have unlimited formal powers, restricted only by custom and common sense. Two house legislatures with separate executives in Washington and the states moderate conflict within and across levels. There are strict limits to what each chamber can do, and neither house can accomplish anything without the other's consent.

The alternative thesis maintains that it is not primarily institutional structure that shapes conflict in each country. Instead, it is culture and history. The United States has a more coherent sense of national identity than does Canada because it fought a war for independence, whereas Great Britain walked away from its New World colony. The United States developed national symbols in a way that Canada did not. Its Civil War was fought to preserve a union, whereas the Canadian confederation came about, and remained intact, largely because of the absence of other feasible alternatives. The strong sense of identity in the

United States made concentration of power in Washington possible: Americans did not distrust each other.   The weaker identification in Canada promoted suspicion, yet also demanded a strong central authority to hold the country together.   An American-style separation of powers system would not work.   The strong state in Ottawa sought to secure powers for itself where the BNA Act was obscure, at least in part to build up a sense of nationhood.   Much of Canadian history is a search for identity (Schwartz 1967).   Whether that would be a pan-Canadian vision as sought by one former prime minister (Pierre Eliott Trudeau) or a "community of communities" as envisaged by another (Joe Clark) has preoccupied Canadians since independence.

These conflicts are clearly reflected in the energy issue.   Until the late 19th century, no branch of the American federal government took any stand on energy policy.   Following the Civil War, with federal supremacy established in law if not in fact, the Supreme Court ruled in favor of *state* regulation of energy.   In 1877 it established in *Munn v. Illinois* the right of state governments to regulate utilities (including electric and gas suppliers) and then (about a decade later) the power of the federal government to regulate firms engaged in interstate commerce. Even as much control over energy (especially electric utilities) remained at the state level, there was a steady and unchecked trend toward greater federal control of energy policy.   Contemporary energy politics in the United States is overwhelmingly focused upon the federal government alone.[3]   The U.S. federal government owns 36 percent of the land in Colorado, 49 percent of Wyoming, 65 percent of Utah, and 87 percent of Nevada; it owns 40 percent of all of the coal in the country and 61 percent west of the Mississippi River, where states own just five percent of such resources (Masselli and Dean 1981, p. 8; Mosher 1981, p. 477). The federal government also controls 80 percent of the oil shale reserves in Colorado, Utah, and Wyoming (Rycroft and Monaghan 1982, p. 86).

Canadian energy policy has been marked by sharp federal-provincial conflicts since confederation.   In the longstanding battle of the federal government to assert some control over the provinces, the Prairie provinces had to fight, sometimes violently, even for local self-government in the late 19th century (Thomas 1978).   Alberta, and Saskatchewan were admitted into the confederation as provinces in 1905, yet they did not obtain control over their natural resources until 1930. Since then the two levels of government have struggled over resources. Over 85 percent of Canada's oil and gas reserves are found in Alberta, and more than 85 percent of these reserves are on provincial land (Harrison 1981, pp. 66-67).

What drives these differences in energy policy? Do constitutional systems or cultural differences matter more? The answer is important because institutional tinkering is a favorite device of political leaders who seek specific policy goals. Americans who worry about policy stalemate on issues such as energy have proposed moving toward a Westminster system.[4] Canadians who seek to maintain provincial autonomy, especially on energy, argue for just the opposite institutional reform. They want a "Triple-E" (elected, equal, and effective) Senate along the lines of the U.S. model. A co-equal second chamber would be a major check on the majoritarian House of Commons. It might even produce divided control of the two houses, since such a Senate would have a heavy bias toward the Progressive Conservative party.

Institutional reform presumably would resolve contentious issues. A historical and cultural account suggests otherwise. You can't keep a good issue down, regardless of institutional structure. It will, like a Phoenix, rise again and again. Just as critically, it may make little sense to worry incessantly about structural reforms. For the very reasons why people don't agree on policy outcomes, they will be unable to consent to institutional solutions that would yield different policies. Do patterns of federalism on energy policy in the two countries provide support for either of these theses?

ENERGY IN THE UNITED STATES

Even as the constitutional legacy of the Civil War set the framework for virtually all federal-state conflicts in the United States, most regulation of energy largely remained with the state and local governments. Natural gas was brought under federal price regulation in 1938; however, a dual system of federal and state regulations remained in effect until 1978, when a federal pricing regime displaced state authority. Oil price regulation was largely a state affair until the 1970s except for controls during the world wars. Energy producing states did secure tax relief for oil, the oil depletion allowance. Pricing was brought under federal control in the 1970s under the Nixon administration's overall wage-and-price regulations. Offshore oil reserves are clearly federal property. Coal, which as noted is largely owned by Washington, is also a federal preserve.

In contrast to Canada, U.S. federal-state energy relations do seem basically cooperative. There is conflict, to be sure, but not anywhere near the level found in Canada.[5] The federal government largely sets energy policy (when it is able to do so). States often must implement the standards established. A few areas of energy policy have traditionally been locally determined. Utility regulation is the prime example. It has historically been a state and local function. Every state has a Public Utility Commission that sets rates for electricity (and other utilities such as telephones) and also sets the standards of operation for utilities. In 1978 the Congress enacted the Public Utilities Regulatory Policies Act, which gave the federal government control over improving the efficiency of electric utilities to increase conservation and providing more equitable rates to consumers. The federal government set the standards, and the states were to see that local utilities achieved them. Many states resented this intrusion of the federal government into this realm, and Mississippi challenged Washington's power all the way to the Supreme Court, which ruled in the federal government's favor under the argument that power clearly came under interstate commerce. The larger story, however, is that by and large the states cooperated quite readily with the federal guidelines, even in the absence of sanctions for meeting the deadlines in the legislation (Thompson 1983).

Historically, the states have largely accepted the role of the federal government in bringing the benefits to constituents. Politicians of all stripes recognized the advantages of the New Deal's Tennessee Valley Authority and the Rural Electrification Administration in bringing electric power to their constituents (Caro 1981, ch. 34). The role of the federal government in the New Deal legitimized Washington as not only a donor of largesse but also as the only level of government that could deal with nationwide problems. The states, rather than resisting centralization of authority over power issues, came to see Washington as a source of additional revenues. By 1970, the critical question on environmental regulation had shifted from who would control effluent standards (a role that had been ceded to Washington both because spillover effects could not be avoided across borders and because the states simply did not have the funds to do the job themselves) to how to extract more money from Congress (*Congressional Quarterly* 1970).

In the mid-1970s states sought out federal assistance on energy conservation (Regens 1980). Once the Supreme Court ruled that the federal government could regulate utilities and once states accepted the role of Washington as the provider of many benefits, it was only a matter of time before the most tendentious aspect of state utility regulation shifted to the capital. The Federal Power Act of 1920 directed the states to give preference to public over private utilities when license renewals were under consideration. In 1986, bolstered by heavy spending by private utility political action committees, the Congress reversed this almost 70-year-old policy. What is most surprising is that there was no outcry from the states over this usurpation of a role Washington had largely left to them. The legislation passed the House of Representatives by voice vote under suspension of the rules, which requires two-thirds assent for enactment (Davis 1986).

States often took the lead when the federal government had not acted. In 1979 President Carter had not been able to convince the Congress to enact standby set-aside programs for gasoline retailers in the event of a supply emergency. His Energy Department, under urging from many states, gave governors the authority to implement such programs in their own states (Light 1980). States have also engaged in lobbying efforts in Washington on energy legislation (Light 1976, 1978). Action on energy in the United States is thus largely a federal affair.

FEDERAL CONFLICT IN AMERICAN ENERGY POLICY

States *do* fight the federal government and each other. Energy-producing states such as Montana and Wyoming have imposed severance taxes on coal (Nelson 1983, p. 179) in clear violation of the spirit if not the letter of free interstate commerce. Altogether, 34 states collected severance taxes on nonrenewable resources as of 1981. In that year, the Supreme Court ruled that such taxes are legal unless Congress votes to outlaw them (Hagstrom 1981). Alaska collects royalties from private companies that produce oil in the state. In 1976 the state enacted a constitutional amendment to secure these rents through the Alaska Permanent Fund. The resources of these funds, which constitute 25 percent of the state's royalty income, have since 1982 been returned in grants of up to $1,000 to each citizen. By 1987, the fund's value had grown to $7.6 billion (Turner 1987). Yet, the accumulation of these resources exaggerated rather than quelled Alaskan hostility toward the federal government.

In 1980 Alaskans voted by 50.6 percent to 49.4 percent to approve a referendum sponsored by Libertarians to establish a Statehood Commission "to study the status of the people of Alaska within the United States and to consider and recommend appropriate changes in the relationship of the people of Alaska to the United States."[6] The Statehood Commission, not surprisingly, rejected any attempt to declare independence and instead issued a fairly mild set of recommendations designed to enhance the status of all states (not simply Alaska) in the federal union as well as to redress some specific Alaskan grievances with Washington (Alaska Statehood Commission 1983).

Washington promised at statehood (1958) to turn over to Alaska ownership of 102,950,000 acres of lands under the Bureau of Land Administration's control and 400,000 acres of national forests. Many Alaskans were outraged over the Carter administration's Alaska Lands bill, which set aside large portions of land that could not be explored for energy to protect the environment. The Alaska Statehood Commission (1983, p. 23) noted that federal actions since 1966, in part related to native American claims, effectively froze the transfer of land back to the state. Another Libertarian initiative, on the 1982 ballot, demanded Alaskan control of all federal lands. It secured a 73 percent majority, but little came of the initiative.

The Alaskan initiatives are perhaps the most extreme manifestation of a larger movement in the American West, the "Sagebrush Rebellion."[7] Like the Alaskan movement, the Sagebrush Rebellion was a protest against federal control of land and natural resources. Much western ire was dissipated in 1981 when Ronald Reagan was elected president and appointees such as James Watt (Secretary of Energy) and Anne Gorsuch Burford (Environmental Protection Agency) took positions that western conservatives found appealing (Mosher 1981).

Federal-state conflict has been most severe on issues relating to the energy development versus the environment. Acid rain is one such concern, but even more prominent is nuclear power and nuclear waste. Initially, the nuclear program was established for military purposes and of course fell exclusively under federal control. Civilian nuclear power is still regulated by the Nuclear Regulatory Commission, but states, under the Clean Air Act amendments of 1970, maintain the power of environmental regulation of any such facilities. States have taken a variety of approaches to nuclear power, including several (California, Connecticut, Iowa, Maine, and Wisconsin) that set standards for waste disposal at such high levels that it is virtually impossible for any plant to gain federal approval (Sylves 1982, p. 9). Nuclear power plants have become hot political issues in several states on both environmental and fiscal grounds: New York, New Hampshire, and Washington are perhaps just the most prominent examples of states in which plants have faced both environmental objections and bankruptcy.

The issue of disposal of nuclear wastes is even more contentious. It is the classic example of the "NIMBY" ("Not In My Back Yard") syndrome in which people want to avoid any adverse consequences of governmental actions. Congress in 1982 finally enacted the Nuclear

Waste Policy Act, which provided for the establishment of two waste disposal sites, one in the East and one in the West. The act, however, provided for a state veto power that could only be overruled by both houses of Congress within 90 days (Davis 1987). Several states, including South Carolina in the East and Idaho in the West, have either barred the importation of hazardous wastes (not restricted to nuclear wastes) or even banned the transport of such disposals through their states. The constitutionality of both types of action is questionable, but it might very well become politically even more dangerous for politicians who seek elective office to impose such facilities upon any jurisdiction.

Despite such local initiatives, control of nuclear policy clearly rests with Washington. In 1987 the Nuclear Regulatory Commission permitted the licensing of nuclear plants in the absence of state and local initiatives on emergency evacuation plans (prompting challenges by states such as Massachusetts). In the same year the Congress overrode its own 1982 policy and selected Nevada as the western site for nuclear waste disposal without the state's consent. The Supreme Court in 1972 upheld federal supremacy over the states in regulating nuclear power plants, although it also permitted California in 1983 to impose a moratorium on new plant construction on economic rather than environmental grounds (Zimmerman 1988). The Environmental Protection Agency in 1990 permitted North Carolina to impose hazardous waste disposal regulations stricter than those of the federal government (Weiskopf 1990). Nuclear energy is an exception to the general rule that energy policy in the United States has shifted from the states (where regulation of oil and gas began) to Washington, even as the constitutional power clearly rests with the federal government. The institutional division of powers cannot stop the steamroller of political interests.

THE WAR OF EACH AGAINST ALL

American energy policy has long been characterized as marked by ideological conflict (see, *inter alia*, Kalt 1981, Wildavsky and Tennenbaum 1981, and, for a summary, see Uslaner 1989b). On electric utilities, the conflict has been between public and private power. On coal, the battle lines were drawn over wages and mine safety between producers and union miners. On nuclear power, the issues were energy development versus environmental regulations. On oil and natural gas, the struggle has been between producers and consumers over price controls and tax breaks. Most studies of energy politics indicated that constituency interests played at best a minor role in such conflicts (for a notable exception, see Sanders 1981). There was little conflict between the federal government and the states because the battles were largely the same at each level (see Prindle 1981, on energy politics in Texas). Moreover, the arenas of oil and gas, coal, nuclear power, and electricity largely did not intersect to produce cross-cutting cleavages. Each had its own distinct left-right cleavages, and the fuels were not generally seen as competing with each other.

By the mid-1970s all this had changed. The twin energy crises of 1973-74 and 1979 led to a new era of competition among fuels and to a very different type of politics in each market. Environmental concerns heightened during this decade, changing the contour of politics on several of these fuels (especially coal and oil). Left-right cleavages were replaced by a war of each against all. Constituency politics reigned supreme as debates over such issues as natural gas pricing became increasingly complex. On some energy issues, such as nuclear power, the conflicts did focus on which government ought to control decision making. But by this time the focus of energy policy had largely shifted to Washington. Most of the conflicts pitted region versus region and one sector of an industry against others rather than Washington versus the states and localities.

Regionalism in energy politics did not produce a crisis in federalism. Many industries were divided so they did not speak with a single voice in the capital. This was particularly true of coal, where eastern and western producers often had conflicting interests, and even within the West there were sharp conflicts over environmental concerns (Mecham and Krogman 1982). Even in producing regions such as the West, energy resources are "localized," and there is no sustaining ideology in the region to support the demands of the producers (Light 1978). Consider the politics of natural gas in the late 1970s and early 1980s.[8] A severe gas crunch led the Congress in 1978 to enact the Natural Gas Policy Act. That legislation partially decontrolled natural gas and brought the federal and state regulatory mechanisms under a single regime. However, to get sufficient support for the legislation, the Congress had to agree to establish a 27-tier price system for different categories of natural gas. By 1982, the regulatory regime of the NGPA had led to an even stranger anomaly: rising production and rising prices. The Congress considered both complete decontrol and recontrol legislation. The House was so stymied that no legislation reached the floor. The Senate defeated by almost identical two-to-one margins both proposals.

The 1978 legislation tore apart traditional coalitions, especially those between major producers (who owned most gas still under price controls through the NGPA) and independents (who owned the majority of gas already freed from controls) as well as between interstate and intrastate pipelines and distributors and the pipelines. Business consumers were split: Some feared price increases, others cared most about security of supply, while yet others favored elimination of government regulations whatever the immediate impact upon their own situations. The battles were exquisitely complex, defying all ideological interpretations and most logic. By the 1970s, then, the cleavages on American energy policy were cross-cutting. There was so much confusion in federal energy politics in part because there was no clear-cut division state-by-state. The same conflicts that defeated both natural gas proposals in 1982-83 largely decimated Carter's energy program in 1977 and led to the uncoupling of his synthetic fuels program in the early 1980s (Uslaner 1989a).

A STRAIGHT FIGHT IN CANADA

In contrast to the convoluted politics of energy in the United States, energy battles in Canada were far more straightforward. The conflicts over energy are very much straight fights between the two strategies of development that dominate all Canadian politics. The approaches of "province-building" versus "nation-building" symbolize competing visions as to what Canada is to become (Simeon 1980). The centralizers have sought to build national institutions, generally seeking protection for Canadian industries against external competition in the hope that such firms will serve the goal of fostering a sense of national unity (Uslaner 1989d). Important examples of this approach are protection for cultural industries even under the Free Trade Agreement with the United States, the principle of "universality" designed to guarantee a minimum standard of living to all Canadians, and "equalization" payments from the federal treasury to poorer provinces. The province-building approach, in contrast, uses the strong state to achieve provincial goals. Quebec's language legislation that mandates French-only signs and restricts the rights of Anglophones in education is a prominent example of this approach.

These two strategies come into sharp conflict on energy. Canada is a major energy producer and exporter. The great bulk of the oil and gas (as well as synthetic fuels) reserves are found in Alberta, and most reserves are the property of the provincial government (Norrie 1988, p. 9). Whose energy is it, anyway? The nation-building approach of recent Liberal governments maintains that the energy belongs to all Canadians. In 1975 Ottawa established Petro-Canada as a government-owned national oil company. In 1980, the Liberal government proposed and enacted the most wide-ranging energy legislation in North American history (see below) that arrogated much decision-making power on energy to the federal government.

The provinces, and especially Alberta, maintain that the BNA Act (and, indeed, its successor, the Constitution Act of 1982) gives ownership of natural resources to the provinces. Alberta views its energy resources as its "special birthright," much as people in the American West (and especially Alaska) see their energy. While nation builders see Canada's large supply of energy as a cushion to shield Canadians from the types of conflict that overtook the United States, province builders see energy reserves as their way out of economic underdevelopment. They resent claims by other Canadians who want to keep these resources in the country and prefer free trade on energy. Albertans sometimes remark that the national oil company really stands for "Pierre Elliot Trudeau Rips Off CANADA." In contrast, residents of central and eastern Canada refer to Albertans as "blue-eyed sheiks."

The contemporary energy conflict in Canada has its roots in the historical battles between Ottawa and the provinces over control over natural resources.[9] The structure of conflict has dominated debate over energy to such an extent that separate spheres of controversy with regard to specific fuels have not developed in Canada as they have in the United States. Additionally, coal has a considerably smaller share of the Canadian than of the American energy mix and thus this fuel did not loom large in energy politics; while hydroelectricity is a much more important energy source in Canada, it is produced entirely by provincial Crown corporations exempt from federal taxation and thus not in the firing line of federalism issues.

The immediate trigger for the current round of federal-provincial energy conflict was a decision in 1973 by Alberta that permitted the province to set oil and gas prices within the province and to determine production levels. The next year the federal government disallowed the deduction of provincial royalties from federal income taxes. In an action similar to that of the United States, the federal government also introduced price controls on energy as OPEC prices skyrocketed. By the second energy crisis, the country was facing two alternative visions as to what to do.

"MADE IN CANADA"?

The minority Progressive Conservative government proposed in 1979 an 18-cent-per-gallon gasoline tax to enhance the move toward world prices. The government's budget was defeated in the House of Commons, and the 1980 federal elections revolved largely around the energy issue (Uslaner 1989c), giving victory once again to the Liberals who immediately proposed the National Energy Program (NEP). This policy established a "made in Canada" price designed to protect Canadians against world prices, established a wide range of taxes on domestic production and subsidies to Canadian firms for exploration, increased federal energy royalties while slightly decreasing provincial revenues, established a goal of 50 percent Canadian ownership of all oil and gas production by 1990, and reserved to the Crown (Petro-Canada) an automatic 25 percent interest in energy development in the "Canadian lands" in the northern territories. The NEP established federal dominance over energy policy. It explicitly established nation building as its goal.

Not surprisingly, Alberta and some other provinces reacted in a sharply negative manner to the NEP. Alberta restricted its own energy output and stopped development of several synthetic fuels projects. A constitutional confrontation over what the applicable provisions of the BNA Act were ensued until the two governments finally reached an accord in September 1981 that largely eliminated many of the taxes despised by Alberta, raised prices slowly over time until they finally were to reach world levels (a key goal of Alberta), but kept in force the "Canadianization" provisions of the NEP. What was critical, however, was the victory of Ottawa on the key constitutional issue that the federal government had the right to regulate energy prices. Alberta had the support of Manitoba, Saskatchewan, and British Columbia, all of which were producers of either oil, gas, or hydroelectricity. The Atlantic provinces also had disputes with Ottawa over offshore oil resources, but they were primarily consuming provinces and thus stood by the sidelines even as pursuing their own disputes separately. Quebec, with its own agenda on language and cultural rights, should have been a strong defender of province building, but like Ontario (the sole strong defender of Ottawa) was a consuming province.

Despite these diverse interests, the conflict over the NEP was very clearly structured. The federal Liberals strongly stood behind nation building, the Progressive Conservatives behind province building. The one represented consumers, the other producers. The Liberals represented eastern and central Canada, the Tories the western part. One stood for a strong federal state, the other for provincial power and greater reliance upon the market. Indeed, even the constellation of interest groups was quite limited: in both 1973-74 and 1979-81 the energy battles largely represented *only* producer and consumer interests (Berry 1974, Toner and Doern 1986). The environmentalists did not become involved in this energy dispute, the energy industry itself was united, and, unlike in the United States, business consumers were not split but saw themselves simply as consumers. There were no cross-cutting cleavages because there were only two sides to the issue. What we had was a straight fight between the left and the right, between two competing visions as to what Canada was to become. When the Progressive Conservatives replaced the Liberals following the 1984 election, it was hardly surprising, then, that they largely repealed the NEP.

The world view of Alberta was that of Alaska writ large. In the same year (1976) that Alaska established its Permanent Fund, Alberta announced formation of its Heritage Savings Trust Fund (AHSTF). From an initial endowment of $1.5 billion (Canadian) the fund was expected to grow to ten times that amount by 1990. While Alaskans returned their booty to citizens of the state, Albertans invested some of theirs in loans to other provinces in a strategy the provincial government hoped would give them political leverage against Ottawa (Doern and Toner 1985, p. 44). While Alaskans toyed with the idea of secession, many western Canadians have thought quite seriously about it. Approximately one-quarter of Westerners express at least mild support for the idea of an independent West (Johnston 1986, p. 53). Separatists in the Western Canada Concept Party won a seat in the provincial Legislative Assembly; in 1989 another western protest party with an otherwise murky message, the Reform Party, actually won a by-election for the federal House of Commons after winning 15 percent of the vote in the 1988 federal elections in Alberta.

Energy, then, is a lightning rod for attitudes toward what Canada is to be. As with Alberta, other provinces see their energy resources as a bulwark against federal domination and as a mechanism to build up their own economic well-being. Even after the Canadian Supreme Court ruled that offshore oil belonged to the federal government, Newfoundland refused to sign an accord with Ottawa. British Columbia expects to make major gains in hydroelectric power sales as a result of the Canadian-American Free Trade Agreement. The same is true for Quebec, which sees the development of energy from the James Bay (valued at $50 billion for 1987 and half of 1988 alone) as a key element in establishing a viable Quebecois economy that some separatists see as providing the economic leverage that could make Quebec a viable independent country (Burns 1988).

WHO GOVERNS?

The energy issue in Canada reflects the larger conflicts in that society. The struggle over the patriation of the Constitution involved many of the same conflicts involved in the NEP battle. The confrontation over the Meech Lake Accord, designed to gain Quebec's assent to the Constitution, ultimately came down to a battle between that province and Newfoundland. These two provinces have battled each other over the energy resources of Labrador, which have been ceded to Quebec even though the area is part of Newfoundland (Claiborne 1990).

The energy issue in the United States mirrors the worst in American politics, a war of each against all that is *not* politics as usual. Tempers flare over energy policy in both countries. Some Canadians and Americans each talk of secession. It seems, then, as though one crosses the border in either direction and sees pretty much the same thing.[10] Americans and Canadians drive the same cars, eat the same food, even (through cable television, now available to 80 percent of Canadians) watch the same television shows (American). It should hardly be surprising that political movements cross the border as well, as witnessed by environmentalism, abortion, the religious right, and many others.

But such a view is too facile. When some Canadians talk of secession, or at least of alienation, they mean it. Canadian political science students read such texts as *Must Canada Fail?*, *Unfulfilled Union*, and *Canada in Question*. American political science students read such texts as *Government by the People* and *A More Perfect Union*. Americans who brandish thoughts of splitting the union are either at the very edges of the political spectrum (or beyond it) or are confident enough that no one will take them seriously so that they can engage in some good-natured tomfoolery.[11] Texans were truly irate at oil and gas price regulations in the 1970s when they put bumper stickers on their cars welcoming energy shortages in the Northeast stating: "Drive Faster. Freeze a Yankee!" But they had no long-standing animosity against their brethren. Nor did Alaskans really intend to secede. If they had done so, someone would have taken notice at the time. Instead, the 1980 referendum went by almost completely unnoticed.[12] Canadians, on the other hand, are preoccupied with questions of national unity.

All of the talk of national unity in Canada suggests support for an institutionalist perspective. Canadians try to put Humpty Dumpty together again with structural glue. For the very reason that redesigning the machinery of government has become such an obsession, it is unlikely to succeed. The core of Canada's problem lies in its weak sense of national identity. The proposed reforms, from the Meech Lake Accord to the "Triple-E" Senate, weaken national institutions at the expense of the provinces. The former gives each province a veto over Constitutional and other issues, while the latter weakens the House of Commons as the institution of majority rule in the country. They thus legitimate rather than fix the identity crisis. In contrast, U.S. citizens are hardly preoccupied with federalism issues. Since the 1960s and the civil rights struggle states' rights issues have faded into the background.

To be sure, Americans *do* have preferences on institutional structures. A 1987 Gallup poll found that 37 percent of Americans trusted local government officials most, whereas 22 percent selected state government, and just 19 percent the federal government; 46 percent said the federal government had too much power over other levels, while 37 percent believed it had the right amount of power (Associated Press 1987). Much of the distrust of the federal government and the glorification of local government can be attributed to the general American distrust of centralized power and bigness in general (see Lipset and Schneider 1981). Yet this wariness of big government has not hampered the centralization of policy making.

The salient issues in U.S. energy policy generally do not center upon the most appropriate level of government. Natural gas pricing involved so many actors and such high stakes that the termination of state-level regulation got lost in the Washington fray. Even when issues of federalism do become prominent, as in severance taxes and nuclear power, there are few clear lines of ideological cleavage with respect to federalism issues. The nuclear power issue finds opponents of the technology pressing for greater local control. Normally such liberals are supporters of greater centralization. The issue is *not* centralization of power, but rather the environmental hazards of nuclear energy.

If institutional design explains the nature of conflict and the resulting outcomes, structural reforms should alter each. In the United States groups pressing for stronger nuclear regulation persisted even as they must have been aware that they were unlikely to prevail on constitutional grounds. In Canada the dispute between Newfoundland and Nova Scotia, on the one hand, and the federal government on the other over control of offshore oil resources did not end with the Supreme Court decision establishing federal supremacy. Progressive Conservative Prime Minister Brian Mulroney's province-building approach effectively overturned federal sovereignty by transferring virtually all royalty payments to the two provinces.

The Canadian and American party systems reflect the bifurcation of the federal and subnational energy regimes. The West has long been almost completely alienated from the party system in federal politics (at least prior to 1984). The Liberals are weak in the Prairies and in British Columbia. In 1980 they held just 1.3 percent of the parliamentary seats in the West and less than 1 percent of the provincial Legislative Assembly seats in that region. In contrast, the Democrats had slightly under half of the congressional seats in the West, more than half of the governorships, and about 44 percent of the state legislative seats in the American West. In Canada there is a clear relationship between partisanship and attitudes on energy. There is no such linkage in the United States. In the United States the party systems at the federal and state levels are the same, even if the election results are not. In Canada voters often split their partisanship (Uslaner 1990). In only one province, Ontario, is the constellation of provincial parties the same as that found in the federal parliament. In British Columbia neither major federal party seriously contested recent provincial elections (until the Liberal "breakthrough" in 1991). No set of structural changes in the Westminster system or the electoral system is likely to alter these fundamental political dynamics (Wilson 1983, pp. 173-174).

The rapid transferability of conflicts from one level to the other in the U.S. reflects the integration of the political system. State legislatures often serve as the training ground for the best candidates for Congress (Jacobson and Kernell 1981). In Canada, on the other hand, there is very little of this type of elite circulation; federal and provincial party organizations do not generally work together and sometimes even see themselves as competitors (Smith 1975, pp. 331-332; Whitaker 1985). Federal and provincial parties maintain separate fund-raising efforts, and candidates for the federal Parliament, at least in Ontario, overwhelmingly have neither served in the provincial Legislative Assembly nor even sought election to it (Johnston 1985, p. 153; Williams 1985, p. 312). Indeed, federal officials may actually prefer to deal with provincial governments controlled by opposition parties since this reduces competition between the two tiers of each party for personnel and resources (Whitaker 1985, p. 155).

The tensions between federal and provincial party systems in Canada reflect not so much questions of institutional design as they do longer-standing cultural differences among Canadians. The federal system does not integrate the disparate elements of the "mosaic" into a "melting pot." No institutional mechanism seems capable of doing so. The U.S. system, in contrast, is becoming *more*, not less, nationalized. Competitive two-party politics has spread to most states, providing for the first time a base of state legislators who climb the ladder to become congressional candidates.

These behavioral and organizational differences between the two countries are explicable by cultural, not structural factors. The clear sense of national identity in the U.S. permits a wide range of interests and ideologies to flourish, even to (as in the case of energy) thwart each other. The weak sense of nationhood in Canada forces many issues into questions of identity, and ultimately into conflicts with much clearer (albeit higher) stakes than in the United States. This is certainly the case with energy.

It is far from clear, however, that Canada performed worse than did the United States on energy policy. After all, at the national level in the United States, the decade of the 1970s was marked by what Goodwin (1981, p. 679) called a "preference for inaction" on energy policy. Canada did at least enact fairly comprehensive, if controversial, legislation. When the other side (the Tories) won the 1984 federal elections, it did just what we would expect of a strong party system: it largely repealed the NEP. The American and Canadian responses to the energy issue reflected the more fundamental patterns of conflict in each society. Americans were badly divided about energy, and the conflicts were an exquisite montage of the diversity of the society and its economic base. There was little in the 1970s to hold Americans together, so the policy initiatives came apart. Natural gas and nuclear power plants and waste show how badly divided the United States can become on a key policy area. Yet there is enough of a common thread in the American psyche so that even in the face of massive policy failure there is an underlying commonality to how conflict is shaped at the federal and state levels. The federal bargain reflects this deeper-seated unity. Canadian energy politics in the 1970s set the stage for a full-fledged debate over national identity, including the protection of French culture and language in Quebec. The lack of an acceptable solution, either institutional or political, precipitated the crises of the 1980s and 1990s. The energy crisis passed into political oblivion in the United States; it translated into crisis in Canada.

NOTES

The support of the General Research Board of the Graduate School and of the College of Behavioral and Social Sciences of the University of Maryland—College Park, the Embassy of Canada for Faculty Enrichment and Research Awards, and the Everett McKinley Dirksen Congressional Leadership Research Center are greatly appreciated, as are the assistance of Magda Ghaneima and the comments of Jonathan Lemco. This chapter was originally prepared for the Conference on Comparative Federalism: Changing Theory and Practice in the Adaptive Canadian and American Federal Systems, the Nelson A. Rockefeller Center for the Social Sciences, Dartmouth College, June 22-25, 1989.

1. Language, of course, is at least as good an example in Canada. It may threaten to become so in the United States should Puerto Rico be admitted as a state. Several states have already mandated English as the "official language."

2. For a discussion of these explanations, see Uslaner (1990).

3. A listing of sources here would take us too far afield here. See the bibliography in Uslaner (1989a). Also of note is the comment of John Chubb, one of the leading students of both energy and federalism. When I asked him for citations on federalism and energy policy, he commented tersely that there simply is not very much.

4. See James L. Sundquist, *Constitutional Reform and Effective Government* (Washington: Brookings Institution, 1986).

5. Thompson (1983) argues that federal-state energy relationships are largely cooperative rather than conflictual, while Aron (1979) takes the opposite perspective. To a considerable extent, these different viewpoints reflect the areas being studied (public utilities by Thompson and nuclear energy by Aron).

6. I am grateful to my colleague Mavis Mann Reeves for bringing this referendum to my attention and to Barbara Whiting of the Division of Elections, Office of the Lieutenant Governor of Alaska, for providing the results of this referendum and that of 1982.

7. The Alaskan movement was popularly called the "Tundra Rebellion."

8. This discussion of natural gas follows Uslaner (1989a), ch. 5.

9. This section closely follows Uslaner (1989a), ch. 7.

10. Obviously, not everything is the same in the two countries. When one crosses the border into Quebec, one enters a somewhat (although hardly completely) different world.

11.   In contrast, Canada, true to its British heritage (following such entities as the Raving Loony Monster Party), has its own party (the Rhinoceros Party) that is explicitly not serious.

12.   No student of federalism I spoke with, other than my colleague Mavis Mann Reeves (who informed me of the referendum), had heard of the secession proposal, and not until I reached someone in the Alaska government could I find out very much about it.

REFERENCES

Alaska Statehood Commission. 1983. *More Perfect Union: A Plan for Action*. Juneau.

Aron, Joan B. 1979. "Intergovernmental Politics of Energy." *Policy Analysis*, 5: 451-471.

Associated Press. 1987. "Poll: Federal Government Esteemed Least," *Washington Post* (September 8): A21.

Berry, Glyn R. 1974. "The Oil Lobby and the Energy Crisis," *Canadian Public Administration*, 17: 600-635.

Burns, John F. 1988. "Quebec Utility Looks South for Growth," *International Herald Tribune* (June 2): 11, 15.

Cairns, Alan C. 1968. "The Electoral System and the Party System in Canada," *Canadian Journal of Political Science*, 1: 55-80.

Caro, Robert A. 1981. *The Path to Power*. New York: Random House.

Claiborne, William. 1990. "New Snag Develops in Canadian Pact," *Washington Post* (June 11): A17, A20.

Clarke, Harold D., Jane Jenson, Lawrence LeDuc, and Jon H. Pammett. 1984. *Absent Mandate*. Toronto: Gage.

Congressional Quarterly. 1970. "States Need More Federal Funds to Combat Pollution," *Congressional Quarterly Weekly Report* (April 10): 972-974.

Davis, Joseph A. 1987. "Nuclear Waste: An Issue That Won't Stay Buried," *Congressional Quarterly Weekly Report* (March 14): 451-456.

_____. 1986. "More Than Money Behind Private Power Win," *Congressional Quarterly Weekly Report* (June 28): 1473-1477.

Doern, G. Bruce and Glen Toner. 1985. *The Politics of Energy*. Toronto: Methuen.

Doran, Charles F. 1984. *Forgotten Partnership: U.S.-Canada Relations Today*. Baltimore: Johns Hopkins University Press.

Goodwin, Craufurd. 1981. "The Lessons of History." In C.D. Goodwin, ed., *Energy Policy in Perspective.* Washington: Brookings Institution.

Hagstrom, Jerry. 1981. "The Severance Tax Is the Big Gun In the Energy War Between the States," *National Journal* (August 29): 1544-1548.

Harrison, Rowland J. 1981. "The Constitutional Context of Canada's National Energy Program." In Earl H. Fry, ed., Energy Development in Canada. Provo, UT: Brigham Young University Canadian Studies Program.

Hofstadter, Richard. 1955. *The Age of Reform.* New York: Random House.

Jacobson, Gary C. and Samuel Kernell. 1981. *Strategy and Choice in Congressional Elections.* New Haven: Yale University Press.

Jackson, Edgar L. 1980. "Attitudes of Albertans Towards Energy and Associated Issues." In Edgar L. Jackson and Leslie T. Foster, eds., *Energy Attitudes and Policies.* Cornett Occassional Papers, number 2. Victoria, British Columbia: Department of Geography, University of Victoria.

Johnston, Richard. 1985. "Federal and Provincial Voting: Contemporary Patterns and Historical Evolution," pp. 131-178 in David J. Elkins and Richard Simeon, eds., *Small Worlds: Provinces and Parties in Canadian Political Life.* Toronto: Methuen.

_____. 1986. *Public Opinion and Public Policy in Canada.* Toronto: University of Toronto Press.

Kalt, Joseph P. 1981. *The Economics and Politics of Oil Price Regulation.* Cambridge: MIT Press.

Lanoutte, William J. 1982. "Canadian Electricity May Be Cheaper, But It Doesn't Come Free of Problems," *National Journal* (May 22): 910-912.

Light, Alfred R. 1980. "The Governors' Push for Emergency Energy Powers," *Publius*, 10: 57-67.

_____. 1978. "Drawing the Wagons into a Circle: Sectionalism and Energy Politics," *Publius*, 8: 21-37.

_____. 1976. "Federalism and the Energy Crisis: A View from the States," *Publius*, 6: 81-96.

Lipset, Seymour Martin and William Schneider. 1981. *The Confidence Gap.* New York: Free Press.

Malcolm, Andrew. 1981. "Pleasing Both Sides, Court Just Sharpens Canada Crisis," *New York Times* (October 4): F4.

Masselli, David Charles and Norman L. Dean, Jr. 1981. *The Impacts of Synthetic Fuels Development*. Washington: National Wildlife Federation.

Mecham, Milo and Marian Krogmann. 1982. "The Coal States and Energy Policy." Presented at the 1982 Annual Meeting of the Midwest Political Science Association, Milwaukee, April.

Mosher, Lawrence. 1981. "Reagan and the GOP Are Riding the Sagebrush Rebellion--But for How Long?" *National Journal* (March 21): 476-481.

Norrie, Kenneth. 1988. "Energy Revenue Sharing: Issues and Options." *Energy Options* paper. Ottawa: Energy, Mines, and Resources Canada.

Nelson, Robert H. 1983. *The Making of Federal Coal Policy*. Durham: Duke University Press.

Prindle, David E. 1981. *Petroleum Politics and the Texas Railroad Commission*. Austin: University of Texas Press.

Regens, James L. 1980. "Energy Conservation and the States: Approaches to Implementing National Policy," *Publius*, 10: 47-56.

Rycroft, Robert W. and James E. Monaghan. 1982. "National Security Policy: Synfuels and the MX System." In J.W. Regens, R.W. Rycroft, and G.A. Daneke, eds., *Energy and the Western United States*. New York: Praeger.

Sanders, M. Elizabeth. 1981. *The Regulation of Natural Gas*. Philadelphia: Temple University Press.

Schwartz, Mildred. 1967. *Public Opinion and Canadian Identity*. Berkeley: University of California Press.

Simeon, Richard. 1980. "Natural Resource Revenues and Canadian Federalism: A Survey of the Issues," *Canadian Public Policy*, 6: 182-191.

Smith, David E. 1975. *Prairie Liberalism: The Liberal Party in Saskatchewan*. Toronto: University of Toronto Press.

Sniderman, Paul M., H.D. Forbes, and Ian Melzer. 1974. "Party Loyalty and Electoral Volatility: A Study of the Canadian Party System," *Canadian Journal of Political Science*, 7: 268-288.

Sylves, Richard T. 1982. "Nuclear Power and the States." Presented at the 1982 Annual Meeting of the American Political Science Association, Denver, September.

Thomas, Lewis Herbert. 1978. *The Struggle for Responsible Government in the Northwest Territories*, 1870-97. Second ed. Toronto: University of Toronto Press.

Thompson, Edward III. 1983. "The Rapid Transformation of Intergovernmental Energy Relations," *Publius*, 13: 97-111.

Toner, Glen and Francois Bregha. 1981. "The Political Economy of Energy." In M.S. Whittington and G. Williams, eds., *Canadian Politics in the 1980s*. Toronto: Methuen.

Toner, Glen and G. Bruce Doern. 1986. "The Two Energy Crises and Canadian Oil and Gas Interest Groups: A Re-examination of Berry's Propositions," *Canadian Journal of Political Science*, 19: 467-493.

Turner, Wallace. 1987. "Alaska Governor Proposes State Use of Oil Fund," *New York Times* (February 21): 5.

Uslaner, Eric M. 1989a. *Shale Barrel Politics*. Stanford: Stanford University Press.

_____. 1989b. "Is American Energy Politics Ideological?" *The Energy Journal*, 10: 55-75.

_____. 1989c. "Looking Forward and Looking Backward: Prospective and Retrospective Voting in the 1980 Federal Elections in Canada," *British Journal of Political Science*, 19: 495-513.

_____. 1989d. "Energy Policy and Free Trade in Canada," *Energy Policy*, 17: 323-330.

_____. 1990. "Splitting Image: Partisan Affiliations in Canada's 'Two Political Worlds'," *American Journal of Political Science*, 34: in press.

Vogel, David. 1986. *National Styles of Regulation*. Ithaca: Cornell University Press.

Weiskopf, Michael. 1990. "EPA Upholds State on Tougher Environmental Laws," *Washington Post* (June 2): A4.

Whitaker, Reginald. 1985. "Party and State in the Liberal Era." In Hugh G. Thorburn, ed., *Party Politics in Canada*, fifth ed. Scarborough, Ontario: Prentice-Hall.

Wildavsky, Aaron and Ellen Tennenbaum. 1981. *The Politics of Mistrust*. Beverly Hills: Sage.

Williams, Robert J. 1985. "Ontario's Political Systems: Federal and Provincial." In Hugh G. Thorburn, ed., *Party Politics in Canada*, fifth ed. Scarborough, Ontario: Prentice-Hall.

Wilson, John. 1983. "On the Dangers of Bickering in a Federal System." In *Political Support in Canada: The Crisis Years*, ed. Alan Kornberg and Harold D. Clarke. Durham: Duke University Press.

Zimmerman, Joseph F. 1988. "Regulating Atomic Energy in the American Federal System," *Publius*, 18: 51-65.

Chapter 4

Energy Policy and the Environment

Rodney D. Schmidt

Since World War II, hydrocarbon development has played an increasing role in the Canadian, American, and world economies. Continuous change in world energy markets coupled with the development of new technologies has necessitated frequent reevaluations of national energy programs in many oil- and gas-producing nations. The period began with fears of oil shortages, followed by two decades in which the discovery of new, cheap oil sources in the Middle East drove prices down and challenged the global predominance of expensive North American oil. Also, dramatic increases in oil price and supply occurred for a sustained period, followed by an abrupt fall in price in the 1980s. Many attribute this rollercoaster in price and supply to the fact that a handful of large oil producers in the Persian Gulf dominate the market.

Of equal importance for energy policy has been the structural evolution of this market. Prior to 1960 (and arguably up to the early 1970s), the world oil market was dominated by the seven large multinational oil companies. By the early 1970s, however, important changes in host country rules on taxation and payment of royalties as well as in actual extraction decisions, began to take form. The direct result was that exporting governments played an increasing role in energy supply and price decisions. The new OPEC "cartel" was at least perceived to have real powers with respect to setting world oil prices.

Throughout the 1970s the world economy was subjected to a number of unexpected and unwelcome oil price shocks, which most analysts tied directly to the power and influence of the OPEC cartel. In response to the price and supply volatility of this period, the oil market experienced another important structural reformation: the emergence and rapid growth of short term markets. In particular, spot market sales and futures trading in oil have come to dominate the delicate business of the international oil market. Consequently, energy policies in Canada and the United States have been subject to much debate, modification, and, at times, rather fundamental alteration in an effort to keep stride with the rapidly changing world energy market. Further fueling the energy policy debate in North America are the immense size of the combined Canadian and U.S. energy bases and production potentials, the economic and political rewards of exploiting them, and, more recently, the environmental ramifications of hydrocarbon development.

With these forces at play in the world petroleum industry, and given the high stakes involved in energy development, energy policy has been pushed to the forefront of regional and federal public policy concerns in both countries since 1960. Growing scarcity of conventional world energy reserves, increasing U.S. dependence on oil imported from the Persian/Arabian Gulf, growing environmental pressures, and the size of the North American hydrocarbon base will ensure that energy will continue to dominate public policy debates in both the United States and Canada for years to come. Furthermore, since Canada is both an importer and exporter of petroleum and petroleum-based products as well as an exporter of natural gas, and because U.S. dependence on imported hydrocarbons is expected to increase, the volatility of energy prices and supplies in the world market has direct effects upon the shape of energy policy in North America. These effects have been exhibited most clearly in the nature of the energy pricing and taxation regimes over the past 30 years, as well as in bilateral agreements (witness the energy stipulations in the Canada/U.S. Free Trade Agreement [FTA]).

Adding to the complexity of developing sound energy policy, environmental and energy policies have begun to overlap significantly in recent years with regard to hydrocarbon development. As a consequence of this overlap, future problems for Canadian and American policy makers will include resolution of fiscal, regulatory, trade, and possibly even jurisidictional matters. Clear examples of the trend include America's attempts to resolve issues related to development of the Alaska National Wildlife Refuge (ANWR) (which was affected by the *Exxon Valdez* oil spill), the recent interest in Canada regarding the Environmental Assessment Review Process (EARP), and discussion over the appropriate route of the Trans-Alaska Gas pipeline. In sum, the realities and patterns of hydrocarbon demand and supply in North America, coupled with the force of the Green movement worldwide, have added a new dimension to the energy policy debate in North

America. The new dimension entails the implication of energy and environmental interests in similar, and in some instances, identical policy questions: those regarding the optimal development of the hydrocarbon base. Hence, a host of social welfare issues are brought to the forefront.

This chapter considers the rationale for government involvement in the energy sector. The objectives of energy taxation and pricing policy are examined in the context of the social welfare questions that are raised when environmental and energy development concerns are meshed. Justification for a government role is related to objectives regarding energy security and environmental preservation. The limits of this role are framed in terms of socially optimal policy results as well as in terms of the micro- and macroeconomic effects that result when the fiscal tools available to the government (i.e., taxation and pricing) are employed. The following discussion is relevant not only to Canada and the U.S. sovereign entities, but also to both countries in the context of their bilateral linkages and relations.

THE ROLE OF GOVERNMENT

Many governments take an active role in their respective energy sectors. In the U.S., for example, energy-related matters demand a great deal of attention from specialists in the areas of energy, national security, economics, policy, and from political participants themselves. The growing importance of energy as a policy concern in the United States has in the past been framed primarily in terms of the implications for national security. While it would require a discussion beyond the scope of this chapter to determine whether or not this is the driving concern in the formulation of energy policy, there certainly appears to be an active role for government if energy is important to a nation's security. Nonetheless, due to the finite nature of oil and natural gas reserves and considering the fundamental role that both play in modern economies, concern over energy security opens a door for active government participation in the energy sector.

A second justification or rationale for a government role concerns the revenue-gathering responsibilities of any public authority. To the extent that any government is the rightful owner of these resources, the general public has a vested, legal right and an obligation to set the terms of access to these resources.[1] In essence, then, the government is the "landlord" (to the extent that it is the representative of the people), and some involvement in decisions related to the development of these resources is justifiable if not inevitable.[2] As supervisor or landlord, the government must be concerned with capturing a high level of resource revenue so that the rewards of a rich resource base can be shared among the general public.[3] This is not to suggest that government intervention should necessarily be aimed at expropriating income derived from resource development. Rather, it could be argued that intervention or participation in resource development should be intended to ensure that an appropriate portion of the resulting market returns are captured for the benefit of the general public.[4] This may be achieved in the least distortionary fashion by levying taxes on the economic profit earned from resource depletion so as not to interfere with investment and production decisions. This approach assumes that the forward and backward economic linkages are fairly strong in the energy industry. Thus the benefits of a healthy, growing energy industry would flow through to the economy as a whole, benefitting all sectors. Furthermore, if the authorities wish to include directly all individuals in the economic income derived from resource depletion, a lump-sum transfer of the revenues accrued from taxing economic profit is generally the least distortionary means of doing so.

Third, a governmental role in the resource sector might be justified whenever the market fails to ensure the most efficient exploration, development, and conservation of these resources. This can be an unenviable and difficult task since it may require the government to develop an information base that is better than that which most participants within the industry possess. While this is not impossible, many would argue that the participants within a particular market or industry possess related information and knowledge that, if not superior, is at least as good as that of a participant outside the respective market. As Begg (1982) points out, it is certainly possible to specify more general models in which there is sufficient disaggregation to allow different groups to have different information and form different expectations.[5] Already we have simple examples when individuals in different industries or markets know more about their own market [than others do].[6]

This suggests, on the one hand, that there is a very limited scope for government in this capacity, when government is *not* a player within the market. On the other hand, where market imperfections of either an endogenous or exogenous nature are present, a policy designed to influence corrective behavior within the domestic industry so as to create an efficient rate of development and structure of production may justify government participation.

Finally, a role for government in energy policy is defendable when energy development clearly poses implications for the environment. Drilling a well, constructing a pipeline, transporting hydrocarbons by ocean vessel, and so on, are all of concern to a government conscious of the well being of its territory of jurisdiction. Consequently, the energy debate and the environmental debate have been fused, further complicating the art of establishing consensus on the appropriate pattern for development of the hydrocarbon base in North America.

In sum, the rationale for government participation in the energy sector is linked to government responsibility concerning the promotion of efficient resource exploitation; the maximization of resource revenues through the taxation of profits (ideally, in the least distortionary way); the assurance that energy security, in the interest of national security, is met; and the preservation of the ecosystem. Immediately discernible within this context is the fact that the goal of maximizing resource revenue can conflict with that of ensuring efficient resource development and use depending, for example, on the time frame of reference used, while goals related to national energy security may conflict with either of these depending upon what type of policy is considered as one which promotes energy security. Similarly, environmentally sound energy policy adds another echelon of complexity to policy making. To see this, one must consider the primary tools available to government to achieve these potentially conflicting objectives.

FISCAL TOOLS

Apart from outright expropriation or nationalization of an industry, the tools available to the government are its constitutional right to levy taxes and its political right (i.e., in terms of its popular electoral support as government) to regulate prices.[7] With these tools, the government is to satisfy the policy objectives outlined above. First reflex may be to suggest that, as theory prescribes, the number of policy goals cannot exceed the number of instruments for policy to be successful; therefore, these energy objectives require either revision or additional instruments. This, however, need not be the case and will depend upon the ability to achieve a number of policy objectives with a policy configuration that uses fewer instruments. For example, it is conceivable that energy security and environmental objectives can be achieved simultaneously under the correct policy configuration. This will be further addressed later.

Through levying taxes and controlling resource prices, then, the government is able to maximize and stabilize resource revenue. The distortionary nature of a tax depends upon where the tax is levied. Economic theory suggests that taxes on production beyond the taxation of economic profits will alter production decisions, resulting in an inefficient allocation of resources, and possibly, a suboptimal time path and structure of production. Rowse (1988) argues that the revenue losses associated with this type of taxation are unlikely to be recouped over the long run since the annual production level of the source diminishes over time.[8] Thus, not only does this approach to taxation result in an efficiency loss due to its effect on production decisions, but it will also ultimately reduce the long-run value of resource revenues to the government.[9]

At the macro level, this could have a long-term adverse impact upon the government budget deficit if government purchases do not decline adequately to offset revenue losses. The adverse effects of an expanding government budget deficit on interest rates, and therefore on domestic investment and the balance of payments, are too familiar in the present world economy. The Petroleum and Gas Revenue Tax (PGRT) in Canada and the Windfall Profits Tax (WPT) in the United States are examples of such taxes. In order to avoid this sort of problem, taxes must be based on profits rather than on gross revenues.

As a means of passing on the benefits of an abundant resource base, price regulation can also be used to hold prices at a level below that which would have otherwise occurred in the marketplace. While controlling prices insulates the domestic user from world price volatility and stabilizes resource revenues (at least in the short run), it carries with it a number of efficiency and equity related side effects. At the micro level, artificially low (or high) prices tend to adversely affect decisions on production and consumption, thereby generating a redistribution from one group in society to another. The "fairness" of such a policy, an expressed concern of many energy policy makers (including those who drafted the National Energy Programme [NEP] for Canada in the early 1980s), is immediately brought into question as one group benefits at the expense of another. Furthermore, the economy suffers from an overall efficiency loss resulting from artificially set prices, hence inflicting a burden on the society (see Scarfe, 1981).[10]

The macroeconomic consequences are no more favorable in the event that the country of concern is both an importer and an exporter of the good (as Canada is in petroleum). Holding prices below the world level encourages, in this case, a level of consumption greater than would have occurred otherwise and, therefore, increases reliance on imported oil as domestic sources are depleted. This in turn creates a drain on the balance of payments and necessitates larger foreign borrowing and higher real interest rates to attract these borrowed funds.[11] Higher interest rates in turn further suppress domestic investment not only in energy but in all sectors of the economy. In addition to the inefficient employment of resources at the microeconomic level and the adverse investment and balance-of-payments effects at the macroeconomic level, price controls may negatively affect long-term resource revenues if these effects take root structurally (e.g., in the form of preferences regarding consumption). Since artificially low prices affect consumption decisions in the short term (and in the long term, if they have a structural impact), pricing policy has direct environmental ramifications.

Carefully constructed taxation and pricing policy are clearly critical to simultaneously achieving the goals of maximizing resource revenue and ensuring equal sharing in the benefits of resource development without generating undesirable externalities. While the rationale for active government participation in the development of resources can be justified, the use of these mechanisms to influence energy development is constrained by their respective microeconomic and macroeconomic effects. Consequently, finely tuned taxation and pricing policy should,

1)   extract a fair share of the economic rent related to resource development without distorting optimal production and consumption decisions,

2)   provide incentive to develop resources in an environmentally sound fashion (e.g., fiscal disincentives to pollute/fiscal incentives to utilize environmentally "clean" technology or procedures), and

3)   facilitate energy security objectives.

The remainder of the chapter focusses on the means of satisfying these energy policy objectives considering first, the relation between fiscal policy and energy security, and second, the relation between fiscal policy and environmental protection.

FISCAL POLICY AND ENERGY SECURTIY

History has shown that economies in North America are affected by shocks in world oil markets. To the extent that endogenous hydrocarbon resources can be utilized to help insulate economies from such events, it is fair to say that a nation's energy security can be enhanced by policy that promotes efficient hydrocarbon development while maximizing the inter-temporal benefits to the society from resource exploitation. For market economies like Canada and the U.S., it can be argued that energy security is closely tied to the optimal timing and structure of resource exploration, development, and production. This, in turn, is intricately linked to the rate of capital formation in an industry, which is itself a function of investor perceptions (both domestic and foreign) of the stability of the respective political/economic environment. Policy that fluctuates between regulation and deregulation of prices or that suggests government is willing to change rules on taxation for an industry in a retroactive fashion is likely to inject a sense of uncertainty regarding the stability of the energy policy environment. Uncertainty in this sense can have an impact on investment. This is a particularly important consideration in formulating tax policy. To reduce the degree of tax-related uncertainty and consequently the associated political risk, government tax policy should focus only upon the expropriation of a "fair share" of economic profit while simultaneously shouldering an equally "fair share" of the associated development risk, the risk of failure. This would signal to the industry that the government's intentions in its energy policy are confined to the efficient collection and redistribution of resource income.

In this context, an increase or decrease of the tax rate on profit accrued from oil production is likely to be less controversial since government could demonstrate that profits accruing to producers justified such action (or the onus could be shifted to industry to demonstrate the opposite). Furthermore, industry reaction time to a tax increase (decrease) would be improved since uncertainty regarding the intended effects of the tax shift would be reduced. Investment could be expected to respond according to market forces and not to political uncertainty.

Understanding the critical issues for decision makers in the energy sector is also significant for effective policy formulation. For example, the treatment of the risk/reward tradeoff associated to petroleum exploration and production (E&P) is extremely important for the investment decision in the petroleum industry. As an illustration of this, consider briefly the treatment of this tradeoff in the U.S. versus that in the U.K. Under the fiscal configuration in the U.K., the marginal rate of taxation on production is approximately 84% while in the U.S. it is roughly 35%. However, equally important from the perspective of an investor, the risk (costs) shared by the U.K. government in a failure (a dry hole) is significantly higher than that in the U.S. This feature of fiscal arrangements in the U.K. is extremely important and demonstrates an understanding of the nature of investment constraints in the industry. That is, dry hole risk is the primary risk in E&P since the level of capital at risk for the exploration phase is extremely high. Given the capital intensity of most E&P ventures and given a standard drilling success rate in the range of 25%, most explorationists face strict budget constraints. This imposes a significant value (or premium) on the degree to which government shares in the risk associated to exploration activity.

Consequently, in determining optimal production profiles, the tradeoff between the per barrel capital at risk relative to the expected per barrel payout of a venture is critical. As a result of their respective tax frameworks, the per barrel payout relative to the per barrel capital at risk for a typical E&P venture is much lower in the U.K. than it is in the U.S. The treatment of risk (costs) and returns in the U.K. appears to be designed to extract a good portion of the economic rent realized from hydrocarbon production while simultaneously ensuring continued investment in additional resource development.

Concerning price regulation, it is not clear that either the control or decontrol of prices has more than a neutral effect upon an industry in terms of climatic stability. Under controlled prices, uncertainty related to world price volatility is reduced. This may foster a greater sense of stability and thereby positively influence investor perceptions, investment, and security. On the other hand, prices fixed below world levels could decrease the rate of new investment in the industry since lower prices make some investments no longer economically feasible at the margin. While this does not necessarily have direct implications for perceptions regarding the stability of policy, it does suggest that the domestic industry would be less developed than it might be if the higher world market price had prevailed domestically. As a result, domestic capacity and production would be lower and the reliance on imports greater, thereby increasing vulnerability in the event of a disruption.

It may be argued, however, that price fixing facilitates energy security objectives by leading to a relatively greater rate of capital formation in the domestic industry when domestic prices are higher than world prices. In fact, investment in the domestic industry would likely accelerate dramatically if world prices were expected to remain below the fixed domestic price for a reasonable length of time. Investors would naturally channel a greater proportion of investment towards the higher-priced region and sell oil on the domestic market. This expansion of industry capacity would further insulate the domestic economy if import supplies were disrupted. Energy security, in this case, could be enhanced by the use of price-fixing policy.

While the conceptual exercise in this respect is fruitful, the problem lies in the practicability of the latter option. In Canada, for example, the most common objective of fixing oil or natural gas prices during the past 25 years has been to fix them lower than international prices to reduce the burden on consumers. Further, the implicit assumptions in holding domestic prices below world prices are: 1) there exists an infinite or at least an abundant and diversely located supply of the resource in question so that prices will not rebound quickly, and 2) the costs of doing business in the domestic industry of the country or territory in question do not fully reflect these higher prices.

In an effort to help ensure energy security, the U.S. has opted to create a mechanism aside from taxation and price setting. Through government stockpiling of oil in the Strategic Petroleum Reserve, the U.S. hopes to offset the price and supply effects that might be expected in the event of a major disruption. While this policy does result in a direct cost to society as a whole in the form of management and storage costs, it is not clear that it is designed for the purpose of redistributing resource income, nor does it carry with it the same efficiency consequences of certain pricing and/or taxation regulations. It might be argued that this approach will fuel a perception of stability among investors, since it conveys the message that a stable energy supply environment is not only an expressed desire but a distinct government policy objective. To the extent that this sort of policy contributes to moving the industry toward an optimal timing and structure of production (i.e., the development pace that simultaneously maximizes the economic and social value of the resource base), resources are developed and extracted most efficiently, long-run resource revenues are maximized, and energy security is enhanced. Arguably, however, a policy of stockpiling is likely to have limited to no impact whatsoever on the optimal timing and structure of production.

ENERGY POLICY AND ENVIRONMENTAL PROTECTION

Recently, the environment has entered the higher echelons of policy consideration. Rapid and continued urbanization, population growth, and the advent of the "throw-away" culture have driven most societies into a corner. The only path out seems to be concrete action on the environment. The most potent implication of this environmental reality is the far-reaching nature of policies designed to protect the environment. Whether one is considering social programs, such as development of facilities in a virgin area for care of the elderly, or the exploitation of a natural resource, environmental implications can and will play an larger role in the decision process. Clearly, as concern over the preservation and deintoxification of the earth's ecosystem intensifies, decisions in business and government will necessarily be more responsive to environmental demands.

Before we examine the implications of this development for policy, it should be noted that environmental concerns are not likely to fade. The reason for this stems from the fact that once the environment is damaged, it is not easily repaired. Furthermore, once the environment is damaged beyond the point of rejuvenation, especially in a densely populated area, the welfare of those within it is directly affected. The environment has a direct impact on social welfare of individuals and governments today, regardless of whether or not it was previously a factor. The pollution and environmental problems that many societies and governments currently face are examples of this phenomenon.

A case in point, and a very good illustration of the environmental impact on energy policy, is Taiwan. Faced with severe pollution and environmental erosion, Taiwan has abruptly shifted the direction and emphasis of its energy policy. The roles of coal and nuclear energy are painfully being downplayed, while those of cleaner fuels, such as natural gas, are taking priority. Although the change in policy was somewhat influenced by major technological progress in the transportation of natural gas and its use in electricity generation, the economics of fuel substitution alone do not yet justify the move to increase imports of natural gas, especially with an abundance of coal in the region. There is clearly a sufficient, if not necessary, environmental cause for a shift to the use of cleaner fuels in Taiwan.

The nature of the problem of environmental preservation in the context of energy exploitation is one of market failure. It presents a classic welfare economics problem: the marginal private cost (benefit) and the marginal social cost (benefit) of a resource development are not necessarily identical. Externalities can arise from "jointness" in consumption or production, i.e., when the behavior of one agent affects the consumption or production of another.[12] Development of the hydrocarbon base can thus be thought of as a "double jointed" problem since environmental considerations may affect both individuals' and firms' welfare. Furthermore, the effect on welfare may also be of varying degrees of importance across these agents.

If environmental considerations are a factor in some cases and not in others, or if they appear therein in varying degrees of importance, then the extent to which oil and gas development affects agents will vary and could be either substantial or negligible in many cases. Consequently, it is extremely difficult to formulate rules or policy that maximizes social welfare. Attaining this policy objective when market failure occurs becomes a complex issue. Economic and business interests must be balanced with environmental considerations even though the two are not necessarily always compatible. This problem brings us closer to the heart of the issue: the existence of externalities in hydrocarbon exploitation places a definite limit on the scope in which private companies can freely function if social welfare is to be maximized.

When evaluating the social welfare ramifications of hydrocarbon development, the results can vary depending upon whether the analytical framework is static or dynamic. The same criteria that are applied in a static environment may not be fully applicable in a dynamic framework.[13] This is especially true of a dynamic growth sector such as the petroleum sector. One reason for this is the uncertainty of the future.[14] A second, more important reason is that growth itself tends to offset errors in judgment and management.[15] That is, short of the conditions necessary for an environmental emergency, there is undoubtedly some rate of economic growth that, if generated by the development of the petroleum base, would allow the industry to violate at least some conditions with impunity.[16] As a result, static welfare economics conclusions may not afford suitable standards by which to appraise a dynamic sector such as petroleum, especially if free enterprise establishes a higher rate of efficient economic growth.[17] Since the implications of dynamics must be considered, the limitations on free competitive enterprise may be significantly different, and the externalities generated by the process may be evaluated in an alternative context. In sum, policy designed to maximize welfare in a dynamic energy sector framework is a function, among other things, of environmental considerations, sectoral and economic growth, and energy availability.

This indicates a justifiable role for allocative policies (tax/subsidies, regulation, and/or public production decisions) by governments where externalities in hydrocarbon development exist. By participating in the energy sector, a government could achieve potential improvements in social welfare with the appropriate policies. Policy that would correct for all distortions and market failures would be optimal. However, if corrective policy that addresses all distortions in a market is not a practical alternative, the "second best" criterion could be considered.

Under second-best, policy making takes the conditions in those sectors of the economy outside its mandate as given. The problem with the second-best approach is that in many cases these givens do not necessarily correspond with what may be optimal.[18] As a practical matter then, there is no method of guaranteeing that piecemeal policy will improve social welfare. Unfortunately, in practice most public-sector decision making is best characterized by the methods of the second-best approach.[19]

One approach to policy making that may help to circumvent some of the difficulties associated to the second-best approach is that of evaluating efficiency gains from small policy changes in a distorted economy. Best known as the "nth-best" approach, this method examines the efficiency consequences of a very small change in, for example, some set of distortions.[20] In some respects, this may be one of the most practical means of addressing the environmental component in energy policy, even though it does possess limitations. First, local rather than global information on the relevant objectives and constraints is needed for the nth-best approach.[21] As such, the nth-best method provides a mechanism to formulate energy policy so as to address environmental requirements that may differ from one context to another. Such differences may be related to the nature and history of sectoral development in an area (e.g., consider the different environmental implications of hydrocarbon exploration and production for a region versus those related to refining and petrochemical development). Under the nth-best approach the practical information requirement for policy making reduces to a specific local rather than a global need.[22]

Second, use of nth-best methods implies no need of global rules for optimal policy. This reduces the magnitude of the policy problem to one of gathering and evaluating local information. Finally, because one is limiting the scope of policy evaluation to the effects of an incremental change in a selected set of distortions, a criterion for evaluation can be derived.[23] Nevertheless, the limitations of the nth-best approach should not be neglected. The problem of evaluating efficiency vs. equity effects of a policy adjustment is not fully resolved.[24] Even where compensation is used to meet the latter, consistently ranking different policy states remains a problem.[25] Furthermore, even if policymakers can overcome these difficulties, there is no guarantee that this process of gradual improvement will converge on a global optimum for policy choice.[26]

For any government concerned with preserving or protecting the environment, fiscal tools and regulatory powers are certainly the means of generating incentive for industry and business to behave in an environmentally sound fashion. The sensitivity of deploying certain fiscal mechanisms or regulatory limits on hydrocarbon development for environmentally driven purposes is similar to that when energy security goals are considered. It is rooted in the microeconomic and macroeconomic implications that the uses of taxation, pricing policy and regulation have on sectoral and economic growth. The problem that arises when environmental objectives are commingled in energy policy with those of energy security and optimal industry development is one of identifying the means of addressing the externalities generated during resource development. While the fiscal tools and powers of the government are certainly confiscatory in nature, the economic and social welfare conclusions of their respective use are bounded practically and politically. Consequently, a policy that incorporates environmental considerations into hydrocarbon exploitation is required to maximize social welfare in a dynamic framework, but constrained by a number of factors—including the institutional limits of public policy decision making.

CONCLUSION

Continued demand growth and reliance on conventional hydrocarbons to satisfy consumption needs in North America will keep energy policy at the heart of economic and political concerns. The gradual depletion of conventional resources on the continent will fuel these forces in both Canada and the United States. Considerations of national security will ensure that reliance on foreign energy sources will keep North America's attention on questions of hydrocarbon development for some time. Complicating the scenario for energy policy today and in the future will be questions concerning the preservation and continued survival of the North America environment. These forces pose a fundamental problem to policymakers aiming to maximize social welfare: policies must balance the implicit trade off between the economically optimal time path and structure of hydrocarbon development while also achieving environmental objectives.

Given the limited tools available to policymakers, not to mention the microeconomic and macroeconomic implications of their respective use, the matter of delineating policy to achieve simultaneously energy security and environmental preservation, becomes a stiff task. The limitations on general policy rules are practical in nature since one is forced to contend not only with potentially conflicting interests but also with uncertainties regarding the criteria for maximizing social welfare. While the most desired policy is clearly that which comes closest to maximizing social welfare, these practical constraints can impede progress and steer policy making in different directions. Consequently, policy designed according to nth-best methods (i.e., where very small policy changes are evaluated) is one possible, albeit limited, option for policy makers wrestling with the constraints and objectives of energy policy in Canada and the United States.

NOTES

1. R. G. Wirick, "Managing Canadian Energy Demand and Supply," in E. Carmichael and C. Herrera, eds., *Canada's Energy Policy and Beyond* (Toronto: C. D. Howe Institute, 1985), p. 72.
2. Ibid.
3. Ibid.
4. Ibid., p. 71.
5. David K. H. Begg, *The Rational Expectations Revolution in Macroeconomics* (Baltimore: The Johns Hopkins University Press, 1982), p. 69.
6. Ibid.
7. This assumes that treating the development of hydrocarbons purely as a public good question is not an option.
8. John Rowse, "Depletable Resource Recovery Profiles and Efficient Resource Allocation," Department of Economics, University of Calgary, Discussion Paper No. 108 (1988), pp. 16-17.
9. Ibid.
10. Brian L. Scarfe, "The Federal Budget and Energy Program, October 28, 1980: A Review," in *Canadian Public Policy* 7, no.1 (1981), p. 3.
11. Ibid.
12. Robin Boadway and Neil Bruce, *Welfare Economics* (New York: Basil Blackwell Inc., 1984), p. 112-113.
13. It can be argued that, in the long run, guaranteeing the preservation of the environment will only enhance future economic and business prospects for a society since these are conditional on the physical welfare of its agents, at the least.
14. J. P. Gould and C. E. Ferguson, *Microeconomic Theory* (Homewood, Illinois: Richard D. Irwin, Inc., 1980), p. 462.
15. Ibid.

16. Ibid.
17. Ibid.
18. Boadway and Bruce, op. cit., pp. 131-133.
19. Ibid.
20. Ibid., p. 133.
21. Ibid., pp. 133-34.
22. Ibid.
23. Ibid.
24. Ibid.
25. Ibid.
26. Ibid., p. 134.

Chapter 5

Environment, Free Trade, and Canada–U.S. Relations

John E. Carroll

In recent years, every Canadian has confronted a dilemma that is unknown to Americans. That dilemma consists of a choice: to support a strong, politically independent Canada in which most of the real decisions affecting Canada's future are made in Ottawa, Toronto, and other of Canada's major cities and centers of governance, and thereby live with a "weaker" economy (i.e., higher unemployment, lower material living standard) or to endure a strong political dependency on Washington and Wall Street and thereby enjoy a "stronger" economy and a more materially rich life-style with greater consumption possibilities.

Canadians appear to vacillate between these two choices. When the pendulum swings too far toward U.S. dominance, resentment builds and the pendulum swings back. Likewise, when the pendulum swings too far toward Canadian nationalism and greater political independence, fear and frustration take over and the desire seems to grow again for greater integration with the United States. Today, in the second term of the Progressive Conservative government of Brian Mulroney and with the installation and implementation of the first free trade agreement in the history of Canada-U.S. relations, the pendulum has swung far in the direction of integration with Canada's southern neighbor. This follows a period in the late 1960s and through the 1970s of greater Canadian nationalism, as evidenced by the strong rallying around Prime Minister Trudeau, the passage and implementation of the Foreign Investment Review Act (FIRA), curbs on U.S. ownership in Canada, and numerous cultural and other measures to foster a separate Canadian identity.

A DILEMMA CHARACTERISTICALLY CANADIAN

Peering more broadly at the whole of Canadian history, one can see a nation that gave up its colonial status with Great Britain very slowly, that endured a very strong British presence in (some would say dominance of) its economy well into the present century, and that willingly accepted a dominant U.S. presence (and U.S. ownership over its natural resources) for much of the post-WW II period. It was not until the early or mid-1970s that Canada began, under Prime Minister Trudeau and important provincial government leadership, to feel its oats as it were, to experience an individual sense of destiny, a singular identity, to feel in control of its own future.

Canada, given its rather small population on an enormous land mass with great natural resource wealth, exhibits a frontier mentality with respect to natural resources, with respect to development of those resources, to industrial development, and to matters of scale and proportion. This kind of mentality also developed in the American West. However, there is a feeling in many parts of the United States that the time for a frontier mentality has gone. We now find a "spaceship mentality," which accepts the notion that there are limits to growth and size. This spaceship mentality, while not unheard of in Canada, is not as deeply embedded in the national psyche, given Canada's aforementioned landmass-to-population ratio. It is natural that Canada embraces a form of expansive mentality, a mentality to match, perhaps, its expansiveness of land and resources. In a country feeling its (independent) oats after a long period of external economic and, to a degree, political domination, it is doubly natural for such a mentality to take hold.

CHANGING PLACES

Because of the vociferousness and longevity of the bilateral acid rain debate, many Americans, and perhaps Canadians as well, will be surprised at this depiction of a somewhat environmentally insensitive Canada and a relatively more environmentally sensitive United States. And yet, prior to 1978, the first year of the acid rain debate, Canada, in terms of transboundary environmental relations, had seemed to be the sinner, and downstream/downwind U.S. locales were increasingly regarding themselves as the ecologically victimized, the sinned against. Megascale and largely energy-related developments along the southern border of Canada, that nation's development corridor as it was coming to be called, threatened or gave the perception of threatening relatively pristine northern U.S. environments, such as the Boundary Waters Canoe Area in Minnesota, Flathead Lake in Montana, Lake Champlain in Vermont and New York, or already highly polluted U.S. environments that, it was perceived, could take no more.

An increasing U.S. emphasis on environmental issues, such as wilderness preservation, especially after the first Earth Day (1970), was inevitably clashing with Canada's economic and political coming of age. Further evidence of a difference in attitude between the two countries was (and still is) the ambient air quality and water quality objectives approach to pollution control espoused by Canada, versus the more purist air quality and water quality standards approach embraced by the United States. The former involves consideration of and acceptance of the natural diluting capacity of bodies of water and masses of air, a perhaps more pragmatic approach to the less practical but more pristine U.S. approach of set maximum and average acceptable effluent and discharge standards at the pollutant emission site, regardless of the condition or capacity of the recipient air or water.

The two approaches are incompatible and each reveals a national philosophy: Canada's natural view (given its relatively small number of people [27 million], large land mass, and vast resources) that resources are there to be used; and the increasing U.S. sense that American ecosystems have had enough, regardless of absorption capacity, and that it is now time to control pollution at the source.

In actual practice the two nations are not quite as far apart as it would seem, since U.S. talk about preservation is often just rhetoric, and a more utilitarian philosophy often prevails in real behavior. The one caveat to this generalization, however, is the greater U.S. access to and willingness to use the courts to stop or delay government, a technique that does have some effect in closing the gap between preservationist rhetoric and practical reality, especially when that preservationist rhetoric is clearly embedded in the law.

Canada-U.S. environmental relations, like economic and political relations, have swung from one side to the other. At various times and places each nation has had opportunity to play the role of the sinner and the sinned against. In recent decades, and especially in the 1970s, Canada has often played the role of sinner for reasons aforementioned. But by the late 1970s, with acid rain emerging on the scene, the pendulum swung in the opposite direction, and the two nations were as two ships passing in the night. Canadian concern over acid rain and the damage it could cause to Canada's natural ecosystem and economy has been so vigorous, so steady, and so longstanding (from 1978 to the present) that most people today who have any familiarity with Canada-U.S. environmental relations now think of the much-larger United States as the sinner and Canada as the sinned against. In its sharp concerns over acid rain, Canada has been mirroring the Swedish and general Scandinavian situation of a decade before: a highly vulnerable country (Canada, Scandinavia) downwind of toxic acidic air pollutant emissions from nations upwind (the United States, the United Kingdom, continental Europe), with no control and little influence over the external emissions damaging its territory.

There are a number of good reasons why Canada should be and, in fact, has been very much concerned over the issue of acid rain:

- Canada is a highly vulnerable territory (i.e., chemically and geologically unbuffered against incoming acid pollution, whether through wet or through dry deposition);

- it is in a position downwind of enormous acid pollution emissions coming from the United States (more than 50 percent of Canada's acidic deposition comes from the United States);

- it has a highly educated population very well aware of the problem and its ramifications; and

- it is economically dependent on the wild natural environment (for tourism), and this resource is directly vulnerable to damage, or is perceived as vulnerable.

Canada does have an Achilles heel on this question, given its own dependence on metal smelting and the role that such smelting plays in generating pollution emission (and is, in fact, responsible for some small quantity of acidic pollution crossing the border southward and doing damage in the United States). But Canada, seeking recognition as a world leader among the nations vulnerable to acid rain, has had to protect its credibility by taking strong and costly action to curb its own emissions. This it has done. In contrast, the United States is recognized, along with the United Kingdom and the hapless and highly polluting Eastern European nations, as among the world leaders responsible for acid rain damage to itself as well as to others. As luck would have it, however, there is further imbalance between the United States and Canada gravitating against significant U.S. action to rectify the problem: the United States sees itself as less vulnerable to ecological damage, does not endanger a large element of its national economy by enduring the problem, and is not as interested in the question or as willing to pay the cost of doing something about it as is its northern neighbor. Thus, the imbalance and the political and diplomatic as well as environmental problem has persisted for a dozen years, and will certainly persist, particularly at the ecological level, for some considerable time.

THE REAL ISSUE

The highly publicized national and international debate over acid rain and transboundary acidic pollution has clearly cast Canada into the environmental victim role and the United States into the environmental culprit role. What this scenario hides, however, is that the United States and Canada are quite equal when it comes to their more important combined role relative to the rest of the world. Both Canadians and Americans are consuming the energy and natural resources of the planet and the planetary ecosystem itself at a per-capita rate much higher than that of the people of any other nations. U.S. figures for 1980 indicated that the United States comprised 6 percent of the planet's population and was widely accepted to be consuming about 38 percent of the world's energy and natural resources. More recent figures indicate that Americans constitute 5 percent of the world population and consume more than 25 percent of the world's resources. (The lower population and consumption figures represent a relative increase in the population of other nations and some decline, as well, in the U.S. economic role in the world.) And, although the Canadian population is only 10 percent that of the United States, the Canadian per-capita consumption figure is slightly higher. The important point to note, however, is that the two nations, separately or in combination, far outpace the rest of the planet's population in matters of consumption. They are thus responsible for far more than their share of global impact and global depletion, and lead the world in this area.

Realization of such should signal to the reader the relative insignificance of their bilateral relationship environmentally when compared against this much more significant context, which argues forcefully that they share quite equally (relative to population size) with respect to the rest of the world. This is the real issue. They are both, environmentally speaking, sinners of great magnitude, and it makes the characterization of either as sinned against rather nonsensical. Both have major (if not overwhelming) responsibility for the problems of climatic change, holes in the ozone layer, deforestation (tropical as well as temperate), desertification, and oceanic contamination, among others. This does not negate the role played by European countries of both East and West, Japan, and others, but rather to acknowledge the considerable absolute impact of one large industrial North American country, the United States, and, more important, the per-capita consumption figures represented in both the American and Canadian societies. Accusation of guilt or innocence between these two nations pales when compared to the much more significant global picture, and the role of the two great North American industrial economies and societies within that whole.

FREE TRADE AND THE PROBLEM OF CONSUMPTION

What do these things have to do with free trade? On September 23, 1988, the *Globe and Mail* of Toronto, Canada's largest national newspaper, published my remarks:

> Free trade across borders equals increased consumption of goods
> and services. Increased consumption of goods and services
> equals increased industrial activity and thus increased emissions
> of pollutants into both air and water. Increased air pollution
> emissions leads to increased acid rain. Canada, in opting for
> free trade, has opted, knowingly or unknowingly, for increased
> acid rain. And this from a nation which has prided itself
> throughout the 1980s as a leader among nations in the battle to
> reduce acid rain.

Preposterous, you say? This may seem preposterous to the reader not accustomed to making such linkages. But it is true nevertheless. Who supports free trade in the Canada-U.S. bilateral relationship? Both national governments, many (though not all) state and provincial governments, and a very large proportion of national and multinational banks, business firms, and other such institutions support free trade. Would such institutions support a trade strategy that led to less consumption, less production, and thus less business activity? Highly unlikely. It is because free trade rationalizes the economic relationship and leads to what is on net increased business and industrial activity, not less such activity, that it is embraced by virtually all the powers that be with the exception of those that are competitively direct losers. Increased pollution (and acid rain) resulting from increased production and consumption of goods and services is simply another cost of free trade to be joined to various other costs and then measured against the various benefits. This is not designed as an argument against free trade but as merely a call to recognize its role in the environmental calculation. Needless to say, it would be well nigh impossible to assess with any precision the specific net difference in pollution emission with or without reduction in trade barriers, but there can be no doubt that they are increased, and perhaps increased significantly.

When the Mulroney government came to power in 1984 and espoused free trade with the United States as the top priority issue in Canada-U.S. relations, Canada could no longer afford to maintain the vigor of the acid rain complaint, which had been an authentic irritant in the bilateral relationship. Acid rain as a diplomatic issue then became a bit risky. Little did anyone realize at that time that Canada was not only sacrificing its claim to environmental purity and acid rain leadership on the altar of free trade but that it was also in fact risking an increase in transborder pollution. As a result, it not only further endangered its acid-vulnerable ecosystem but its credibility as environmental leader as well. All of this speaks to a reduction in meaning of a border between these two nations as both implicate themselves as well as each other in the quest for higher levels of economic development. Not only does the will not exist to reduce acid-causing emissions, particularly in the United States, but there is some evidence of will in both countries to cause an increase in those emissions to achieve other ends that remain to this day higher ends, higher purposes.

ENVIRONMENTAL AND BILATERAL IMPLICATIONS

What all of this implies for the environment in the next few years is continued deterioration. In spite of all the public attention, the public debate, the results of continued research, and the organized efforts of environmentalists both within each nation and transnationally, there is no real sign of emission reduction in sight. It is true that the rhetoric, especially in the early 1980s, has been very strong. But perhaps we can agree with the telephone company when it tells us that talk is (and has been) cheap. Action to match such talk has been entirely lacking. The will to address directly the problem through emission reductions rather than by conducting more research is simply not there, and presumably will not be there until the situation gets worse. The argument is sometimes made that we do not know enough about pollution impacts to justify the expense of reducing emissions. If that is so, then do we know enough to justify increasing them (which we have been doing)? And cannot the argument be turned around and the point made that, if we do not know enough to reduce emissions, then do we know enough to maintain them at present levels? No, we know what we want: to be able at least to maintain present levels of emission, and perhaps to increase them somewhat. In knowing what we want, we know enough to make the argument fit our ends. In the near term, therefore, the environment will continue to deteriorate.

What does all this imply for Canada-U.S. relations, and particularly for environmental relations, in the next few years? It implies that the environment will not be a significant irritant, not because it is not deteriorating—for it is—but because the balance between the circumstance of each nation is evening out. Without a fair degree of imbalance, or at least perceived imbalance, there is no diplomatic problem. Both nations are committed by their actions to higher economic development goals, and importantly in ways that are increasingly integrated. Such integration creates a climate wherein the bilateral relationship remains smooth. This climate will likely remain stable until such time as the Canadian people feel undue influence in their affairs coming from south of the border, at which time they will once again become nationalistic. Rifts will then recur in the relationship. The pendulum is ever swinging in one direction or the other, toward greater Canadian independence or toward greater Canadian dependence.

The economic consequences of these events are promising in the short term (and as we conventionally measure such things in terms of jobs, prices, availability of greater quantities of consumer goods and services at lower cost, etc.). They are not, for broader global economic reasons, good in the longer run, given enhanced tendency toward personal indebtedness, reduced savings, and other matters that threaten global (or at least Western) economic destabilization. The real costs can be measured only in the erosion of the foundation of humanity, that is, the erosion of the ecosystem upon which we are all dependent.

Perhaps the great lesson that this North American experience provides to Europeans is the consequence of economic integration. Although integration has its advantages, whether in the form of free trade in North America or in the form of an integrated economy and common currency in post-1992 Europe, it also has clear costs. Often these costs can be environmental, especially as long as the tools of integration are used primarily to enhance economic development. As long as the dash to economic development, as that phrase is conventionally interpreted, continues in the traditional unidirectional manner, the environment is at risk and will continue on the path to deterioration until such time as it is no longer able to support the human species. The health of bilateral relations, of diplomatic relations, on the contrary, is much more dependent upon binational balance, or at least the perception of binational balance, and is not related directly to environmental deterioration. Free trade and economic integration, while containing potential to put the environment at risk, lend themselves to reduction of damage to diplomacy, to bilateral relations between these two North American neighbors.

Such linkages between free trade and production of pollution are rarely made and almost never thought about. The average person thinks of international trade as simply rationalizing a naturally imbalanced system of resource and human skills distribution, enabling human societies to have many things they could not otherwise have, and at cheaper cost. Fair enough, and such is indeed a traditional rationale for free trade. But this is a much more insidious (from the ecological and perhaps from the social and psychological perspective as well) end result (and I would argue purpose) of free trade: to encourage greater net consumption, perhaps at levels well beyond the real needs of people (although the latter, what constitutes the real needs of people, is always a personal and individual judgment). As stated above, increased consumption, increased consumer demand, for whatever reason, increases production of goods and services, increases the use (and burning) of energy (including principally nonrenewable forms), causes by-product air, water, and all other forms of pollution, and fulfills what many in other societies are increasingly calling unnecessary needs. If free trade does these things, then a Canada-U.S. free trade agreement not only causes more pollution in North America within each nation but more transboundary pollution as well, and, irony of ironies, more acid rain within and across the borders of both Canada and the United States. The latter circumstance may be consistent with U.S. recalcitrance on doing something about acid rain, but it is certainly ironic in its apparent opposition to Canada's otherwise consistent attempt to reduce acid rain emissions. Joint action toward free trade is evidence that both nations view their interests and their role in the world as very much the same, as indeed reality indicates it is, regardless of rhetoric over acid rain or, for that matter, rhetoric arguing on behalf of a separate identity for Canada. On perceived larger issues such as free trade (and national defense, etc.), sameness and mutual identification clearly prevails.

A SIMILARITY OF INTEREST AND SOME DIFFERENCES

What we may thus conclude is that the interests of the United States and Canada appear identical. Through its behavior on free trade and in other ways, Canada has made a clear decision to assume a commonality of interests and to act accordingly. And it might be suggested that other external circumstances, globally and intercontinentally, will probably make even less significant what Canada-U.S. differences there, in fact, really are.

Further, today's world is full of enormous strains on sovereignty, not the least of which are international and global environmental stresses, whose effect and whose resolution cannot be accommodated within the confines of traditional notions of the nation-state. These stresses create considerable uncertainty about what the future holds for the nation-state, for national security, and for environmental security. In the case of Canada, such uncertainty is further compounded by the failure of the Meech Lake Accord and the renewed threat of Quebec's breaking away from Canada as a whole, as well as what this would do to the Atlantic provinces, which would be separated from the rest of Canada by Quebec. These problems are not directly related to environmental issues, but they will influence the future course of events, making even more speculative what might be coming down the pike in our increasingly unstable ecological, economic, and geopolitical milieu.

Policy prescriptions, given global ecological realities (which we are still most reluctant to accept, given the threat they represent to the direction of growth and the course of development and progress as we have come to define these terms), can only be those that relate to significant reduction in consumption and reduction in demand for all types of natural resources, including energy resources. This holds whether or not such significant reduction is or is not currently politically feasible. (Most would hold that it is not at this time.)

POLICY PRESCRIPTION

A central conclusion of this chapter is that, in terms of the environment and free trade, future policy and diplomatic differences between Canada and the United States are as nothing compared to the environmental, energy, and natural resource differences that exist between these two North American nations combined and the rest of the world. There will always be differences between the United States and

Canada, environmental and otherwise, but, as has been discussed, these two nations are traveling down essentially the same path. As a result, it seems that the gap between North America and the Third World, and between North America and the rest of the industrial world when it comes to per-capita energy and resource consumption, will persist. Policy prescriptions must take account of these realities and respond accordingly.

Policy prescriptions that would close the gap between the per-capita energy and resource consumption of Canada and the United States as a whole on the one hand and the rest of the industrial world on the other, are of the highest order of importance. So are policy prescriptions that reduce the role that these combined North American industrial nations are playing relative to consumption of their fair share relative to the share available to the two-thirds of humanity who occupy the so-called Third World. Also key are policy prescriptions aimed at rectifying the imbalance between humanity and the planetary ecosystem relative to global change, to climatic change, to damage to the ozone layer, to global deforestation (tropical and temperate), to soil depletion and desertification, to oceanic contamination, and to air and water quality deterioration.

Clearly, all of these policy prescriptions would reduce, in a significant way, the per-capita energy and natural resource consumption that now characterizes both North American industrial nations. Just as clearly, they would threaten the contemporary life-style of mainstream North Americans living on both sides of the Canada-U.S. border. They would also raise uncomfortable values, ethics, and moral choice questions. Yet it is only through a change of values that crucial environmental problems can be addressed.

This chapter raises a linkage between free trade and provision of the means to live an ever-more consumptive life-style than exists at present. If such linkage exists in reality, and I believe it does, then free trade appears to exacerbate rather than to resolve the problem. It would not be correct to assume that this chapter advocates protectionism, for protectionism does not necessarily result in an improved environment, either. What is needed, therefore, is to address directly the problem through policy prescriptions that directly aim at the aforementioned high levels of per-capita consumption.

Such policy prescriptions can work only if they accomplish two ends: to remove subsidies that either encourage fossil fuel consumption or discourage consumption of recyclable materials, and to promote more energy-efficient domestic and work arrangements. Only through using such a combination of incentives and disincentives can Canada and the United States really address the problem. The same prescriptive policy could be endorsed for both nations; and, coincidentally, such an approach would reduce or eliminate differences related to various transboundary environmental problems.

Such policy prescriptions have not been politically realistic up to this time. Nonetheless, increasing scientific and public concern over climate change, holes in the ozone layer, forest destruction, and increased public recognition of the need for life-style changes may make such approaches politically more feasible. And current heightened concerns over instability in the Middle East, especially if extensive loss of North American lives should ever ensue, increases the realization in North American society of the true cost of the oil consumption habit, given that half of that habit is fueled by imports. Hence, circumstances, ecological and political, may well contribute to changed realities in the near future. With such a change in reality, much may be achieved vis-à-vis energy and environmental conservation that has not heretofore been achievable. With such an achievement these two great North American industrial nations may begin to take their rightful place within the broader community of nations. Reduction in conflict, both within North America and between North America and other world regions, and, as well, between North America and the ecosystem of the planet, will result. Such constitutes true rationalization of social and economic opportunity, and the underpinning, therefore, of trade that is truly free.

Chapter 6

The Political Communication Systems of Environmental Groups: A Canadian–American Comparison

Mary Ann E. Steger, Nicholas P. Lovrich, Jr., John C. Pierce, and Brent S. Steel

Public policy disputes increasingly turn on scientific and technical issues. Those issues challenge the public's capacity for understanding and influencing the course of government action (Nelkin 1979). Environmental politics, for example, is one policy area in which the public is likely to be at a disadvantage when trying to exercise informed influence. Environmental interest groups, in their lobbying efforts, often serve as important mechanisms for pressing the public's concerns in this scientifically and technically complex policy area (Milbrath 1984). This role of interest groups is especially important when one considers the information-sharing function those groups perform in modern, postindustrial democracies, what A. Paul Pross defines as policy-relevant "communication" (1986, p.88) and Jeffery M. Berry terms "educating the public" (1984, p.5). In their role as information sharers, environmental interest groups constitute a critical link between their members and policy-making elites.

This chapter examines the political communication systems of environmental groups in the province of Ontario and the state of Michigan. Two related questions are explored: How do environmental groups engage in political communication in the environmental policy area? What is the nature of organizational communication with government officials in the environmental policy area? Both questions deal with the information-sharing activities of environmental organizations; the first focuses on the structure of these activities, and the second on the political uses of this information. It is expected that information-sharing activities as well as the political uses of information-sharing will be affected by the organizational characteristics of the environmental groups, the distinctive political cultures of the United States and Canada, and the political differences associated with parliamentary and presidential structures of government.

THE CANADIAN AND AMERICAN CONTEXTS

Canada and the United States are both postindustrial democracies with a common legacy. Even so, the two nations have distinct political cultures (see Gibbons and Nevitte 1985, Horowitz 1966, Presthus 1974, Lipset 1985) and different structures of government. The Canadian political culture is broadly thought to be more organic and collectivist in nature than its American counterpart, while the American political culture is seen as reflecting a Lockean individualistic conception of society (Lipset 1985). The Canadian policy-making system has been characterized as closed rather than open, with structures that tend to be hierarchically organized and based only to a limited extent on a pluralistic, competitive approach to decision making (Presthus 1974, Pross 1975). As a result, there is less of an attempt by Canadian elites to generate public support for policy issues than there is in the American system. In contrast, the American policy-making system reflects a pluralistic, competitive approach to decision making; the emphasis is on conflict-oriented techniques directed toward arousing public opinion to achieve political objectives (Pross 1975, p.19).

Robert Presthus (1974, pp. 212-213) summarizes the interaction between political culture and system structure as follows:

> [In Canada] the decisive factor is probably the organic conception of society and the deferential patterns of authority which underline the assumption that leaders will act in the community interest without public scrutiny. The parliamentary system, with its centralization of policy decision and quasi-participative system, is the logical institutionalization of this conception of society. Equally, the diffusion of power institutionalized in the American separation of powers system is similarly apposite to the major underlying conceptions of the American political culture, including an historic fear of government.

This comparison leads to the conclusion that environmental groups in Canada and the United States operate in quite different cultural and political systems as they act to influence policy making. Students of interest groups tend to believe, of course, that such groups represent "political communication mechanisms capable of adapting to the policy system in which they are located" (Pross 1975, p. 27).

The environmental policy-making systems of Ontario and Michigan—the two research sites of this study—reflect the centralized versus fragmented nature of their respective national-level political systems. In Ontario, power is centralized in the majority party (or coalition) government, which acts through the premier and the cabinet and controls the legislative assembly. Two cabinet ministers are concerned with environmental issues, the Minister of the environment and the minister of natural resources, and both maintain control over policy making in their respective areas. The chief administrative officers in these ministries, however, are deputy ministers appointed by the premier. The Environmental Assessment Board is a major actor in provincial environmental policy making, but the decisions made by the board can be overruled by the cabinet. In Michigan, power over environmental policy making is dispersed among various elected and appointed officials, including the governor, the Senate and House of the Michigan legislature, the Joint Committee on Administrative Rules (which must sign off on any administrative rule), the Air Quality Control Commission (a body appointed by the governor that issues permits and notices of noncompliance to industry), and the Michigan Department of Natural Resources.

Cross-national differences in the structure of the policy process and in government institutions are likely to affect groups' access as well as the strategies and tactics they use to influence decision makers and to communicate information. The fragmented structure of the American system allows for access at many points, both at national and state levels of government (Jones 1984). In the more hierarchically organized Canadian system, access is restricted. Thus, in his comparative study of welfare reform in Canada and the United States, Christopher Leman (1980, p.158) made this observation:

> [The] two countries differed sharply in the extent to which outsiders had access to knowledge and power in welfare debates. U.S. experts, media, and interests participated actively in debates on welfare policy, unlike their Canadian counterparts . . . While U.S. policy-making circles were remarkably porous to the entry of outside participants, Canadian circles seemed hermetically sealed.

Consequently, in the Canadian policy-making system, interest groups must adapt to a process of elite accommodation (Presthus 1974), while the American groups must operate in an open and competitive system.

GROUP ACCESS AND TACTICS IN ONTARIO AND MICHIGAN

To explore how cross-national differences in political systems and political culture may affect environmental group access and tactics, interviews were held with twenty-four government officials and directors of prominent environmental organizations in Ontario and Michigan.[1] Since all interviewees were promised anonymity, none of the comments mentioned below is attributed to its original source.

Policy-making elites in Ontario agree that the provincial government, meaning the premier and cabinet, is very important in environmental policy making. The government creates policy, establishes regulations, and is viewed as having broad administrative discretion. Ontario elites believe that the environmental minister's office is very well connected to the environmental community, and that groups are in regular contact with the ministry. Most environmental organizations lobby various ministers (as well as other government officials) by letter, and a few have representatives that meet personally with cabinet ministers and their deputy ministers. Many groups also have regular contacts with members of the legislative assembly, usually through letters, newsletters, and meetings. As one might expect in a system emphasizing elite accommodation, the Ontario interviewees believe that groups taking a conciliatory rather than a confrontational approach are most effective in their contacts with government officials. Environmental groups rarely have access to civil service employees in the ministries, and it was reported that some ministry staff resent environmental organizations because they are seen as having the ear of the current minister.

There is little coordination and centralization of policy-making power evident in the Michigan elite's picture of the state's environmental policy system. The state legislature is considered to be one of the most prominent actors, but it seldom speaks with one voice on environmental issues. Policy proposals that manage to obtain bipartisan support are subject to rules made by the legislature's Joint Committee on Administrative Rules (JCAR). Elites in Michigan view the committee as the key obstructionist element on environmental issues because of its pro-industry bias viewpoint. Several interviewees accused JCAR of letting this bias influence its decisions on administrative rules. Given the power of this committee, agency personnel are said to withdraw rules they know will not pass JCAR review.

The interviewees in Michigan agree that no one policy actor has enough power to centralize decision making on environmental issues. Group leaders, consequently, feel they must maintain contacts with as many actors in the policy process as possible. Most statewide groups have developed relationships with people in the governor's office, top-level and mid-level people in the Department of Natural Resources, and members of the relevant legislative committees. In addition, interviewees report that some environmental groups are asked to make recommendations to the governor's office on appointees to the Air Quality Control Commission.

It is not surprising that cross-national political system differences would affect how policymakers and interest group leaders see the proper role of organized groups. The Ontario interviewees believe that, in Canada, groups serve a watchdog function and that their primary role is to educate the public and government on issues. Groups in Michigan also are viewed as providers of information, but they are considered to be only one among many competing voices; utility companies, industry, chambers of commerce, and labor are also in the choir in question. Interviewees in Michigan believe that groups need to develop political power to be effective. This might be accomplished in several ways, including having staff in the state capital who have regular contacts with state officials, showing legislators that the group's position is backed by a large membership, and getting involved directly in electoral politics in the form of either initiative or candidate support.

As expected, the elites interviewed in Michigan and Ontario confirm that group tactics are different in the two political systems. In Ontario, as in Michigan, environmental groups engage in a variety of tactics, but the Ontario groups are seen as pursuing active, quiet involvement in the policy process. In contrast, environmental groups in Michigan must be visible and powerful in order to compete in Michigan's highly fragmented power structure. One elite informant believes that the questions period held regularly in the legislative assembly presents the most effective opportunity for influence for groups in Ontario. There is no analogue for the question period in a presidential system.

A tactic that is considered important in both countries is the use of the media, especially the press. An important caveat concerning media use in Ontario was offered by one informant, who observed that the media play a less important role when environmental organizations are granted access to government and believe that their viewpoints are heard. If the provincial government does not allow this access, the use of the media becomes more important. A major difference in tactics between Ontario and Michigan environmental groups involves the use of court suits. Canadian groups are not permitted to sue the Crown, and this restriction results in a less adversarial relationship between interest groups and government in Ontario than in the United States. In Michigan, of course, court suits filed by environmental groups are a common phenomenon.

GROUP CHARACTERISTICS AND RESOURCES

Environmental organizations in Michigan and Ontario must adapt to two different political cultures and systems as they perform their information-sharing role and try to influence environmental policy making. Cross-national differences in group tactics should be evident, but "the intensity of interest group organization . . . . and the attending practice of lobbying [in Canada and the United States] are . . . . different only in degree" (Presthus 1974, p. 213). This difference in degree is probably related to the organizational characteristics and resources of these groups as much as it is affected by cultural and system differences. There will be a gap between the communication and influence capabilities of well-financed, skilled, organized groups and those with fewer resources (Canadian Study of Parliament Group 1989).

Environmental organizations may be categorized as citizen groups (King and Walker 1989), amateur groups, and theme-oriented or issue groups (Canadian Study of Parliament Group 1989). They are not usually considered to be as well financed and as skilled as are groups representing business or professional interests. There is, however, significant variation in the monetary, membership, and organizational resources found among environmental groups in both Ontario and Michigan. Many groups have professional, full-time paid staffs, enjoy substantial numbers of dues-paying members, attract significant numbers of volunteers, collect considerable funding from sources outside the group, and maintain national or provincial/state affiliations.

The type of membership a group has, individual versus organizational, may affect the group's ability to influence policy. Environmental groups usually have more individual members than organizational members when they are compared with groups in the profit-making sector (King and Walker 1989). The type of membership found in a group may be as important as the typical monetary resources associated with interest groups: a large annual budget and the ability to finance full- and part-time staff members. Environmental organizations with institutional members have the potential to communicate their positions across a broad spectrum of society. If their organizational members include business and government groups, they may be perceived as more representative and powerful than groups having only individuals as their membership base.

The network in which an environmental organization is found may also affect its ability to communicate and exercise influence. Groups can increase the strength of their environmental message by being part of a coalition, but one opinion is that a "coalition is only as strong as its weakest link" (Canadian Study of Parliament Group 1989, p. 4). In addition, groups may be networking with their parent organizations-national or provincial or state affiliates. These affiliations allow groups with few resources to benefit from the greater resources of the national provincial or state affiliate.

THE ONTARIO AND MICHIGAN STUDY OF ENVIRONMENTAL GROUPS

The Sample of Groups

An organizational profile was included in a mailed questionnaire survey conducted in the summer and fall of 1987 of directors and members of environmental organizations in Ontario and Michigan. Separate lists of environmental groups in the province and the state were developed from several sources: (1) contacts with directors of organizations that participated in an acid rain survey conducted by these researchers in 1986; (2) personal interviews with government officials and environmental group leaders in 1987, which were summarized above; (3) mailing lists provided by coalitions of groups and groups that had a chapter form of organization; and (4) an extensive catalog of groups in Ontario prepared by the Ontario Environmental Network.

All of Michigan's 71 known state and local environmental groups, including affiliates of national organizations, were contacted. Of the several hundred environmental organizations active in Ontario, a representative cross-section of 98 groups was chosen. The larger number of groups in Ontario reflects a plethora of newly formed, locally based associations. Such groups were previously in evidence in Michigan, but more recently many such groups have folded into or have been replaced by larger groups. From this initial contact, 63 Ontario groups and 43 Michigan groups agreed to distribute survey questionnaires to their members, their staff, and to members of their respective boards of directors. In Michigan, 23 of the 43 participating groups (53 percent) completed detailed organizational profiles; in Ontario, 38 of the 63 participating groups (60 percent) returned their completed profiles.

Measure of Organizational Resources

Group leaders (voluntary or paid) were asked to provide information on a range of organizational characteristics, and measures were created to represent the following list: the presence or absence of a paid staff;[2] the size of the group's annual budget;[3] the number of volunteer workers upon which the organization can call;[4] whether the group has individual memberships; whether the group has organizational members (environmental groups, clubs, civic organizations, governments, research, business, or labor organizations);[5] the extent to which funds are raised from dues;[6] the extent to which funds are raised from external sources;[7] whether the group is organized into chapters; whether there is a national or provincial/state affiliation;[8] and whether the group has a tax-exempt status.

Table 6.1 reports the results of a principal components (varimax rotated) factor analysis of the measures of organizational characteristics, with the indicators for type of organizational members omitted. Three quite distinct dimensions appeared for the 11 organizational characteristics. The first dimension was defined by four measures of the groups' financial resources: size of the annual budget, extent of external funding, presence of a paid staff, and tax-exempt status. The second dimension related to human resources—whether there are chapters (which have their own members), the number of volunteer workers, individual memberships, and the proportion of funding raised from member dues. The third dimension contained provisions for organizational memberships and the presence of affiliations at the provincial or state or national levels; this dimension represents the network resources of groups.

MEASURES OF INFORMATION USE AND GOVERNMENT CONTACTS

Measures also were created from the following information reported by group leaders: external sources of information;[9] types of information sources;[10] the means used to communicate with members;[11] the staff time devoted to information transmission;[12] frequency of interaction with

Table 6.1

**A Principal Component (Varimax Rotated)
Factor Matrix of Measures of Group Resources**

Group Resources (N=61)	Factor 1	Factor 2	Factor 3
Size of Annual Budget	.83524	.01798	-.10365
Extent of External Funding	.81708	-.02482	.05581
Paid Staff (1=yes;0=no)	.73049	-.15692	-.22121
Tax Exempt Status			
(1=yes;0=no)	.66264	.19025	.12727
Organized into Chapters			
(1=yes;0=no)	.18209	.68397	-.25315
Number of Volunteers	.19227	.67746	.21098
Individual Members			
(1=yes;0=no)	-.40016	.64235	.21596
Percent Raised from Dues	-.39511	.53442	-.16593
Groups as Members			
(1=yes;0=no)	.08243	-.12960	.79508
Provincial/State Affiliation			
(1=yes;0=no)	-.33674	.07665	.65347
National Affiliation			
(1=yes;0=no)	.34579	.32187	.42643
Eigenvalue	2.99836	1.85163	1.42997
Percentage of Variance	27.3	16.8	13.0

Cumulative Percent = 57.1

national, provincial/state, and local government officials;[13] services provided to elected officials and career civil servants;[14] and methods used to influence governmental policy making.[15]

CROSS-NATIONAL SIMILARITIES AND DIFFERENCES

Difference of means tests were performed on all of the measures described above to assess country effects. There are very few noteworthy differences among the measures of organizational characteristics, sources and types of information, and means used to communicate with members. Only one organizational characteristic—the percent of group funding that was raised by membership dues—has a statistically significant t-value, with environmental organizations in Ontario raising higher average amounts from dues than do groups in Michigan. Among the measures of types of information, Michigan groups use legal and economic resources to a greater degree than do their Ontario counterparts; the same pattern emerges in the use of newsletters, with groups in the U.S. state using this means of communication more than those in the Canadian province.

Table 6.2 presents mean values among Ontario and Michigan groups on five measures of government contacts: interactions with provincial/state officials, types of legislative and bureaucratic services provided by these groups, and types of information provided to elected officials and career civil servants. These are the only categories of group activities in which significant differences appear.

All significantly higher values are associated with the Michigan environmental groups. The Michigan groups contact state officials more-frequently than do those in Ontario, and this pattern is consistent for the measures of interactions with elected officials, top- and mid-level agency personnel, and legal and scientific experts. Given the fragmentation of power in the American political system, more-frequent contacts with all types of government officials by Michigan groups was expected.

There are no significant mean differences for three of the legislative services listed in Table 6.2. Environmental organizations in both nations provide information to their respective legislative bodies and build public support for proposals at relatively high levels (mean levels ranged from 0.61 to 0.70 on these measures), and engage in similarly low levels of campaign activity (mean values were 0.08 and 0.09). Differences, however, are evident when testifying at hearings is considered, with the Michigan groups more likely to engage in this activity than are groups in Ontario.

The environmental groups in the U.S. state provide two bureaucratic services, voicing support for agency policies and making recommendations on high-level appointees, at higher mean levels than do their Canadian counterparts. Both activities involve a more political, policy-relevant interaction with state agency personnel than the bureaucratic services in which Michigan and Ontario groups are similarly active (serving on advisory bodies and providing information on attitudes). This active political involvement on the part of the Michigan groups suggests that they are adapting to their state's political system. Cross-national differences also appear in the types of information groups provide to elected officials and to career civil servants. Michigan groups are more likely to communicate scientific and political information to both elected and bureaucratic officials than are their Ontario counterparts. This pattern also includes the communication of technical information to bureaucratic officials by the American groups.

Table 6.3 reports country percentages for the methods groups use to influence governmental policy making. The groups in this U.S. state are, again, actively involved in all types of lobbying activities to a greater degree than are the Canadian groups. Presthus (1974, p. 218) reported similar findings and drew the following conclusion:

> The historic benefices for the private sector have made lobbying less of a functional requisite in Canadian politics, i.e., governmental elites have less frequently had to be convinced of the propriety of accommodating group claims, compared with the United States.

The groups have only two relatively similar lobbying methods, namely, contacting cabinet ministers in Ontario/submitting reports to the governor's office in Michigan, and organizing political protests.

Country differences were expected on two other lobbying methods. Ontario groups were believed to be engaged in quiet techniques, such as letter writing, to a greater degree than were those in Michigan; the reverse was expected in the use of court suits. The greater American propensity for adversarial court proceedings is evident among the Michigan groups; 30 percent of them have filed court suits, compared with only 11 percent of the Ontario groups. However, the Michigan groups also write more letters (70 percent) than do their Canadian counterparts (58 percent).

Sixty-one percent of the Michigan groups have testified before legislative committees, compared with just 47 percent in Ontario. The Canadian environmental groups engage in this form of lobbying, but not

Table 6.2

Cross-National Differences (Difference of Means Tests) on Measures of Interaction with Provincial/State Officials, Legislative and Bureaucratic Services, and Types of Information Provided to Elected Officials and Career Civil Servants

	ONTARIO GROUPS (n=38)	MICHIGAN GROUPS (n=23)	
	Mean	Mean	t-Value
Frequency of Interactions with Provincial/State Officials			
—Elected Officials	3.19	3.91	-2.60**
—Top-Level Bureaucrats	3.17	4.22	-3.65***
—Mid-Level Bureaucrats	3.19	4.52	-5.21***
—Legal Experts	2.03	2.78	-2.62**
—Scientific Experts	2.67	3.74	-3.68***
Legislative Service Provided			
—Testify at hearings	0.42	0.70	-2.16*
—Provide legislative information	0.61	0.65	-0.36
—Build public support	0.61	0.70	-0.71
—Campaign support	0.08	0.09	-0.11

Bureaucratic Services Provided			
—Serve on advisory bodies	0.63	0.82	-1.72
—Provide information on attitudes	0.58	0.74	-1.29
—Support agency policies	0.42	0.74	-2.57**
—Recommendations on appointees	0.18	0.61	-3.48***
Types of Information Provided to Elected Officials			
—Scientific information	0.39	0.70	-2.37*
—Technical information	0.26	0.43	-1.34
—Legal information	0.24	0.39	-1.23
—Political information	0.50	0.78	-2.35*
—Economic information	0.42	0.43	-0.10
Types of Information Provided to Career Civil Servants			
—Scientific information	0.34	0.70	-2.82**
—Technical information	0.26	0.57	-2.36*
—Legal information	0.24	0.43	-1.56
—Political information	0.42	0.74	-2.57**
—Economic information	0.39	0.43	-0.30

*** p ≤ .001; ** p ≤ .01; * p ≤ .05

Table 6.3

Cross-National Differences in Methods Used to Influence Government Policy Making

Methods Used to Influence Government Policy Making	Percentage Using Method	
	ONTARIO GROUPS (n=38)	MICHIGAN GROUPS (n=23)
Briefs to parliamentary committees (ONT) or testifying before legislative committees (MI)	47%	61%
Briefs to cabinet ministers (ONT) or submitting reports to the governor's office (MI)	50%	52%
Appeals to executive assistants of cabinet ministers (ONT) or appeals to agency personnel (MI)	42%	74%
Briefs or appeals by outside experts —lawyers, former officials, scientists, etc.	21%	44%
Contacts with government regulatory bodies	55%	74%
Filing lawsuits	11%	30%
Instigating a letter-writing campaign	58%	70%
Building coalitions with other groups	55%	70%
Releasing information through the mass media	63%	70%
Organizing political interests	21%	26%

to the same extent as do groups in the United States. This finding is explained in Graham White's (1989) analysis of the Ontario legislative assembly. He reports that the provincial legislature has increased its capacity to act as a policy-making body within provincial government in the past several decades through a series of reforms and concludes that "interest groups in Ontario, particularly those of greater size and influence, are increasingly seeking to legitimize their positions . . . . by appearing before legislative committees" (p. 259).

Lobbying agency personnel is a method used extensively by environmental groups in Michigan (74 percent), but much less among the Ontario groups (42 percent). In the interviews that were held with government officials and group leaders in Ontario the opinion was offered that access to civil service employees is not common in the province. These results suggest that contact with ministry personnel is certainly less common in Ontario than are the same types of contacts in Michigan.

RELATIONSHIPS BETWEEN GROUP RESOURCES AND INFORMATION ACTIVITIES AND GOVERNMENT CONTACTS

Tables 6.4, 6.5, and 6.6 report the bivariate relationships among three sets of group resources: monetary, membership, and network, and the following variables: number of external sources of information; types of information; the means used to communicate with members; staff time devoted to the transmission of information; the frequency with which groups interact with national, provincial/state, and local officials; the number of services provided to legislators and career civil servants on the provincial or state level; and the number of lobbying techniques used by these groups.

In general, there are more noteworthy relationships (gamma of 0.40 or better) among variables in the monetary resources category than in the other two categories (see Table 6.4). Furthermore, a large annual budget, external funding sources, a paid staff, and tax-exempt status are associated more strongly with the sources and types of information, contacts with members, and the staff time spent on communicating than with the various types of interactions with government officials. As one might expect, the results suggest that environmental groups with substantial monetary resources have the ability to increase each of the following: external sources of information, types of information, staff time spent on information transmission, and the various means groups use to communicate with members and contributors.

Table 6.4

**Relationships Between Monetary Resources and Measures
of Information Activities and Government Contacts**

| | Monetary Resources of Groups | | | |
Information Activities and Government Contacts	Annual Budget	External Funding	Paid Staff	Tax Exempt
—Number of External Information Sources Used	.52*	.38	.57	.40
—Number of Types of Information Used	.44	.59	.36	.25
—Number of Means Used to Inform Members	.41	.57	.62	.57
—Staff Time Devoted to Information Transmission	.35	.60	.21	.40
—Frequent Interaction with National Officials	.29	.06	.40	.19
—Frequent Interaction with Provincial/State Officials	.40	.34	.37	.33
—Frequent Interaction with Local Officials	.20	.17	.03	.36
—Number of Services Provided to Legislators	.26	.25	.29	.46
—Number of Services Provided to Civil Servants	.15	.19	.10	.11
—Number of Methods Used to Influence Government Policy Making	.14	.19	.15	.04

* Numbers presented in this table are gammas.

Table 6.5

Relationships Between Member Resources and Measures of Information Activities and Government Contacts

Information Activities and Government Contacts	Chapters	Member Resources of Groups		
		Volunteer Number	Single Members	Percent from Dues
—Number of External Information Sources Used	.34*	.18	-.66	-.18
—Number of Types of Information Used	.03	.15	-.08	-.22
—Number of Means Used to Inform Members	.29	.60	-.28	-.05
—Staff Time Devoted to Information Transmission	-.01	-.03	-.44	-.04
—Frequent Interaction with National Officials	-.04	.15	-.41	-.08
—Frequent Interaction with Provincial/State Officials	.04	-.04	.05	-.35
—Frequent Interaction with Local Officials	-.22	.16	.53	-.36
—Number of Services Provided to Legislators	.06	.20	.20	-.08
—Number of Services Provided to Civil Servants	-.22	.17	.15	-.27
—Number of Methods Used to Influence Government Policy Making	.39	.11	-.05	-.11

* Numbers presented in this table are gammas.

Table 6.6

Relationships Between Resources Based on Group Memberships/Affiliations and Measures of Information Activities and Government Contacts

Information Activities and Government Contacts	Resources Based on Group Memberships and Affiliation		
	Group Members	Provincial/ State Affiliate	National Affiliate
—Number of External Information Sources Used	.11*	.01	.27
—Number of Types of Information Used	.27	-.18	.00
—Number of Means Used to Inform Members	.30	-.33	.72
—Staff Time Devoted to Information Transmission	.11	-.17	.18
—Frequent Interaction with National Officials	.10	-.75	.05
—Frequent Interaction with Provincial/State Officials	.23	-.21	.22
—Frequent Interaction with Local Officials	.29	-.04	-.34
—Number of services Provided to Legislators	.36	-.19	.06
—Number of Services Provided to Civil Servants	.55	-.07	.32
—Number of Methods Used to Influence Government Policy Making	.10	-.05	.31

* Numbers presented in this table are gammas.

Table 6.7

**Relationships Between Types of Organizational Members and
Measures of Information Activities and Government Contacts**

Information Activities and Government Contacts	Environ-mental	Club	Civic	Govern-ment	Research	Business	Labor
—External Sources	.11*	-.03	.48	-.11	-.30	-.05	.12
—Information Types	.08	-.31	.25	-.38	-.29	.16	-.12
—Means to Inform Members	.48	.45	.61	.40	.19	.39	.08
—Information Time by Staff	-.01	-.16	.37	.21	.21	.17	.09
—Interaction—National Level	.57	-.01	.48	.06	.40	.35	.88
—Interaction—Provincial/State Level	.50	.16	.71	.55	.49	.45	.40
—Interaction—Local Level	.40	.10	.71	.68	.58	.39	-.06
—Legislative Services	.53	.25	.65	.26	.36	.50	.29
—Bureaucratic Services	.66	.28	.73	.50	.70	.71	.31
—Methods of Governmental Influence	.43	.01	.52	-.06	.26	.15	.16

* Numbers presented in this table are gammas.

These same monetary resources affect relatively few of the interactions groups have with governmental officials. Having a paid staff is somewhat associated with frequent interactions with national officials; a large budget leads to somewhat more frequent contact with provincial/state officials; and a tax-exempt status is weakly related to an increased number of services provided to legislative officials. It appears that monetary resources increase a group's capacity to generate and communicate information, but these resources do not, by themselves, promote the transmission of environmental information to government officials.

Membership resources—chapters with members, volunteers, individual memberships, and money raised from member dues—would appear to influence few information activities and government contacts (see Table 6.5). Groups with individual members reduce their ability to rely on external sources of information, have less staff time for communicating and educating, and interact less frequently with government officials on the national level. However, these groups do increase their contacts with local-level government officials. The only other noteworthy correlation involves volunteers—groups with larger numbers of volunteers use more means of communication with members.

When network resources (having group members, provincial/state and national affiliations) are correlated with information activities and government contacts, only three noteworthy relationships emerge (see Table 6.6). Groups with national affiliations increase the number of ways they can communicate with members, and having group memberships is related to a higher number of services provided to career civil servants. The last is an inverse relationship; groups with a provincial or state affiliation have fewer contacts with national officials.

Many of the environmental organizations in this study have group members of various types such as other environmental groups, social clubs, government associations, civic groups, research organizations, business concerns, and labor unions. Table 6.7 reports the relationships among seven categories of organizational members and measures of information activities and government contacts. The seven categories are related to many of the contacts environmental groups have with government officials at all levels, but the category of organizational membership is not highly associated with sources and types of information. Environmental groups and civic organizations are two categories of group membership related to most of the measures of government contacts. What is interesting is that having research organizations as members increases the number and type of government contacts. Research organizations improve an environmental group's credibility in communicating scientific and technical information to government officials.

CROSS-NATIONAL DIFFERENCES IN RELATIONSHIPS AMONG COMMUNICATION ACTIVITIES AND CONTACTS WITH GOVERNMENT OFFICIALS

While there are few country differences on the various measures of organizational resources, country effects are evident in the analysis of group contacts with government officials (see Table 6.2). This part of the analysis explores additional country differences in the relationships between the measures of communication (which includes time spent on transmitting information) and the various types of government contacts. The results are reported in Table 6.8.

The patterns of these relationships for the Ontario and Michigan environmental groups are very different. In Ontario, both high numbers of external sources and types of information are associated with all of the following: frequent interactions with government officials at the national, provincial/state, and local levels; large numbers of services provided to legislators and civil servants; and the use of many types of lobbying methods. In Michigan, the number of external sources used by the group has high and noteworthy correlations with only two measures of contacts: services provided to legislators and civil servants. Similarly, the number of information types is moderately correlated with services provided to legislators and lobbying methods in Michigan. Environmental groups using a wide variety of means to communicate with members in Michigan also have frequent contacts with national-level officials and provide many services to legislators and career civil servants. In Ontario, in contrast, the number of means used to communicate with members is related to frequent contacts with government officials on both the provincial and local levels, but not on the national level. Finally, groups in Ontario that spend considerable amounts of staff time on informational activities tend to have frequent interactions with national officials. Their counterparts in Michigan, in comparison, have frequent contacts with state officials and use a variety of lobbying techniques if their staff devote large amounts of time to informational activities.

Table 6.8

Relationships Between Measures of Group Information Sources, Types of Information, Contacts with Members, and Time Spent on Informational Activities and Measures of Contacts with Government Officials by Country

Contacts with Government Officials		Group Information Source and Types, Contacts with Members, and Information Time			
		External Sources	Information Types	Means Used to Inform Members	Time Spent by Staff on Information
—Frequent Interaction with	ONT	.61*	.63	.21	.43
National Officials	MI	.32	.37	.56	.18
—Frequent Interaction with	ONT	.59	.85	.42	.35
Provincial/State Official	MI	-.06	-.16	.11	.49
—Frequent Interaction with	ONT	.50	.77	.63	.20
Local Officials	MI	-.20	-.27	-.45	.24
—Number of Services Provided	ONT	.61	.69	.15	.22
to Legislators	MI	.86	.48	.45	.18
—Number of Services Provided	ONT	.45	.53	.21	.15
to Career Civil Servants	MI	.65	-.08	.56	-.06
—Number of Methods Used to Influence	ONT	.83	.81	.33	.30
Government Policy Making	MI	.38	.47	.11	.49

* Numbers presented in this table are gammas.

THE COMBINED EFFECTS OF ORGANIZATIONAL RESOURCES, INFORMATIONAL ACTIVITIES, AND COUNTRY ON GOVERNMENTAL CONTACTS

The final step in this analysis is the assessment of the combined effects of organizational resources, informational activities, and country differences on government contacts.   Four additional measures of government contacts are used in this part of the analysis. Three variables were created representing interactions with elected officials, top-level agency personnel, and mid-level agency personnel across all three levels of government: national, provincial/state, and local.[16] In the previous analyses, interactions with officials at each level of government were treated separately. A fourth measure combines three of the government lobbying activities: appearing before legislative committees, contacts with cabinet ministers or the governor's office, and appeals to assistants of cabinet ministers or agency personnel.[17] This is a summary measure of the contacts groups in Ontario and Michigan have had with their respective legislative and executive officials.

Table 6.9 reports the cumulative and relative effects of three sets of variables on the measures of contacts with national, provincial/state, and local officials. The three sets of independent variables are: (1) measures of organizational resources (budget size, a paid staff, individual and organizational members, and number of volunteers); (2) informational activities (number of external sources, number of means used to inform members, and time spent in communicating information); and (3) country differences (the variable representing country was coded 0 for Ontario and 1 for Michigan). These independent variables explain very similar percentages of the variance for each of the three types of government contacts—the adjusted R^2 values   were 0.22 for contacts with elected officials and 0.28 for contacts with top-level agency/ministry personnel.

Informational activities have independent impacts in each of the three equations, but none of the organizational resources has independent effects on these measures of contacts with government officials. The indicators used for country differences, external sources of information, and the means used to communicate with members are positively related to contacts with elected officials at the national, provincial/state, and local levels of government. When contacts with top-level bureaucrats is the dependent variable, the means used to inform members is the most important variable.   Finally, two informational activities (external sources and the time spent on communicating information) are positively associated with interactions with mid-level bureaucrats in the third equation.

Table 6.9

Multiple Regression Analysis Results: The Combined Effects of Measures of Organizational Resources, Informational Activities, and Country on Measures of Contacts with Government Officials at the National, Provincial/State and Local Levels

	Contacts with National, Provincial/State, and Local Officials		
	Elected Officials	Top-Level Bureaucrats	Mid-Level Bureaucrats
Adjusted R^2	0.27	0.28	0.22
F Statistic	2.98**	3.32**	2.62*

STANDARDIZED REGRESSION COEFFICIENTS:

Organizational Resources

Size of Annual Budget	-.02	.02	.11
Paid Staff	.09	.09	.06
Individual Memberships	-.03	-.05	.20
Organizational Members	.01	.09	-.01
Number of Volunteers	-.12	-.08	.05

Informational Activities

External Sources Used	.30*	.23	.30*
Means to Inform Members	.38**	.44***	.01
Time Spent on Informing	.12	.21	.30*

Country

Ontario=0; Michigan=1	.22[a]	.09	.20

*** $p \le .001$; ** $p \le .01$; * $p \le .05$; [a] $p = .08$

Table 6.10 reports the cumulative and relative effects of these same independent variables on slightly different measures of government contacts: the number of services environmental groups provide to legislators and to agency personnel (see Table 6.2 for the types of services included), the combined lobbying efforts that are directed at both legislative and executive officials, and the total number of lobbying activities used by the Michigan and Ontario groups. There is more variation in the cumulative effects of organizational resources, informational activities, and country on the four dependent variables. The adjusted R^2 values for the four equations are as follows: 0.14 when legislative services was the dependent variable, 0.31 for the provision of bureaucratic services, 0.28 in the equation for combined legislative and executive contacts, and 0.22 for total lobbying activities.

Two organizational resources (group members and individual members), all three informational activities, and country have positive, independent effects in at least one of the equations. Country has an independent impact on the provision of services to provincial or state career civil servants when controlling for the remaining independent variables in this equation. These results suggest that *involvement in one or more informational activities leads to increased levels of service provision and a wide variety of lobbying techniques.* In addition, having organizations as members and country effects help explain variation in the provision of services to career civil servants, and having individual members is positively associated with increased legislative and executive lobbying activities.

SUMMARY AND CONCLUSIONS

This study has explored the political communication systems of environmental groups in Ontario and Michigan. The policy-making elites we interviewed and the information provided by environmental group leaders on their organizations verified our expectations that structural and political/cultural differences between this U.S. state and Canadian province have a considerable impact on the interactions between environmental interest groups and government. In general, the environmental groups in this study appear to have adapted well to their respective political settings. Elites and publics attempting to understand and influence environmental policy via interest groups must remain sensitive to that adaptation.

Table 6.10

Multiple Regression Analysis Results: The Combined Effects of Measures of Organizational Resources, Informational Activities, and Country on Measures of Legislative, Executive, and Bureaucratic Contacts

	Legislative Services Provided	Bureaucratic Services Provided	Contacts— Legislative/ Executive	Total Lobbying Activities
Adjusted R^2	0.14	0.31	0.28	0.22
F Statistic	2.20*	3.88***	3.55**	2.87**

STANDARDIZED REGRESSION COEFFICIENTS:

<u>Organizational Resources</u>

Annual Budget	-.01	.05	-.06	-.09
Paid Staff	.02	-.05	.10	.04
Individual Members	.18	.10	.30*	.14
Group Members	.13	.24*	.09	.08
Number of Volunteers	.08	-.03	-.11	——[a]

	Legislative Services Provided	Bureaucratic Services Provided	Contacts— Legislative/ Executive	Total Lobbying Activities
Informational Activities				
External Sources	.40**	.30**	.36**	.41**
Informing Members	.04	.26*	.16	.19
Time Spent	.14	-.01	.29*	.19
Country				
Ontario=0; Michigan=1	——[b]	.28	.09	.14

*** $p \leq .001$; ** $p \leq .01$; * $p \leq .05$

[a] Coefficient was too small to be recorded in this form.

[b] This variable was not in the equation presented; when this variable was entered, the F statistic was not significant.

One major finding is that environmental groups in Michigan visibly interact with government officials to a greater degree than do groups in Ontario. These Michigan groups, in comparison to their Canadian counterparts, have more-frequent contacts with all types of state-level officials, including elected officials, top- and mid-level agency personnel, and legal and scientific experts in government. Access in a political system "is determined by where power lies in the system" (Presthus 1974, p. 220); consequently, group leaders in Michigan recognize the fragmented nature of power in their system of government and interact with all actors involved in the environmental policy-making process.

The centralization of power in the Ontario parliamentary system produces noticeable differences in cross-national bureaucratic contacts. Contacts with career civil servants in ministries are less common in Ontario than are these same types of contacts in Michigan. In the U.S. state, career civil servants are one of several important targets of group lobbying efforts; in Ontario, mid-level bureaucrats are approached less often by group representatives. This finding is consistent with Leman's (1980) conclusion that bureaucrats in the United States are more independent and more free to pursue policy goals than are their counterparts in the Canadian parliamentary system. Although information has been referred to as the "most valuable benefit legislators receive from interest groups" (Presthus 1974, p. 215), there are cross-national differences in information-based legislative contacts. Members of the Ontario legislative assembly currently play a more prominent role in policy making than they did in the past, but they are not considered as important by groups in Ontario as were members of the state legislature in Michigan. White (1989, p. 255) drew the following conclusions about group interactions with the Ontario legislative assembly:

> Interest group leaders often make public presentations to legislative committees not so much because they believe that they can affect policy, but because they wish to justify themselves to their membership. Nevertheless, lobbyists do take the legislature and its members seriously as contributors to the policy process.

Ontario group leaders who were a part of this study do not ignore legislative contacts, but they do not give them the same importance as do environmental group leaders in Michigan.

Although cross-national differences are evident in contacts with government officials, there are few significant differences between the

Ontario and Michigan groups on measures of organizational resources. These results suggest that monetary resources and, to a lesser degree, people resources increase a group's capacity to generate and communicate information, but affiliations with other organizations, surprisingly, do not. Moreover, these monetary, human, and network resources are not associated with increased government contacts. Only one set of group characteristics is related to government contacts, and that is type of organizational members. Groups with organizational memberships are more likely to interact frequently with government officials at all levels of government, provide a range of services to legislators and bureaucrats, and use a variety of lobbying strategies.

Another conclusion involves the role environmental groups play in the two policy-making settings and the tactics employed by groups to transmit policy-relevant information. Here the consensual Canadian system stands in sharp contrast to the competitive American system. Although groups in both systems provide information on environmental issues to government and to their members and contributors, the Ontario groups are not as actively engaged in lobbying as are the Michigan groups. Among the groups in the Canadian province, only those that engage in many types of informational activities interact regularly with government officials and lobby extensively to influence environmental policy decisions. Many groups in Ontario may pursue a less obvious, quieter involvement in politics when compared with their American counterparts. Group leaders in Michigan, on the other hand, seem to realize that in order to be effective competitors to private-sector interests, their organizations must be visible and active to catch the attention of state decision makers.

Finally, this chapter highlights the importance of informational activities for groups in both political systems. Groups that depend on a variety of external sources to compile information and use a wide array of types of research information, including scientific and technical, legal, political, and economic, are groups that regularly contact government actors, provide services to these officials, and use a broad range of lobbying techniques. This cross-nationally applicable finding is equally valid for the means groups use to communicate with members and contributors. Having newsletters or magazines; holding meetings, workshops, or courses; preparing videotapes, films, or reports; or releasing information through the mass media also increase group contacts with government officials.

Consequently, the activities environmental groups use to engage in political communication are very important in explaining the nature of group communication in the environmental policy area. Groups with sizable budgets and paid staff members can increase their communication activities. Nevertheless, it is political system and political culture differences that are most pronounced in this study. Interest groups must accommodate their strategies and activities to the characteristics of the political system in which they operate and to the prevailing political and cultural values of that system. It appears that the Michigan and Ontario groups we studied have done this. Furthermore, it would appear that the information age has indeed penetrated the dynamics of environmental interest group life. It has done so in similar ways in two postindustrial nations of considerably different political cultures and institutional arrangements.

NOTES

An earlier version of this chapter was prepared for delivery at the 1990 Annual Meeting of the Midwest Political Science Association, April 5-7, Palmer House, Chicago, Illinois

1.   Interviews and a mail survey of environmental group leaders and members were conducted in the summer and fall of 1987. The study was supported primarily by a grant from the Canadian Embassy, under the auspices of the Canadian Studies Faculty Research Program. The work was also supported in part by funds provided by Washington State University and Oakland University. The authors gratefully acknowledge this support but take full responsibility for all statements and conclusions reported herein.

The 13 individuals interviewed in Michigan included representatives from all significant state governmental bodies and statewide environmental groups actively involved in the environmental area of policy making. The 11 individuals interviewed in Ontario also included the relevant government officials, but only leaders from a representative cross-section of the types of groups involved in this policy area could be included given the large number of environmental organizations active in the province.

2.   Both full-time and part-time staff were considered in the creation of the measure representing the availability of a paid staff. Groups having no paid staff were coded 0 and those with a paid staff were coded 1. Twenty groups (53 percent) in Ontario had paid staff; 12 Michigan groups (52 percent) had paid staff.

3. The size of the groups' annual budgets ranged from a low of $200 to a high of $6 million (mean = $252,006; sd = $27,663). Because of this variation, budget amounts were placed into categories of low (up to $2,000), medium ($2,200 through $100,000), and high ($118,000 through $6 million). These categories were coded 1, 2, and 3.

4. The number of volunteers associated with these groups ranged from 0 to 1,000 (mean = 139; sd = 246). These values were placed into three categories: few (0 through 20), average (25 through 60), and many (100 through 1,000), and coded 1, 2, and 3.

5. Information was compiled on seven types of organizational members, and separate variables were created for each type. Groups having such members were coded 1; those not having these types of members were coded 0. The types included other environmental groups (23 of the 61 had environmental groups as members), clubs (16), civic or community organizations (16), governments (15), research organizations (9), businesses (18), and labor groups (8).

6. The percentage of group funding raised from dues ranged from 0 to 100 (mean = 53; sd = 39). In the cross-tabulation analyses, these values were placed into three categories coded 1 (0 through 25 percent), 2 (30 percent through 75 percent), and 3 (80 percent through 100 percent).

7. Three items were combined to create the percentage of funds raised from sources external to the group: the percentages raised from foundations, government sources, and corporations. Thirty-three groups raised no money from any of these external sources; consequently, these groups were coded 0, and groups with some funding from external sources were coded 1.

8. Group leaders were asked if their groups were affiliated with a national organization (1 = yes; 0 = no), and leaders also were asked if their groups were affiliated with a provincial or state organization (1 = yes; 0 = no).

9. Group leaders were asked to indicate whether their organizations used any of the following external sources to compile information on environmental problems: (1) affiliates or offices of the organization; (2) other environmental organizations; (3) scientists or experts in universities or research institutions; (4) lawyers or legal experts; (5) elected government officials or their staff; (6) nonelected government personnel; (7) others. The number of external sources used was counted across these seven types (mean = 4.39; sd = 1.95). For

this study, the number of external sources was categorized as follows: 0 through 4 = 1 (26 groups); 5 through 7 = 2 (35 groups).

10.   Four types of research information were listed: scientific or technical, legal, political, and economic, and leaders indicated whether their groups used these types. Number of types of research information used was counted across the four types (mean = 3.25; sd = 1.23). Forty-one groups used all four types of information (coded 2); the remaining 20 groups used no sources or up to three (coded 1).

11.   Many ways of communicating with members were listed: a newsletter, magazine, periodic membership meetings, special reports or pamphlets, workshops or short courses, videotapes or films, community or regional newspapers, radio, television, and other forms. The number of means of communication was counted across these nine forms (mean = 4.92; sd = 1.89). Thirty-eight groups used one to four forms (coded 1); the remaining 23 groups used five to nine forms (coded 2).

12.   The percentages of total staff time devoted to three activities—educational activities, political activities, and scientific or technical research—were combined to create the measure of staff time spent on informational activities (mean = 46.98; sd = 38.57). These percentages were placed into three categories coded 0 (no staff time), 1 (5 percent through 75 percent), and 2 (80 percent to 100 percent).

13.   Group leaders were asked how frequently representatives from their organizations interacted with a set of national-level government officials, which included elected officials; heads of departments, divisions, agencies, or commissions; mid-level bureaucratic personnel; legal experts; and scientific experts. They were also asked how frequently organizational representatives interacted with the same sets of officials both on the provincial or state level, and on the local level. Five response categories were listed, with endpoints of "never" (coded 1) and "often" (coded 5), and a midpoint of "occasionally" (coded 3).

For the measure of frequency of interaction with national officials the two categories at the "often" end of the scale were counted across the five types of officials (mean = 0.87; sd = 1.31). Thirty-eight groups had no frequent interactions with national-level officials (coded 1); the remaining 23 groups had frequent interactions with from one to five of these officials (coded 2).

The measure of frequency of interaction with local officials was constructed in exactly the same manner as the measure for contacts with national officials (mean = 1.28; sd = 1.50). Twenty-nine groups had no frequent interactions with local-level officials (coded 1); the remaining thirty two groups had frequent contacts with from one to five of these officials (coded 2).

The 61 environmental groups had most of their contacts with officials at the provincial or state level; consequently, for this measure, only the "often" category was counted across the five types of officials (mean = 1.03; sd = 1.44). Thirty-four groups did not interact "often" with any provincial or state officials; 27 did not have contacts that were "often" with the five types of officials.

14. Four types of services were listed that groups could provide to members of the provincial parliament or state legislature: testifying at hearings, providing information on pending legislation, building public support for legislative proposals, and campaign support. Similarly, four types of services that groups could provide to provincial or state civil servants were listed including participation in public advisory bodies, providing information on public attitudes, support agency policies, and recommendations on appointees to high-level posts. Leaders were asked to indicate which of these services were provided by their organizations, and the number of services promoted was counted separately across the categories listed for legislators (mean = 1.87; sd = 1.32) and across the categories listed for bureaucrats (mean = 2.23; sd = 1.49). Both measures--legislative services and bureaucratic services--were recorded as follows: no services = 1, one or two services = 2, and three or four services = 3.

15. Ten methods used to influence government actions or policies were listed: (1) briefs to parliamentary committees or testifying before legislative committees; (2) briefs to cabinet ministers or submitting reports to the governor's office; (3) appeals to executive assistants of cabinet ministers or appeals to agency personnel; (4) briefs or appeals by outside experts; (5) contact with government regulatory bodies; (6) filing court suits; (7) instigating a letter-writing campaign; (8) building coalitions with other groups; (9) releasing information through the mass media; and (10) organizing political protests. The number of methods used was counted across these 10 categories (mean = 4.46; sd = 3.10). These values were recorded as follows: none through three methods = 1; four through 10 methods = 2.

16. To create these three measures, the individual items included in the measures of frequency of interaction with government officials at the various levels of government were used (see n. 13). For the indicator of contacts with elected officials, the items on interactions with elected officials on the national, provincial/state, and local levels of government were combined (mean = 9.36; sd = 2.68).

Similarly, the items in interactions with top-level bureaucrats on all three levels of government were combined for the indicator of contacts with top-level bureaucrats (mean = 9.41; sd = 2.80); for mid-level bureaucrats, the items in interactions with mid-level personnel on all three levels of government were combined (mean = 9.46; sd = 2.71).

17.   The measure of contacts with legislative and executive officials was created by counting across the first three categories of methods (see n. 15) used by groups to influence government actions or policies (mean = 1.54; sd = 1.22).

REFERENCES

Berry, Jeffrey M. (1984) *The Interest Group Society*. Boston: Little, Brown and Company.

Canadian Study of Parliament Group (1989) "interest Groups and Parliament." Ottawa: 12-13 April 1989; Quebec City: 1 June 1989.

Gibbins, Roger and Neil Nevitte (1985) "Canadian Political Ideology: A Comparative Analysis," *Canadian Journal of Political Science* 18 (March): 577-598.

Horowitz, Gad (1966) "Conservatism, Liberalism, and Socialism in Canada: An Interpretation," *Canadian Journal of Public Policy* 32 (May): 143-171.

King, David C. and Jack L. Walker (1989) "The Provision of Benefits by American Interest Groups," Paper presented at the Annual Meeting of the Midwest Political Science Association. Chicago, Illinois.

Leman, Christopher (1980) *The Collapse of Welfare Reform: Political Institutions, Policy, and the Poor in Canada and the United States*. Cambridge, Massachusetts: MIT Press.

Lipset, Seymour M. (1985) "Canada and the United States: The Cultural Dimension." In C.F. Doran and J.H. Sigler (eds.) *Canada and the United States*. Englewood Cliffs, New Jersey: Prentice-Hall.

Millbrath, Lester W. (1984) *Environmentalists: Vanguard for a New Society*. Albany, New York: State University of New York Press.

Nelkin, Dorothy, ed. (1979) *Technological Decisions and Democracy: European Experiments in Public Participation*. Beverly Hills, California: Sage.

Presthus, Robert (1974) *Elites in the Policy Process*. London: Cambridge University Press.

Pross, A. Paul (1986) *Group Politics and Public Policy.* Toronto: Oxford University Press.

_____ (1975) "Pressure Groups: Adaptive Instruments of Political Communication." In A.P. Pross (ed.) *Pressure Group Behavior in Canadian Politics.* Canada: McGraw-Hill Ryerson Limited.

White, Graham (1989) *The Ontario Legislature: A Political Analysis.* Toronto: The University of Toronto Press.

Chapter 7

The Environment/Energy Interface: Social Learning Versus the Invisible Foot

Gilles Paquet

Despite all the pleasant rhetoric at the Houston Summit and the formal negotiations between the United States and Canada regarding acid rain, there is little resolve expressed by the Canadian and American governments to take a strong stand on the energy/environment issues that confront Canada and the United States today. Both governments welcome any additional studies, and negotiated agreements between the two countries are welcome as a progressive approach to the solution of current environmental problems, mainly in response to the intense public concern and media attention devoted to energy and environment issues, but these issues are not very high on the political agenda of either government.

The lack of congruence between rhetoric and action is attributable to the acute economic problems experienced by both countries and, in particular, to the shadow their huge government budget deficits cast on any initiative likely to be costly in terms of public funds. In addition, there is still an immense amount of ignorance and uncertainty about both the *real* energy challenges facing North America and the *real* costs of green-type initiatives suggested by environmentalists. Also, while there is no precise measure of the price the Canadian and American citizens are willing to pay to achieve energy sovereignty and to meet the environmental standards they purport to defend, there has been little evidence to indicate that they are willing to accept important sacrifices. Finally, much of the inertia on the policy front is also a result of the extraordinary tension between the natural myopia of politicians (whose time horizon rarely extends beyond four years) or corporate leaders (whose loyalty is to quarterly earnings and sound bottom lines) and the essentially long-term nature of energy/environment issues.

The recent period of intense negotiations between Canada and the United States leading to the Free Trade Agreement has focused the attention of officials of both countries toward the long-run and strategies for sharing their energy and environmental resources. This continental solidarity might have been expected to increase concern over the prudent use of resources. But this has proved too optimistic a forecast. The only commitments emanating from the Free Trade Agreement discussions on the energy/environment front pertain to a continental sharing of energy in what is still regarded by both parties as the unlikely event of a crisis (risk-sharing amounting to little more than a minimal insurance policy) and to a continuing interest in educating their citizens about the realities and costs of environmental problems.

While policy discussions flounder, political choices still are being made every day by governments, corporations, and citizens to craft effectively an overall policy stance. This de facto policy on both sides of the border puts priority on market mechanisms as the appropriate means both for handling energy production, allocation, and development, and for ensuring viable environmental quality. Experts have argued repeatedly that national policies of a more ambitious sort are unwarranted and would be counterproductive, for the problems are ill-structured, the policy goals are unclear, the technological future is less than transparent, and governments in both countries are still too ignorant about energy and environmental issues to experiment effectively with various policies. Only a substantial deterioration in environmental quality or an increase in energy prices would appear likely to force both countries to question their total reliance on markets and lead them to craft the necessary international and intersectoral arrangements capable of reflecting critical trade-offs on the energy/environment front. In the meantime, there is a policy vacuum.

A POLICY VACUUM

Despite the lack of explicit environment/energy policies on both sides of the border, the casual reader of the popular press has probably developed the impression that the United States did not craft an energy policy in the 1980s while Canada did. This is a result of the attention that accompanied Canada's National Energy Program in 1980. In fact, after the world oil price shock of 1973-74, both the United States and Canada developed temporary policies to cushion their citizens from spiraling world prices. It is only in 1981 that the United States moved away from such arrangements and toward deregulation; Canada did not follow suit until 1985 when a change in government occurred (Watkins 1987). On the environmental policy front, the two countries have been somewhat out of sync, but they are drifting in the same general direction. In the United States, a concerted effort to promote environmental policy strategies was developed in the 1970s but was relaxed in the 1980s. In Canada, the policy thrust was much weaker in the 1970s and today remains largely unfocused.

There are many reasons for these policy choices, and the same underlying forces are likely to continue to influence policies in the 1990s. Taking them into account is crucial if one is to attempt to gauge future policy trends.

Energy

There are a number of reasons why the United States has no effective energy policy: the lack of a stable focus for energy concerns in the American legislative system, the sharp ideological infighting between advocates of public power and the free marketeers, the absence of a strong, coordinated leadership on the issues, and so on. But perhaps the most convincing explanation is that throughout the seventies and eighties there has been a lack of consensus among the American population as to "what ought to be done on energy" (Uslaner 1987). In the absence of government intervention in the pursuit of explicit goals, officials have simply allowed the market to become the main referee. Thus, a de facto market-based energy policy evolved in the United States.

In Canada, a National Energy Program was crafted in 1980 following decades of explicit government intervention on the energy front (Doern and Phidd 1983). Energy had become a vital issue to government officials during the 1980 election, and one could infer from that electoral campaign the existence of a clear national division on this issue. After the election, the newly elected Trudeau government, which received almost all of its support from the eastern and central provinces, imposed a number of important constraints on the energy producers in the western provinces (Doern and Toner 1985). This policy was not the result of a national consensus but rather of a *coup de force* by one of the two national coalitions of interests. However, when Jean Chrétien replaced Marc Lalonde as minister of energy in 1983, the policy climate had shifted as a result of the disastrous consequences of the National Energy Program on investment in the energy sector. A greater willingness to consult and bargain with western energy interests evolved. By the time the Mulroney government ended its first term of office in 1988, any lingering effect of the National Energy Program had evaporated.

In fact, by 1988, both Canada and the United States had built up, at the government-officials level, a rationale for nonintervention in the energy field. In the spring of 1987, the Canadian federal minister of energy, mines and resources, Marcel Masse, all but admitted that there was a policy void when he charged a special committee with the responsibility for consulting the Canadian population to determine appropriate directions for Canadian energy policy. This task force, under the stewardship of Thomas Kierans, submitted its report in 1988 (Kierans 1988; Paquet 1989a). The report urged, in a general way, the adoption of a market approach and the continuation of a policy of nonintervention. There was understandably no follow-up to the Kierans report, for it called for no real public action. "No explicit policy" had become the policy in both Canada and the United States on the energy front.

It would be hard therefore to predict what strategies Canada or the United States would adopt in the event of a new energy crunch, especially given the fact that the recent Free Trade Agreement between Canada and the United States has further reduced the real possibility, and therefore the likelihood, of unilateral efforts to promote a national energy policy on either side of the border.

Environment

Officials in Canada and the United States, as in many other countries, have been conscious of environmental issues for quite a long time. Between 1968 and 1978, some 150 governments created departments of the environment or their equivalent (Roots 1988). Canada and the United States were leaders in this pack: the United States created the Environmental Protection Agency (EPA) in 1970, and Canada created its Department of Environment (DOE) the following year.

This early interest did not fare well through the second oil shock and the early 1980s recession which influenced a systematic downsizing of expenditures on environmental protection (Regens and Rycroft 1989). However, environmental issues have become prominent again since 1987, due mainly to the environment consciousness generated in all quarters (environmental groups, general public, politicians) in both Canada and the United States by the Bruntdland Commission Report—the report of the World Commission on Environment and Development—

which outlined the steps necessary for environmentally sustainable economic development for the planet by the year 2000 and beyond (Brundtland 1987). This awareness has not yet been translated into meaningful policy proposals, however.

The reasons for such inertia are simple: there is a substantial level of soft grass-roots support for environmental policies, but the political costs of action in the face of much ignorance and great uncertainty appear to be much higher than the economic costs of inaction. Political decision making is concerned with short-term cost/benefit analysis, and, in the short-run, tough environmental regulation is bound to hurt many polluting industries and therefore to affect the employment and income of voters. Yet in the longer haul, the losses attributable to environment degradation affecting crops, soils, aquatic ecosystems, forests, and human/animal life are seemingly catastrophic. But at this point, the short-term time horizon of politicians has stacked the deck against longer-term environmental policies.

In Canada, the creation of a department of environment could be regarded as a package of "positional policies" to "signal to affected groups and the attentive public that emerging problems have been recognized and are being dealt with" (Adie and Thomas 1982). But during the subsequent periods of economic difficulties, environmental concerns were displaced by priorities such as budget deficit cutting and international competitiveness imperatives. While the Canadian DOE retains its symbolic value, there is little place for substantial and meaningful action in the current system despite the strong statements of Lucien Bouchard, minister of the environment, until his resignation in the first half of 1990.

Indeed, the fact that the environment portfolio has been handed, albeit temporarily, to the minister responsible for the Treasury Board, Robert de Cotret, would appear to confirm that it no longer represents an autonomous generative policy locus. A "framework for discussion on the environment" has been issued the so-called GREEN PLAN (Bouchard 1990), and a truncated and unsatisfactory national consultation has been hurried through the government over the spring and summer of 1990. Yet the political and economic resources allocated to environmental protection continue to diminish, and whatever momentum might have been injected in the policy-making process by the former minister has all but evaporated with his departure.

In the United States, the terms of the environmental debate have been more explicit as the confrontation developed earlier between ecologists and certain environmentally unfriendly industries. A measure of ethical environmentalism has even emerged (Schwartz 1989) as well as a widespread belief that citizen action should be the primary actor in the protection of the environment. It has also become clear that it will not be acceptable to rely almost exclusively on bureaucratic efforts to solve environmental problems. This dual approach of public and private action has evolved slowly, but in the 1980s there was a shift toward a greater reliance on private protection of the environment as government-initiated environmental protection measures proved less effective than had been anticipated. Public sector policies were sharply criticized as being often motivated more by populist sentiment and pork-barrel politics than by actual environmental concerns (Caldwell 1988; Stroup and Shaw 1989; Fraas and Munley 1989). As a result, "the new breeze blowing in Washington" has tended to promote a myriad of market-based mechanisms to supplement the existing policy framework (Stavins 1989).

THREE ISSUES

These energy/environment dossiers raise complex questions and uncertainty, and potential surprises become possible. The issues are not dealt with adequately by economic theory for they include the complexity of economy-society-environment interactions where resources are not divisible, property rights are nonexistent, market failures are prevalent, and other problems such as uncertainty, public goods, external effects, and irreversibility are omnipresent (Paquet 1990). Perrings has shown that because of the complexity of ill-understood direct and indirect interdependencies, external effects in the socioeconomy are neither anticipated nor taken into account by the price mechanism. This incompleteness of the price mechanism results in the market not being able to detect intertemporal environmental deterioration even though it is physically observable. A great potential for surprises ensues. Without a time perspective that perfectly discounts these surprises or a price mechanism that anticipates them perfectly, the efficiency of the market mechanism in solving environmental problems is doubtful (Perrings 1987).

Three issues are central to the current problems in effectively addresssing environmental concerns: a lack of appreciation of the complexities underpinning the notion of sustainable development, a fundamental myopia about the politico-economic system in dealing with energy/environment issues, and the need for some innovative theory-building if appropriate institutions are to be established.

Sustainability as Resilience

Sustainable development is a difficult concept for economists to deal with. It amounts to development with nondeclining natural wealth (Pearce et al. 1989). This concept is not a static notion: it is not only a process of natural capital conservation and of maintenance of productivity but also a matter of maintaining the stability (a certain constancy) and the resilience (a capacity for the system to maintain its integrity) of the overall ecological system. Both energy and environment issues challenge the stability and the resilience of the system.

Market-based strategies cannot effectively deal with certain irreversible problems. As a result, even though market-type approaches may serve to improve the incentive-reward system in some ways and thereby extend somewhat the time horizon of economic agents, it is unlikely that this will suffice to ensure resilience.

Research by animal ecologists has shed some light on the strategies developed by animals for acquiring system resilience. Vertinsky has noted the uncanny parallel between the successful behavior of animals in the face of uncertainty (the balance and capacity to switch at crisis time between a competitive myopic individual search for efficiency and a collective search for resilience) and the behavior of Japanese companies operating in an environment where the market prevails but that are capable of subjecting themselves to a cooperative framework (through radical state intervention) in a crisis "to secure the collective survival." This duality of private competition in general with a possibility to switch to cooperation and guidance by collective norms in a crisis ensures resilience (Vertinsky 1987).

This model can also be applied to environmental front. The source of system resilience may be manifold. A variety of sources may elicit cooperation in crisis: ethics, "deep ecology," hierarchies of rights and obligations in the context of social norms, and conventions are all more or less effective ways to trigger a switch to different sets of rules in crisis times. But successful switches require a well-developed and operating sociocultural underground within which the market mechanism is nested. Some sort of "social capital" that supports individual actions in normal times but constrains them in critical circumstances is necessary (Coleman 1987). But one cannot expect such social capital to emerge organically, and resilience is unlikely to crystallize without the institutional prerequisites for a smooth coevolution of the economic, social, and environmental systems being put in place (Norgaard and Dixon 1986).

Discounting the Future

The myopia of the price mechanism condemns all evaluations of energy and environment dimensions to be somewhat truncated. Energy and environment issues raise questions of long-run collective needs while the market mechanism effectively monitors only short-run individual preferences. Moreover, sustainable development, i.e., development with nondeclining natural wealth, raises questions about intergenerational comparisons: how should the fate of the next generations be factored in when we make current decisions?

Questions of intergenerational equity are bothersome for economists, for they expose incontrovertibly the fundamental incompatibility between intergenerational equality as an objective and any positive rate of discount which shrinks dramatically the present value of future flows of benefits and costs pertaining to future generations (Diamond 1965). As soon as the rate of discount is positive, this entails a certain myopia and a bias against the future state of the ecological system. This has led many to point to the social discount rate the socially agreed positive rate of discount, as the culprit, because it enforces a certain degree of myopia. A solution has been suggested to reduce the rate of discount and thereby increase the time horizon of decisionmakers. This may not be the right approach. Artificially reducing the discount rate can only introduce yet more distortions as the new rate would ignore time preference and opportunity costs. It would most certainly extend the time horizon and force decisionmakers to take into account more fully some long-run environmental costs, but it would also modify the rate of harvesting of renewable resources and of depletion of nonrenewable resources in ways that may turn out to be both surprising and deplorable.

Tinkering with the discount rate is hardly sufficient. A lower discount rate would not only make long-run costs more relevant to present decisions but it would also give more valence to future benefits in present decisions. Consequently, it is not clear in what way the energy/environment interface would be modified. A more reasonable way to respond to the concerns raised by high social discount rates is to work harder at identifying all the costs and benefits in matters dealing with energy and environmental resources (Pearce et al. 1989).

Institutional Carpentry

In both the United States and Canada, the tools used to identify costs and benefits have mainly been of two sorts: impact analysis and market tests.

Environmental impact analysis is now used worldwide. It requires agencies explicitly to take into account the effects of their policy decisions on the quality of the environment in the hope that taking into account even nonquantified damage assessment before the fact will lead to a change in values and generate more attention to environmental costs even though they may be external to the agency. The concept has now been accepted in more than 30 countries including Canada and the United States. These analyses have served as "an informing and testing of policy," but it is fair to say that it has been much more effective and pervasive in the United States where it is more firmly embedded, if imperfectly embedded in the normal process of planning and decision making (Caldwell 1988). Recent judicial decisions in Canada (in the case of huge dams in Saskatchewan and Alberta) indicate however that this is becoming a more potent tool in Canada.

This being said, the main tendency in both Canada and the United States has been to rely more and more on market-based environmental policies, even if the pace at which both countries have proceeded is quite different. In the United States, the actions by citizen-enforcers have created enough pressure (even though they were not always productive in environmental terms) to allow questions to emerge concerning the best mix of permissible "bounty hunting" and tolerable bureaucratic foot dragging (Greve 1989). In Canada, the move toward market-based environmental policies was much slower: it has been defended on intellectual grounds since the 1960s (Dales 1968), but much of the Canadian economic decision-making structure maintains a preference for public enterprise in these matters (Hardin 1974), and the present government has had to proceed more carefully. But there has been a recent wave of publications in Canada emphasizing the importance of understanding the environment in the economy, i.e., the centrality of market-oriented approaches to environmental problems (Block 1990; Doern 1990). This would appear to indicate that Canada is now rapidly catching up with the United States on this front.

Still, the following cautious statement by the Canadian minister of the environment to a standing committee on environment of the Canadian House of Commons indicates that indecisiveness and prudence are still prevalent:

Energy is a big industry in Canada; energy is almost Canada. It is almost in terms of energy that this country has been built. The modern country of Canada is so blended with energy preoccupations that it is very difficult for us when the time comes to establish a plan for environment, because environment could be perceived as the enemy of energy programs. It is not, and the Minister of Environment is not the arch-enemy of the Minister of Energy. We are not, because we know now that energy consumption must be renewable, sustainable, and protect the atmosphere (Bouchard 1989, 18-12)

Despite much agitation at the task force and committee level, valse-hésitation is the style of the day in government, and there remains a policy void in both countries. Not much work has been done on the construction of either an alternative paradigm to look at energy and environment or of refurbished institutions and attitudinal changes likely to foster the needed adjustments to policy making on these fronts (Daly and Cobb 1989).

In the meantime, citizens in the United States and Canada, indecisive as they may be, have become more restive. While in early 1988 only 4 percent of Canadians thought of environment as the country's highest priority, by mid-1989 94 percent placed the environment at or near the top of their list of concerns (Dyer 1990). The impatience of some Canadians was also relayed in the emergence of Earth First members who were willing to use civil disobedience and even ecological terrorism in pursuit of their environmental goals. In the United States the same tendencies on the environmental front are present, but with a higher degree of impatience and radicalism emanating from deep-rooted environment ethics. In Canada, frustration is still in the incubation phase, but growing quickly.

THE INVISIBLE FOOT AT WORK

While Canadians and Americans may share a soft consensus in favor of effective environmental protection, there is no agreement on how to construct the appropriate private-public action mix to create the sort of resilient system that is desired. There is a great cacophony of voices by different groups and factions on both sides of the border. However, each of these coalitions is slowly being transformed into an action group expending much time and resources to ensure that its point of view will be registered. On the energy front, one notes an even higher level of rent-seeking activity in Canada than in the United States. It is ascribable to the greater dependence on energy of Canada's northern climate requires, but also to the relative importance of energy-related activities both economic and symbolic for regions of the country (Hydro Québec, for instance) (Paquet 1989b).

On both the energy and environment fronts, the voices are as volatile as they are vehement. One is not sure that either government has fairly represented the points of view of its constituents. In many cases, governments have added to the already high degree of false consciousness and anomie. For instance, at the beginning of the 1980s, Canadians regarded energy as a very special commodity and supported a national policy for the sector. By the end of the 1980s, Canadian officials wanted to believe that such a policy was no longer necessary and that the market could now be relied upon to alleviate all problems on this front. This "new" Canadian view was promulgated in the final report of Energy Options and embraced by the Mulroney government officials.

But what was said to the Kierans Task Force by Canadians and what was finally reported was not the same thing. Much cognitive dissonance was injected in the task force process. Canadians still do not feel that energy is a commodity like others, and the "new" Canadian view propounded by the Mulroney government—that there is no need for a national policy—is not widely shared by the citizenry. Polls indicate that Canadian citizens have a much greater concern for conservation and for environmental issues than does their government. They are not necessarily swayed by government officials in the energy field in Ottawa who repeat constantly that "hoarding is not good economics" or that conservation is not critical. For the Canadian public, "energy saved is energy found." Consequently, there has been concern when government-initiated energy conservation projects have all but disappeared and when it has become apparent that the explicit Canadian energy policy is not to have a policy at all (Paquet 1989a).

Indeed, the same sort of concern about "officials" misreading the concerns of the population may be recorded in the United States where, despite the fact that one high-efficiency lightbulb over its lifetime eliminates the need for nearly one barrel of oil, energy efficiency and conservation programs continue to be canceled or downsized (Hirst 1990).

Because of energy misinformation disseminating in Canada and in the United States, there have been negative consequences for environmental action. A hands-off policy on energy limits the possibility of public involvement in environmental policies that might constrain the energy industry. Government policy making on both sides of the border is fragmented. In the United States, cohesive pressure groups already best articulate what environmental policy should be. Yet such groups have not been powerful enough to reinvigorate the conservation movement that would lead North Americans to consume 30 percent less energy than they now do (Stobaugh and Yergin 1983). Nor have they been able to reverse the environmentally malignant energy strategy based on fossil fuels. The progress made on the acid-rain front in 1990 suggests however that one should not discount too readily the power of the environmental groups in the United States: one should remember that the U.S. Environmental Protection Agency was at times the largest regulatory agency both in budget and personnel (Rosenbaum 1985). Canada, after a period of softening environmental drive may also give encouraging signs of some strenghtening of the tonus of environmental policy in spite of all the equivocation and of the federal-provinvial squabbles.

The popular attention focused on and the extent of the litigation associated with environmentalism does not provide optimal conditions for energy competition and cooperation (Vertinsky 1987). There is much waste of resources generated in the energy and environment fields (Buchanan et al. 1980). The invisible foot marches in.

> Adam Smith's invisible hand symbolizes the unseen benefits that economic competition confers on the coordination of economic activity. The "invisible foot" symbolizes the unseen costs the negative welfare effects of competition over distributive shares. (Magee et al. 1989)

The important lobbying activities of the sectors threatened by environmental policies have led to an increased politicization of the EPA context in the United States and of the DOE in Canada. This has had a great impact on the effectiveness of these agencies. The current efforts to neutralize the emergence of a strong environmental policy in Canada owe much to the lessons energy producers learned from the U.S. record over the last decade.

Energy-related projects create jobs, regional development, and growth-generating megaprojects within relatively short periods. Al these features imply a focus on well-identified beneficiaries. On the other hand, the environmental losses are diffuse and likely only to hurt in the long-run. It is not difficult to see why the "invisible foot" may operate effectively: redistributing from environment to energy may not be right in long-term societal opportunity costs terms, but it is quite attractive in the short-run.

In the United States, the energy and energy-related sectors took some time to realize the dangers posed to them by developing environmental concerns: the energy crisis blinded them in the 1970s. In Canada, the energy players are intent on ensuring that current environmental policy making is not defined in threatening terms. The present reactive approach of the Department of Environment— emphasizing the broad responsibility of all citizens for pollution control—is bound to generate more paralysis than progress in government policy-making in Canada, for as Lucien Bouchard insisted before the Standing Committee on Environment, environmental questions challenge "the current life style of our society. We must tap the creativity of Canadians in designing acceptable solutions. Better informed and educated citizens will be better able to make intelligent decisions" (Bouchard 1989, 18).

Such cautiousness does not reveal a weakness of will on the part of the Canadian government, but rather the depth of the issues raised by the energy/environment interface. The Canadian government does not feel either compelled to or able to propose a proactive environmental/policy that would amount to a modification of Canadian life style.

The continental integration of economic forces on energy-based resources leads one to believe that there will be coordinated efforts on both sides of the border to neutralize attempts to promote environmental policies likely to impose high costs on the energy and energy-related sectors. Consequently, one should not be too optimistic in examining the environmental agenda for the next decade. There have been many promises made by many countries especially in terms of reduction of CO_2 emission, for instance. These scenarios call for 20% and 50% reductions in carbon dioxide emissions by 2005 and by 2025 respectively. But this will not be possible without massive progress in energy efficiency and perhaps without a greater reliance on nuclear energy. Yet neither front is very promising at this time in view of the withdrawal of resources allotted to both. Moreover, as energy prices will continue to rise and energy crunches will thus become more probable, energy lobbies will likely grow in both power and persuasiveness. When faced with a trade-off between energy and environment concerns, the Canadian and American public and politicians will thus probably choose to support the energy sector.

SOCIAL LEARNING

An alternative to the litigious chaos of the rent-seeking society is the design of a democratically-rooted policy capable of effecting the necessary switch from competition to cooperation when necessary. This is possible only if governments become learning organizations and if policy-making is reframed in terms of social learning.

Governments as Learning Organizations

Defining a policy requires establishing the basis for selecting certain procedures or adopting certain strategies in the face of different plausible sets of circumstances. This cannot be done by presuming that experts already have all the necessary information, and that it is only a matter of negotiating the technically adapted policy. The information is widely spread in the population and scattered in many expert sub-groups. Reasonable policy-making process must be based on social learning, on mutual learning by experts and clients, on interaction likely to generate a more complete picture of what measures are feasible, acceptable, and implementable.

Attempting to solve the energy/environment problems by using a research organization (Garratt 1987), might appear to be a roundabout and ineffective strategy, but this is not so. The development of a policy stance in the environment/energy field requires policy makers and policy analysts to recognize a central problem: the goals of the policy are either unknown or very ambiguous and the means-ends relationships are highly uncertain and poorly understood (Rittel and Webber 1973; Paquet 1989).

A standard way of looking at policy-making à la Wilensky identifies four elements of policy formulation: (1) goal setting, (2) control, (3) innovation, and (4) intelligence (Wilensky 1967). When the problem is well-structured, policy-making emphasizing (1) and (2) is quite adequate. But when dealing with ill-structured and elusive problems, one must use an alternative approach which necessarily focuses on (3) and (4), emphasizing intelligence as the basis for an innovative learning process.

Friedmann and Abonyi have proposed a policy approach to such problems, based on the analysis of four sub-processes: (1) the construction of appropriate theories of reality, (2) the formation of social values, (3) the gaming that leads to the design of political strategies, and (4) the carrying out of collective action. These four interconnected sub-processes are components of a social learning process summarized in a

Figure 7.1

The Paradigm of Social Practice in Policy Research

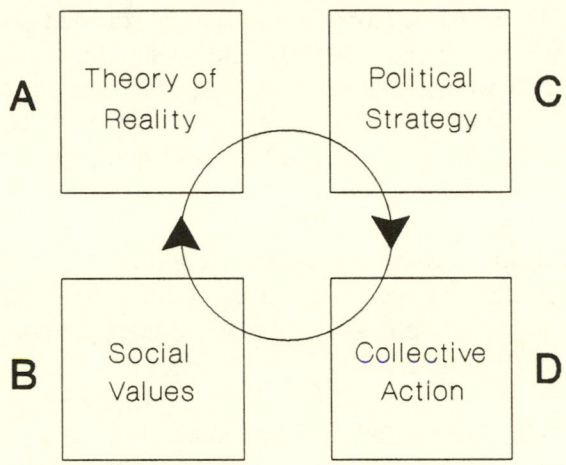

Source: Friedman and Abonyi (1976) p. 88.

graph adapted from Friedmann and Abonyi in Figure 7.1 (Friedmann and Abonyi 1976).

Social values (Block B of Figure 1) provide normative guidance in either the transformation of reality or the selection of strategies for action; they define what is acceptable. Theory of reality (Block A) is a symbolic representation and explanation of the policy environment; it depicts what is feasible. Political strategy (Block C) refers to the political action chosen; it identifies the stable and implementable options. Social action (Block D) deals with the practical measures taken to ensure an effective policy outcome. Together these four sub-processes come to life in concrete situations (Paquet 1989).

A Joint North American Task Force

The long-term costs of the scenario of the invisible foot are very high, but there is no hope that social learning will proceed unless one can force the debate outside the present framework which emphasizes short-run technical and economic efficiency while excluding other considerations. The time may be ripe for a first Joint North American Task Force on Environmental and Energy Resources to reframe the basic questions. If the Free Trade Agreement has made clear that the U.S. and Canada are now to share energy and environmental resources to a greater degree than in the past, a North American coordinated policy on such matters as environment and energy should be sought.

This sort of new regional learning organization is akin to what was recommended by the Advisory Panel on Energy of the Brundtland Commission in 1986 (Iglesias 1987). Such agencies were meant to provide:

> Needed capability to identify and seize opportunities for regional cooperation in financing, developing and exploiting new technologies for energy supply, energy saving, and environmental regeneration.

Both Canada and the United States appear to be converging toward related environmental policies, yet in neither country is there a crisis of great immediacy. Therefore current conditions would permit a Joint North American Task Force on Environmental and Energy Resources to investigate these issues in careful, timely manner.

This would provide an opportunity to create a North American forum to discuss issues that are continental in scope. Presumably, the presence of both Canadian and American environmentalists and energy industry representatives on this Task Force would ensure that the right questions would be asked and that various aspects of the issue would be explored. Moreover, one might count on such a first continental effort to ensure a degree of social learning for all interested parties and the public in general, and for the effort to have enough moral authority—as a result of the wide coverage of its surveying and the extensive amount of knowledge contributed by all the stakeholders for its ultimate recommendations—to be considered seriously by the governments on both sides of the border. Such an initiative would echo the separate initiatives of the Resources for the Future (U.S.) and Resources for Tomorrow (Canada) undertaken some thirty years ago as major efforts to do some stock-taking on the state of national resources and to develop natural resources policies.

A Joint North American Task Force on Environmental and Energy Resources would provide the basis for some harmonization of policies at the North American level on issues that are already commanding some world-level attention. Such an initiative would not only foster a higher degree of North American awareness and due concern in the aftermath of the Brundtland report but also might enable much of the good work that has begun in Canada and in the United States to find a useful outlet likely to materialize in refurbished rules of the game on both sides of the border. For instance, much use might be made of the work done for the National Task Force on Environment and Economy (Canada)—made up of ministers from seven governments, federal and provincial, and the CEOs of seven of Canada's top corporations—in adapting the Brundtland report to the Canadian arena. This has already generated a landmark report (National Task Force on Environment and Economy 1987); in the same spirit, U.S. Senators John Heinz (R-Pa) and Timothy Wirth (D-Colo.) initiated and sponsored Project 88, "a bipartisan effort to find innovative solutions to major environmental and natural resources problems." Also in the U.S., fifty individuals from industry, government, academia, and the environmental community worked on the final report "Harnessing Market Forces to Protect Our Environment-Initiatives for the New President" produced in 1988 (Stavins 1989). Indeed, if a meeting of some 100 senior representatives of corporate and political strategists from both Canada and the U.S. in New York in December 1989 is a harbinger of things possible, battles of words may be soon replaced by calls to link arms at the North American level (Howard 1989).

POSSIBLE STEPS

Social learning cannot occur ex nihilo. It must evolve from a set of basic principles and build on bets on certain promising directions. In the energy/environment world, certain key principles have been put forward by Charles Perrings as the guidelines in any exercise of social architecture. They are (1) the principle of intergenerational equity, (2) the principle of collective property, and (3) the principle of individual accountability (Perrings 1987). These may serve as prime movers in the learning process.

Three Principles

The principle of *intergenerational equity* points to the contradiction between the criterion of intergenerational egalitarianism and a positive social rate of discount. It forces the debate onto a field where means have to be found to extend the time horizon of the present generation if the common inheritance is to be preserved. A small step in this general direction might be taken through the *collective property* of natural resources—energy and environment—and through the astute use of contracts for the use of such resources. This has been accomplished effectively in the world of mines and forestry. Such contracts could prohibit certain practices with proven deleterious effects and institute mechanisms resembling both royalties on depletable resources and taxes on polluters. In order to enforce such contracts, *individual accountability* would need to become an effective norm and mechanisms would need to be designed to ensure that those not meeting contractual obligations will be effectively charged for the damage they have engendered. Given the great possibility of escaping such charges through bankruptcy or the like, the idea of natural resources bonds—reimbursable deposits equal to the maximum possible damage in the event of violation of the rules of the contract—might be used (Solow 1971). The conjectured value of the bond could always be revised upward or downward as experience reveals that more or less destructive methods have been used.

New Norms

These three principles may be effected through a variety of means depending on the basic current values. To the extent that intergenerational solidarity prevails, there may be little cause for hierarchies within the present generation to impose the precedence of longer term objectives like the resilience of the system. Some like Daly and Cobb have chosen to bet on the construction of new solidarities. Others, who are either more cynical or risk-averse, would prefer the State to accept the responsibility for sanctioning some hierarchies in the choices made by the present generation: the precedence of needs over preferences for instance (Frankfurt 1984). Such norms or rules would direct traffic on the forum and ensure, like traffic lights in large cities, a way to orchestrate smoothly the actions of all agents. (Who would claim that the market would do this job better than coercive traffic lights?)

Such norms or rules may be variable according to normal or abnormal times, very much like the way in which instinct guides animals through the switching of rules in critical times such that negotiated conventions based on core values may well be able to arrange such effective switching in human societies. Conventions may be changed according to certain meta-rules, and one of the central roles of the Joint North American Task Force would effectively be to hammer out such meta-rules (Orgogozo and Sérieyx 1989; Paquet 1989).

There is little hope however that such developments will occur organically in Canada or the U.S. on the environment/energy fronts. A reframing of the issues is necessary. Such a reframing in turn requires a revolution in the mind of citizens from both countries. This new consciousness might begin, in the year of the 200th anniversary of the death of Adam Smith, with a recognition of a forgotten portion of his message: competition and markets cannot do everything, and governments should provide "certain public works and certain public institutions, which it can never be for the interest of any individual, or small number of individuals, to erect and maintain". The world of energy and environment calls for such public institutions, and until such a time as it is widely recognized, there is little hope that the requisite social architecture and carpentry will be allowed to proceed.

CONCLUSION

Canada and the U.S. have been groping for market-oriented energy and environmental policies. Recently published reports may serve as a basis for a promising process of social learning on this front (Stavis 1989). However, the market cannot be a panacea. To political and economic actors who focus on energy and environment policy, public goods loom large and, unfortunately, market-place decisions and calculations do not take into account public goods to an appropriate extent (Kash and Rycroft 1984). Social learning will have to lead both governments to return somewhat to some interventionist form of policy-making.

Moreover, what is acceptable, what is feasible, what is stability-generating and what is effectively implementable need not be the same all across North America. Much of the existing diversity may not be rooted so much in fundamental differences or in poor understanding of the issues as in historical circumstances and differing values. An occasion to take stock of the knowledge and values of the energy/environment players in Canada and the U.S. may be useful even if it does not lead to a unified policy, but only to a critical appraisal of current policies and to the elaboration of different but coherent strategies. For example, there may be advantages for both Canada and the United States in developing joint policies on matters of binational concern such as acid rain where the spillover effects from one country to the other are important, but this need not be the case across the board. It should however become clearer to each nation (as social learning proceeds) why and to what extent values and priorities differ, and why explicitly different policies may be desirable.

Some may regard the social learning approach as futile or at least as likely to generate more heat than light. F. Scott Fitzgerald may have been right that no grand idea was ever born in a conference, but, as he aptly added, "a lot of foolish ideas have died there" (Fitzgerald 1945). A Joint North American Task Force might be expected to slaughter foolish ideas in good currency. While the U.S. and Canada determine their own policy options, such a task force could effectively evaluate their potential for success. As Canadian humorist Stephen Leacock has reminded us, Canadians can only be passionate about moderation, one may reckon that any slaughter of foolish ideas and sacred cows at such a conference would likely be civil and humane.

REFERENCES

Adie, R.F. and P.G. Thomas. 1982. *Canadian Public Administration*. Scarborough: Prentice-Hall.

Block, W. 1990. *Economics and the Environment: A Reconciliation*. Vancouver: The Fraser Institute.

Bouchard, L. 1989, October 26. Statement before the Standing Committee on Environment of the House of Commons of Canada, 2nd Session of the 34th Parliament.

_____. 1990. *A Framework for Discussion on the Environment*. Ottawa: Supply & Services Canada.

Brundtland. 1987. World Commission on Environment and Development. *Our Common Future*, Oxford: Oxford University Press.

Buchanan, J.M., Tollison, R.D. and G. Tullock. 1980. *Toward a Theory of the Rent-Seeking Society*. College Station: Texas A & M University Press.

Caldwell, L.K. 1988, Autumn. "Environmental Impact Analysis: Origins, Evolution, and Future Directions." *Policy Studies Review* 8, No. 1.

Coleman, J.S. 1987. "Norms as Social Capital." Ed. G. Radnitzky and P. Bernholz. *Economic Imperialism: The Economic Approach Applied Outside the Field of Economics*. New York: Paragon.

Dales, J.H. 1968. *Pollution, Property and Prices*. Toronto: University of Toronto Press.

Daly, H.E. and J.B. Cobb, Jr. 1989. *For the Common Good*. Boston: Beacon Press.

Diamond, P. 1965. "The Evaluation of Infinite Utility Streams." *Econometrica* 33, pp. 170-177.

Doern, G.B. 1990. *The Economic Imperative: Market Approaches to the Greening of Canada*. Toronto: C.D. Howe Institute.

_____, and R.W. Phidd. 1983. *Canadian Public Policy*. Toronto: Methuen.

_____, and G. Toner. 1985. *The Politics of Energy*. Toronto: Methuen.

Dyer, G. 1990. "Green Report Card on Five World Leaders." *New Environment*. Premier Issue.

Fitzgerald, F.S. 1945. *The Crack-Up*. New York: New Directions.

Frass, A.G. and V.G. Munley. 1989, July. "Economic Objectives Within a Bureaucratic Decision Process." *Journal of Environmental Economics and Management* 17, No. 1.

Frankfurt, H.G. 1984. "Necessity and Desire." Ed. H.G. Frankfurt, *The Importance of What We are About*. Cambridge: Cambridge University Press.

Friedmann, J. and G. Abonyi. 1976. "Social Learning: A Model for Policy Research." *Environment and Planning* A, 8.

Garratt, B. 1987. *The Learning Organization*. London: Fontana.

Greve, M.S. 1989, Fall. "Environmentalism and Bounty Hunting." *The Public Interest* 97.

Hardin, H. 1974 *A Nation Unaware: The Canadian Economic Culture*. Vancouver: J.J. Douglas Ltd.

Hirst, E. 1990, July. "Electricity: Getting More with Less." *Technology Review*.

Howard, R. 1989, December 28. "Call to Link Arms Replaces Battle of Words at Environment Meeting." *The Globe and Mail*, p. A8.

Iglesias, E. 1987. *Energy 2000: A Global Strategy for Sustainable Development*. London: Zed Books Ltd.

Kash, D.E. and R.W. Rycroft. 1984. *U.S. Energy Policy: Crisis and Complacency*. Norman: University of Oklahoma Press.

Kierans, T. et al. 1988. *Energy and Canadians into the 21st Century*. Ottawa: Energy, Mines and Resources.

Magee, S.P., Brock, W.A. and L. Young. 1989. *Black Hole Tariffs and Endogenous Policy Theory*. Cambridge: Cambridge University Press.

National Task Force on Environment and Economy. 1987. *Report*. Ottawa: Canadian Council of Resource and Environment Ministers.

Norgaard, R.B. and J.A. Dixon. 1986. "Pluralistic Project Design: An Argument for Combining Economic and Coevolutionary Methodologies." *Policy Sciences* 19, No. 3, pp. 297-317.

Orgogozo, I. and H. Serieyx. 1989. *Changer le Changement* Paris: Le Seuil.

Paquet, G. 1989. "A Social Learning Framework for a Wicked Problem: The Case of Energy." *Energy Studies Review* 1, No.1.

_____. 1989. "La Grande Offre Publique d'Achat (OPA) des Années 1960 dans l'Électricité au Québec: Petit Essai d'Ethnographie Interprétative." Ed. R. Comeau. *Jean Lesage et l'Éveil d'une Nation*. Sillery: Presses de l'Université du Québec, pp. 282-297.

_____. 1990. "Pour une Approche Co-Évolutionnaire au Développement Viable." (Mimeo).

Pearce, D., Barbier, E. and B. Markandya. 1989. *Blueprint for a Green Economy*. London: Earthscan Publications Ltd.

Perrings, C. 1987. *Economy and Environment*. Cambridge: Cambridge University Press.

Regens, J.L. and R.W. Rycroft. 1989. "Funding for Environmental Protection: Comparing Congressional and Executive Influences." *The Social Science Journal* 26, No. 3.

Rittel, H.W. and M.M. Webber. 1973. "Dilemmas in a General Theory of Planning." *Policy Sciences* 4.

Rosenbaum, W.A. 1985. *Environmental Politics and Policy*. Washington: Congressional Quarterly Press.

Roots, F. 1988. "The Brundtland Challenge: Background and Objectives." Eds. A. Davidson and M. Dence. *The Brundtland Challenge and the Cost of Inaction*. Halifax: The Institute for Research on Public Policy.

Schwartz, J. 1989, Spring. "The Rights of Nature and the Death of God." *The Public Interest* 97.

Solow, R.M. 1971. "The Economist's Approach to Pollution Control." *Science* 173, pp. 498-503.

Stavins, R.N. 1989, Spring. "Using Economic Incentives To Protect the Environment." *Policy Review* 48.

Stobaugh, R. and D. Yergin, eds. 1983. *Energy Future*. 3rd Ed. New York: Vintage.

Stroup, R.L. and J.S. Shaw. 1989, Fall. "The Free Market and The Environment." *The Public Interest* 97.

Uslaner, E.M.   1987, October.   "Energy Politics in the USA and Canada." *Energy Policy* 15, No. 5.

Vertinsky, I.   1987.   "An Ecological Model of Resilient Decision-Making: An Application to the Study of Public and Private Decision Making in Japan." *Ecological Modelling* 38, pp. 141-158.

Watkins, G.C.   1987.   "Living Under a Shadow: U.S. Oil Policies and Canadian Oil Pricing." Eds. R.L. Gordon, H.D. Jacoby and M.B. Zimmerman.   *Energy: Markets and Regulation.*   Cambridge: MIT Press.

Wilensky, H.L.   1967.   *Organizational Intelligence.*   New York: Basic Books.

Chapter 8

Sustainable Development: An Environmental Solution and a Business Opportunity

Colin F. W. Isaacs

For more than two decades, concern for the environment has been perceived as an impediment to business. Environmentalists obstructed the development plans of business, parks and reserves limited the opportunity to exploit resources, and workers were barraged with propaganda telling them that we could have jobs or we could protect the environment, but we could not do both.

A decision by the United Nations General Assembly to establish the World Commission on Environment and Development in 1983 changed that paradigm. In its report the World Commission declared that caring for the environment is good for business.

The commission was chaired by Gro Harlem Brundtland of Norway and made up of 22 political, academic, and business leaders from around the world. Its report, published in 1987 under the title *Our Common Future*, describes in startling terms the environmental problems facing our planet.

Rather than following the "Limits to Growth" approach favored by international agencies and environmental groups in the 1970s, the Brundtland Commission came to the conclusion that increased economic activity on a global scale is a necessary component of the solution to our threatening environmental crisis. It declared that this economic activity must not be environmentally destructive, as so much of our activity has been in the past, but must instead fit within the definition of what it described as *sustainable development*: Development which meets the needs of the present without compromising the ability of future generations to meet their own needs.

WHAT ARE WE DOING WRONG?

Once the problem and its roots are understood, finding a solution becomes easier.   This is particularly true with the problem of the environment.

The Brundtland Commission opens its report with the following paragraph:

In the middle of the 20th century, we saw our planet from space for the first time. Historians may eventually find that this vision had a greater impact on thought than did the Copernican revolution of the 16th century, which upset the human self-image by revealing that the earth is not the centre of the universe.   From space, we see a small and fragile ball dominated not by human activity and edifice but by a pattern of clouds, oceans, greenery, and soils.   Humanity's inability to fit its doings into that pattern is changing planetary systems fundamentally.   Many such changes are accompanied by life-threatening hazards.   This new reality, from which there is no escape, must be recognized—and managed.

This paragraph contains the essence of the problem and the basis for its solution. The problem is humanity's inability to fit its activities into the pattern of natural systems.   The solution lies in the realization that when humanity fits its activities into that pattern of clouds, oceans, greenery, and soils, then it will overcome environmental problems.

There are three fundamental reasons behind our environmentally destructive way of life.

First, until recently, most people did not believe that our pollution problems were serious. Most people thought that environmentalists were greatly exaggerating when they made apocalyptic statements about environmental issues such as acid rain, toxic chemicals, soil depletion, and water pollution. Society will not act on problems that it does not consider to be serious.   Only in the last three or four years have environmental issues become mainstream within our society. Today the concerns of environmentalists are shared by scientists, politicians, the business community, and average citizens all over the world.

Second, for too long we viewed environmental problems as isolated and unconnected, to be fixed either by technological solutions or by closing down the polluting company. We ignored the fact that pollutants can and do spread around the world. We failed to notice that spreading pollution problems over a larger area or moving waste from land to water was only making things worse. In the 1940s and 1950s we tried to solve toxic chemical waste disposal problems by dumping into abandoned canals and swamps. The layer of dirt we put on top was ineffectual; today, lakes and underground aquifers in many parts of the world are contaminated with those toxic wastes. In the 1970s we tried to solve local air pollution problems by building taller smoke stacks. Today we have regional and continental air pollution problems because the taller smoke stacks spread the pollutants over a larger area. In the 1980s we tried to cure air pollution with catalytic converters and top-of-stack pollution control equipment. Today we know that every percentage reduction in efficiency caused by pollution control equipment is causing an increased discharge of carbon dioxide and hence an increase in global warming. Today we recognize the interconnectedness of environmental problems. There is no such thing as "throwing something away" because there is no "away." Moving contaminants from one medium to another or one place to another just adds to the burden that the planet already has to bear.

The concept that environmental problems are conected rather than unconnected can be illustrated by examining the landfill crisis that is now facing many urban areas. Municipal waste landfills are not a serious environmental problem. Certainly we must eventually give up our habit of burying huge quantities of waste in the ground simply because we will eventually take up too much land with garbage, but on any scale of environmental crises, the problems caused by municipal waste landfills have to be ranked quite low. The problem is not really the space that the garbage takes up but the permanent loss of the materials that are not being recycled. Throwing things into garbage dumps is a terrible waste of raw materials: trees, mineral ores, oil, gas, and much more. It is also a waste of the energy that was used to manufacture the things that are being thrown away. It also adds to pollution from industrial plants. A great deal of toxic waste is produced during manufacture of many products. By throwing those products away we are supporting production of even more of that same toxic waste.

Garbage is just one part of the cycle of resource consumption and pollutant generation that is literally wasting the planet. Recycling and waste reduction programs solve not just the problem of where to put the next landfill but also many of our other serious environmental problems. Today we are beginning to understand that environmental problems are interconnected and must be addressed in a comprehensive way starting at the source.

Finally, we have not been giving enough attention to our own impact on the environment. We are always trying to put the blame for environmental problems on someone else. Canadians blame the United States for acid rain, the USSR for the presence of toxic chemicals in the arctic, and Brazil for cutting down tropical rain forests. We must recognize that the fault does not lie with someone else; everyone must share the responsibility. It is true that some people cause more pollution than others. Those of us who live in North America are almost certainly doing more damage to the environment on a per-capita basis than anyone else in the world. Permanent environmental solutions will come only when every member of society in every country takes responsibility for minimizing the environmental impact of his or her own activities. North Americans, and North American industry in particular, have the opportunity and the responsibility to take that leadership role.

We have regarded the earth as if it had unlimited resources and unlimited capacity to absorb waste. Some experts feel that the only way to avoid the permanent destruction of the planet's life-support systems is to put an end to ever-increasing development. The sustainable development concept promotes the view that, although we are approaching the limits of both resources and waste absorption, growth does not necessarily need to be curtailed. Instead, the type of growth must be changed to recognize the constraints imposed by natural systems.

AN INTRODUCTION TO SUSTAINABLE DEVELOPMENT

The concept of sustainable development is now being adopted by many world leaders. The definition of sustainable development is regarded by many people as fuzzy, but analysis of its report can help explain what the World Commission on Environment and Development really meant.

The first key message is that, just as our environmental problems are interconnected, so are they also interconnected with the economy. We have built our economy as if the planet provides resources and absorbs waste without limit. We have regarded natural resources as almost free, not figuring into the equation the replacement costs for nonrenewable resources that will not be available to future generations. We have used the land, water, and air as a free dump, not taking into account the hidden costs of health care and loss of species, water supplies, recreational resources, and much more that will result from the wastes that we have dumped. Cleanup costs, remediation, and the costs of research to overcome problems have been passed on to future generations. It has been cheap to use nonrenewable resources and cheap to pollute. Our economy has supported, indeed encouraged, our polluting habits. We have been using up the earth's capital rather than living off the bountiful interest. Brundtland tells us that we must begin to recognize the long-term costs of environmental pollution and resource depletion in all our economic equations. When we do so, we find that pollution is in fact very expensive. Prevention is much cheaper.

The second message from the Brundtland Report is especially important for environmentalists and for business. Solving our environmental problems does not mean abolishing industry or returning to log cabins with a tallow candle for heat and light. Solving our environmental problems requires healthy industry and a healthy economy, simply because when our economy is growing we can more easily afford to make the hard choices that will allow us to live within the planet's ecological means. People who are living at a subsistence level will take almost any steps, even environmentally destructive steps, in an attempt to survive. People who have risen above the subsistence level are the people who must engage in the process of long-term planning for the survival of the planet.

The third message, one that should be obvious but that seems too often to be forgotten, is that a healthy economy requires a healthy environment. If our environment is collapsing, if our coastal cities are being inundated by rising oceans caused by global climate change, if our drinking water is being contaminated by health-threatening chemicals from leaking dumps, if our farmland is turning to desert, then these situations will soon adversely affect the economy. We will need to spend time, money, and resources in an effort to fix the problems. Some short-term solutions may involve massive relocation of people; others will involve capital spending in a crisis mode. This is hardly the foundation for a healthy economy. It is essential that we maintain our environment if we are to have the healthy society and the strong economy that we all seek for future generations.

The final message from Brundtland is that we must abandon our "react and cure" approach, our emphasis on cleaning up environmental problems after they have occurred. Instead we must adopt a strategy of "anticipate and prevent," seeking out likely environmental problems before we undertake a new activity and modifying it so as to ensure that those environmental problems will not occur. Solving problems after they have arisen is more expensive and less effective than preventing problems before they arise.

The four messages from the Brundtland Commission that essentially define the concept of sustainable development can be summarized as follows:

- pollution is expensive;

- solving our environmental problems requires a healthy economy;

- a healthy economy requires a healthy environment; and

- solving environmental problems after they have arisen is more expensive than preventing them before they arise.

When the definition of sustainable development that the World Commission chose is quoted, it is important to understand the context within which the words are used. Brundtland uses the word *development* to mean improvement of the quality of life for everybody who lives on this planet. *Meeting the needs* is used in a very narrow context: doing no more than meeting essential needs. *Without compromising the ability of future generations to meet their own needs* requires that we allow future generations to have at least the same ability to enjoy the resources of this planet that we have had, without placing reliance on systems or technologies that have not yet been invented. None of these should pose an obstacle to North American business. In the last fifty years business has continued to expand towards global objectives.   With a world population rapidly approaching ten billion, there will be plenty of sustainable development opportunities for business growth.

Implementation of sustainable development is going to require participation by all people and by all sectors. Some of that work has already started. Government, industry, service-oriented businesses, trade unions, educators, homemakers, and many others have a major role to play in assisting the transition to a society guided by the principles of sustainable development.

THE ROLE OF THE CANADIAN GOVERNMENT

The public expects governments to lay down rules for appropriate behavior, including environmental behavior. It is clear from opinion polls that the Canadian public has not been satisfied with the role its governments have been playing in solving environmental problems.

Until the late 1980s neither the federal nor the provincial governments paid much attention to the environment: environment ministers were the most junior ministers in Cabinet; Canada had far fewer environmental laws than did our neighbors in the United States and even fewer than much of Western Europe; pollution controls were negotiated in secret between civil servants and industry, with the civil servants often feeling that their responsibility was more to help business than to meet the public's expectations for tough environmental controls. Around 1987 government's actions and attitudes began to change, but the actual change has not yet been very great. Most environmental activity now being undertaken by governments in Canada could be described as "green rhetoric": speeches and discussion papers dominate the field. However, this rhetoric is setting the stage for future action. Politicians are quickly learning that the issue of protecting the environment is not going away and that supporting it can be profitable in terms of economic activity and voter support.

The federal and provincial governments face economic problems that are likely to impact on their environmental strategies. Salaries for top technical experts are not competitive with those in the private sector. Funding for new programs will almost certainly have to come from new taxes or other revenue programs. The ability of government to operate programs or to offer financial assistance is likely to be very limited in the next five years. However, government is recognizing that the concept of sustainable development can provide it with some opportunities. Environmental success may no longer be measured in terms of dollars spent by government; the opportunity exists for government to provide only the regulatory and economic framework within which sustainable development activities become more profitable than nonsustainable ones.

Each province now has a "round table," a committee of labor, industry, environmentalists, government officials, and others, intended to search for and develop strategies for sustainable development for use in that jurisdiction. A national round table has been formed as well. The round table concept was introduced in the report of the National Task Force on Environment and Economy, a group called together by the Canadian Council of Ministers of the Environment to prepare Canada's response to the Brundtland Commission report. The round table, or multistakeholder consultative approach, has already been applied with almost universal acclaim to the development of legislative and regulatory initiatives at the federal level and in the province of Ontario.

The Ontario round table has been the leader in strategic planning. A recently published document, the *Challenge Paper*, provides strategies and targets for achieving some degree of sustainability in the areas of water, food and agriculture, forests, waste, air, and urban development. The paper is now the basis for a public consultation program that is intended to produce a strategy to achieve sustainable development in the province.

THE ROLE OF INDUSTRY

Industry has been the traditional scapegoat for environmental concerns. Even in the 1970s, when concern about the environment was regarded as something of a fringe issue, most people thought of pollution as the black smoke coming out of factory chimneys. During most of the 1980s, government regulatory efforts focused almost entirely on industry. Chemicals and foods were tested and retested by government. Small groups of consumers engaged in product boycotts to protest environmental damage. Despite all these efforts, environmentally damaging incidents continue, environmental safety is of even greater public concern, and toxic waste is generated in ever-increasing quantities.

Today, industry more than government is leading the "green" revolution. Canadian business can be divided into four categories. Some companies have adopted environmental strategies because their senior officials are convinced of the imperative nature of our environmental problems. Although few fall into this category, it is often the presidents of these companies who are among Canada's environmental leaders. High visibility, a solid environmental program, and an eagerness to involve environmentalists, environmentally conscious consumers, and local communities in decisions are helping these companies avoid problems and reduce the costs associated with confrontation over environmental issues.

One example of a company in this category is Dow Chemical Canada. Under President David Buzzelli, Dow identified itself as a leader in environmental performance in the Canadian chemical industry. Dow was able to achieve local community approval for a new industrial waste incinerator much more easily than normal because of the consultation processes it employed with both the local community and regional interest groups. The company's plan to isolate completely its plant from the neighboring St. Clair River was far ahead of anything required by government regulation. The payback was clear when the company had a visually spectacular fire at its Alberta plant: the incident was almost ignored by the media and by activists because they recognized the company's leadership in environmental matters. Maybe as many as fifty large companies in Canada have now positioned themselves as environmentally altruistic, within the confines of the need to remain adequately profitable.

A second group includes those businesses that recognize that money can be made by responding to the environmental imperative. The concept of "green consumerism," using purchasing power to effect environmental change, means that "green" products such as recycled motor oil, phosphate-free detergents, and nonchlorine-bleached paper are popular with environmentally conscious consumers. Loblaw supermarkets in Canada sell a house brand line of more than 200 environmentally improved products and have clearly been a leader in green marketing. Other manufacturers of consumer and commercial products are now scrambling to get on the green marketing bandwagon. A recent survey identified more than 80 mid-sized to large manufacturers and distributors in Canada who have identified at least one product line as having environmentally preferred characteristics.

The third and most common category comprises those companies that recognize the risks of environmental regulation being applied either to themselves or to any other members of the industry sector. They seek to implement environmental programs in order to avoid these risks. Some are fearful of the government inspector; others recognize that their business could be seriously damaged by public outrage following a spill or incident. Petroleum companies and chemical companies are frequently found in this category. These sectors have been particularly scared by government initiatives that have given the impression that senior executives could go to jail if the company were to be convicted of an environmental offense.

In some instances, the fear of regulation has been turned to positive advantage. A curbside blue-box recycling program was substantially funded by the soft drink industry in Ontario after the government threatened container deposits as the alternative. The original initiative for that program came from Alcan. Aluminum had already been shut out of the Ontario soft drink container market by a government that wanted to protect the local steel industry. Today the recycling program that Alcan and the soft drink companies helped to set up recovers many times the quantity of recyclable material that would have been recovered through a container deposit system.

A final category of business, irrelevant to this discussion, encompasses those companies that are completely unconcerned about the environment. They view current public concern as a passing fad. Three years ago most companies could be described this way, but today most large Canadian companies have some kind of environmental program. Those that are ignoring the environment are primarily small companies. The problem may be more that the owners and managers are preoccupied with running the company and that they have little environmental expertise, rather than a lack of concern.

New environmental initiatives from business are now being announced almost daily; articles concerning the environment appear regularly in our business newspapers and magazines. Those companies that ignore the environment are running a rapidly increasing risk of being left behind or being regulated in an unfavorable way.

Changes made by industry leadership hold more promise for protecting the environment than do our traditional methods of regulating industry. Even if we passed more laws and hired more enforcement officers, pollution from industry would continue. If we drove polluting industry out of Canada, those companies that are intent on short-term gain no matter the long-term cost would simply pollute us from somewhere else. An industry-led approach will ensure that both our environmental needs and our economic needs are met. This is a target that no government has thus far been able to achieve.

THE FINANCIAL AND SERVICE SECTORS

Nonindustrial business, the so-called service and financial sectors, are also beginning to develop environmental strategies. When a bank lends money it may be seen to be encouraging the pollution output by the borrower. If the pollution problem is serious and long-term, the bank is putting its money at risk in both direct and indirect ways. The borrower may get shut down, or at least heavily penalized, by regulators or may go out of business voluntarily, leaving the bank with some measure of liability for the cleanup program. Because polluting companies today are likely to be among the least efficient and least well managed, reviewing environmental performance before investing is wise not just for ethical reasons but also because it provides a window to the company's overall approach to management.

Similarly, when a hotel provides meals or accommodations it has the opportunity to help address the pollution caused by our food production and energy supply systems. Low-energy lighting and water-conserving shower heads reduce the environmental impacts associated with energy production. Careful choice of food providers can encourage our food production system to move away from the most environmentally damaging agricultural practices. There are many areas where attitudes can be changed, economic equations can be changed, and pollution reduction programs can be implemented.

We have traditionally regarded industry as our primary economy while the financial, service, and education sectors have been thought of as secondary. Today it is recognized that every business contributes to environmental damage, just as every person does. Business pollutes because it is a consumer of manufactured goods, because it produces waste, and because it participates in an economic system that does not recognize the cost of pollution.

Labor has traditionally viewed environmentalists as people wanting to eliminate jobs. The residue of that thinking must change, primarily by ensuring that the economic and human aspects of environmental proposals are always addressed. Labor has in fact been in the vanguard of environmental protection, often without realising it. Canada's occupational health and safety programs, among the best in the world, have the same goals as many environmental programs. They suffer from only one failing: they stop at the plant fence. If, working with labor, we can expand our health and safety programs so that they move from inside the workplace to the community and from the community to the planet, we will have excellent environmental protection programs in place around the world.

THE GREENING OF BUSINESS

Today, a company's environmental reputation will be measured against a variety of standards, including:

- regulations and standards established by government;

- participation in environmental initiatives of industry associations;

- the expectations of environmental interest groups;

- the expectations of the public;

- the environmental performance of competitors;

- the expectations of investors; and

- the expectations of communities where company facilities are located.

Clearly, meeting government requirements is essential for almost any organization today. In the environmental area penalties are increasing rapidly, and directors and officers are more and more likely to be held personally liable for their company's activities.

Industry associations, such as the Mining Association of Canada, the Canadian Chemical Producers Association, and the Canadian Petroleum Association, now have in place codes of environmental conduct. The chief executive officers of member companies are required to sign these codes and ensure company adherence to them. In the trucking business strict adherence to a code is now becoming a condition of association membership. Association-led environmental initiatives will be successful only if all members of the association participate; therefore, involvement in both the planning and the implementation phases is essential for any company that does not want to be outdistanced by its competitors.

Many environmental groups operate by making an example of one company or one product. One example is McDonald's, singled out for a campaign first against polystyrene foam packaging and subsequently against disposables of any kind. Products can also be targeted. Disposable diapers have been singled out by many environmentalists seeking either a government ban of the product or a consumer boycott, both based on the alleged environmental damage being caused by landfill sites. No company can afford to have either itself or its products targeted in this way.

Expectations of the public are high, but people are often not well informed. The public wants pollution to stop immediately and it tells pollsters that it is willing to pay, within reason, if this is necessary to stop pollution. Sometimes the public admits to pollsters that it does not understand the complexity of environmental issues. Nevertheless it is the public, more than environmental interest groups, that is driving government to increased environmental regulation. Winning public trust in any industry sector is going to do more to reduce the threat of punitive regulation than will any federal or provincial lobbying effort that an industry sector could mount. Indeed, lobbying may be counterproductive. Environmentally concerned voters view lobbying in a negative light. The industry that has a strong lobbying presence may well find that building confidence with the public is made substantially more difficult because of it.

Today, an increasing number of companies are putting their environmental performance out for public scrutiny in order to achieve competitive advantage. Opinion polls and focus groups make it clear that those who do so are likely to be able to achieve a small but significant increase in market share.

Slowly, but with ever increasing impact, the investment community is becoming interested in environmental performance. Environmental questions now arise regularly at shareholder meetings. So-called socially responsible funds are attracting a growing share of the investment pool. Even conservative investment houses are quickly discovering the very large risk associated with contaminated real estate or out-of-control emissions.

Right-to-know bylaws and restrictions on environmentally damaging operations are becoming more and more common at the municipal level. When community groups target a company for protest activity, they are frequently successful in hurting the company's reputation and sometimes successful in forcing it to move.

Companies that adopt environmental leadership, or "green" strategies, frequently do so for one or more of several reasons.

- to raise overall corporate profile;

- to have greater influence over government policies and legislation that could affect operations;

- to improve employee morale and the company's ability to attract top-quality executive candidates;

- to improve relations or to reduce the impact of bad relations with neighbors and environmental interest groups;

- to improve financial performance; and

- to enhance share value and investor confidence.

Environmental leadership has its disadvantages. Leadership raises expectations for continued performance. Companies that have implemented environmental initiatives are often expected to go even further without proper consideration of economic impacts. If a company initiates a major environmental program and then backs away from it for any reason, the result will be worse employee morale and much worse relations with regulators and with stakeholders than if it had never implemented the program in the first place.

Environmental leadership costs money, at least in the short-term. Although investment in low-waste processes, energy efficiency, recycling, and resource conservation often has a payback of less than two or three years, investment is required to implement the program. Cleanup of existing problems or such potential catastrophes as contaminated sites always costs money.

AN ORGANIZATIONAL GREENING PROGRAM

Corporate greening is rapidly becoming a growth industry. Consultants such as John Elkington in Great Britain and this author in Canada are experiencing a very high demand for services. There are relatively few corporate executives or consultants who have a sufficient understanding of environmental issues to design properly a complete environmental program.

Helpful corporate environmental principles are being developed by a number of organizations: trade associations, nonprofit groups, and governments. The Valdez Principles, developed by The Coalition for Environmentally Responsible Economies, are typical. They include the requirement that a company give priority to protection of the biosphere, sustainable use of natural resources, reduction of waste, wise use of energy, reduction of risk, compensation for any damage caused, and so on. While the Valdez Principles are not appropriate to all circumstances and while some corporations object to individual components, they do provide a framework on which to develop an in-house program of environmentally responsible behavior.

Using the term *green* in reference to the environment is not new. For decades radical environmentalists thought of themselves as green. More recently, European political parties dedicated to the cause of the environment picked up the term *green*. Today the word is widely but loosely used in Europe to describe anything that is more environment friendly than past practice. Green products adorn supermarket shelves, green gasolines contribute to reduced air pollution, and green businesses are good places to invest.

Turning environmental principles into practice is the challenge facing many companies today. A checklist of steps can be very helpful.

First, any company that intends to be green must identify its objective: is it to meet the environmental expectations of senior officials, to increase profit, or to avoid government regulation and the criticism of environmentalists. The strategy that is developed will depend on the objective to be met. It is particularly useful if the company can develop an environmental policy statement. Not only does this ensure that senior management understands the direction it is taking with respect to the environment, but it also helps ensure that all staff comprehend the approach. Just as staff participation is essential to a health and safety program, so is it also essential to an environmental program. Posting a new environmental policy will tell employees, visitors, customers, and shareholders that the company puts a high priority on the environment. The policy statement should set a tone within which all sectors of the company can start feeling comfortable about giving priority to the environment. Imperial Oil, Noranda, Dow, and Lever Brothers are examples of companies with environmental policies.

Second, every company needs to undertake an environmental audit to identify both problems and opportunities. The environmental audit should be directed to the president of the company and must look carefully at every manufacturing process, waste disposal process, product, transportation system, user, and the like. The audit serves two purposes: to inform senior management of the environmental risks faced by the company and to provide the basis for development of an action program, outlining how and when the environmental problems will be eliminated. Within the company it is important to be open—a business cannot pretend that there are no problems. The staff almost certainly is aware of potential environmental problems. The timing of spills or television shows attacking products may catch the company by surprise, but employees usually know what environmental weaknesses exist. The audit provides a mechanism through which the president and board of directors can become informed and can approve the necessary remedial steps.

With audit in hand, the company should develop an environmental action plan. The priority is to eliminate areas of noncompliance. Once the law is satisfied, the priorities will be set according to the environmental policy statement. If the goal is development of a green marketing strategy, priority will be given to product greening. If the priority is corporate image, emphasis may be given to those areas where the risk of incident or of negative publicity is greatest. New programs can position the company as an environmental leader. An action plan is essential if effort is going to be directed in an organized and cost-efficient way. Companies that do not have environmental action plans frequently find that their programs are unfocused, over budget, and abandoned before completion.

Third, every company needs a senior officer in charge of environment. Committees just do not get things done. There should be one person, generally the CEO, who has the ultimate responsibility for formulating the company's environmental policy and for insisting upon adherence to that policy. CEOs tend to overlook their environmental responsibilities; it is important to remind them frequently that they are as much responsible for the environmental performance of the company as they are for the profitability of the company. In addition to the CEO, most companies also need a senior officer in charge of day-to-day environmental affairs. Particularly during the learning phase, the company needs the highest possible level of environmental expertise. A senior vice-president who understands the relationship of the company's activities to broad environmental issues can be a very valuable asset.

Fourth, every company needs an environmental training program for its staff and customers. Canadian industry has begun developing this training, but much more is needed. Environmental education must not be limited to the shop floor. Staff involved in transportation, sales, and reception can be as vital to the company's environmental program as can the plant manager. Customers also need to be trained in how to use the product in an environmentally sound way and in how to dispose of it properly after use.

Fifth, every company needs to monitor, audit, and report on its environmental performance at least annually. It needs to list the progress that is being made on each of the problem areas, adding new problems to the list and deleting the problems that have been resolved. Progress in taking advantage of environmental opportunity should also be reported. Each year companies need to evaluate environmental training programs, making sure that they are moving forward as quickly as possible. A company must never delay action on a potential environmental problem because it thinks it can get away with it for a few more years; those are the problems that will hit the press! In today's environmental climate, caution is the best approach; if the risk is high, change the product or the process. Today, neither an individual company nor the industry sector as a whole can afford leaks either of toxic material or of unflattering information.

Some companies have started reporting their performance to their shareholders and to the public through pages dedicated to the environment in their annual report. A few publish a separate environmental annual report; Dow Chemical Canada is an excellent example.

Sixth, the green company must monitor the evolution of the green agenda. Change in public opinion, in regulatory requirements, in expectations, and in technology is coming at an amazing rate. Major reports on the environment are being issued almost daily. The company that does not keep up is certain to get left behind. Finally, and this may seem more challenging, the green business needs to help build bridges between the various interests. The company that pretends it has no environmental problems, that isolates itself from the rapidly growing multistakeholder consensual decision-making processes, is going to have its concerns go unheard. Many of the financial benefits of corporate greening are only realized if the public knows what the company is doing. More particularly, if the links are there, if the environmental community can see what the company is doing, if the media knows about the programs, if the community knows what is going on, the benefits will be enormous if some glitches do arise.

GREEN MARKETING

Many companies want to have highly visible environmental activities because it really is good for business. There is lots of profit to be made and waste to be eliminated, in areas such as waste reduction, clean technology, and recycling, but green marketing has caught the attention of the consumer more than anything else. The Canadian Green Consumer Guide sold more than 200,000 copies in nine months. It is based on a very successful British book, the Green Consumer Guide, that has been a best seller in that country, having gone through twelve printings and more than 250,000 copies in less than two years. The Green Consumer Guide looks at a wide range of consumer products and services and makes recommendations to the consumer as to the type or brands of products that should be purchased or avoided by consumers wishing to do their part for the environment.

Green consumerism suggests that consumers can use their purchasing power to effect environmental change. It involves using the power of the marketplace instead of government regulation to achieve environmental change, and there is evidence that it does work. A product is usually described as green if it can meet one or more of several criteria. The green product itself may be better for the environment and therefore better for the long-term health of the user. For example, a phosphate-free detergent should be better for the environment than a detergent that contains phosphates. The green product may be better for the environment because less waste is produced during its manufacture, even though the product may be exactly the same. For example, a paper product may be described as green if it is manufactured in very low waste nonchlorine-bleach pulp mill. A product may be green if less waste or pollution is associated with its packaging or with its ultimate disposal. Finally, a product might be described as green if something about it encouraged environmentally less damaging behavior in its users. For example, the cloth diaper is not a new product, but it does encourage families to reuse rather than to throw away.

The company that wants to take advantage of the green marketing opportunity should consider several key points.

First, green marketing must be based on real action. Consumers and environmental groups are already skeptical of advertising claims. If distributors want to maximize effectiveness and minimize the criticism, they must make sure that they can back up all environmental claims by pointing to new actions that have been taken. European consumers are losing interest in green products because of the multitude of unjustified green claims on the supermarket shelf. As a result the British government has introduced legislation to regulate green marketing claims. This may seriously limit the green marketing opportunity.

Second, green products must identify scientifically justifiable environmental gains. Biodegradable plastics ran in to trouble just a few weeks after their launch in Canada because there is no independent evidence that they work when buried in landfills. A study carried out for the Ontario government confirms that the behavior of biodegradable plastics in the landfill is unlikely to differ significantly from that of regular plastics. Already skeptical consumers will not be helped by arguments over the science of an advertising claim.

Third, manufacturers must identify for themselves points where the product is less than perfect and must be prepared to deal with those issues in public debate. When developing a brand of natural source fertilizer that contained composted pulp mill waste, Loblaw Companies recognized that the product might be attacked on the basis that it contained dioxin. In fact, the waste came from the front end of a bisulphite process pulp mill that did not use chlorine, but, to be absolutely sure, Loblaw had independent tests for dioxin and other toxic chemicals carried out on the fertilizer before it was brought to market. That small step proved to have been worthwhile when GreenPeace held a press conference to claim that the fertilizer might contain dioxin. The company already had the test reports in hand to disprove their claim.

Fourth, distributors must not oversell. Not everyone has grown accustomed to environmental marketing yet. Some believe that a product should not be called environment-friendly, or green, unless it is environmentally perfect. This misses the point that environmental perfection does not exist. We all have an impact on the environment just by living. Nevertheless, manufacturers and distributors must all be careful that they understand exactly what it is that enables their product to make environment claims. It is often wise to describe the claims on the package or in the advertising. A new package from Proctor and Gamble, the Enviropak, avoided much criticism by including in its Canadian advertising the fact that it is only the package that has changed and that lightweight packages will make only a very small difference to the waste problem.

Fifth, manufacturers need to have environmental technical help available all the time, both for themselves and for consumers. The world is rapidly becoming an environmentally sophisticated place: the consumer needs help and advice with environmental issues just as with food safety or cooking, while the manufacturer needs to be able to respond, often at short notice, to new scientific information that is pouring out of governments, universities, and laboratories every day.

Sixth, people and companies both make mistakes in the manufacture or labeling of a product. Because the concept of green products is so new, mistakes in this area are almost inevitable. Perhaps the product does not really fit green criteria after all; perhaps its efficacy is less than the consumer will accept. It is essential that, when a mistake has been made, it be acknowledged and corrected as quickly as possible. Only through fast action and honest disclosure of information surrounding the problem will consumer trust in the usefulness of green products be maintained.

CONCLUSION

The concept of sustainable development is so new that implementation strategies are only just being developed. Initially, many environmental organizations and experts were skeptical. Even today a few experts are maintaining that only a "Limits to Growth" approach can effectively prevent serious environmental catastrophe. The 1970s "Limits to Growth" approach would almost certainly mean reducing industrial and business activity if it were to be applied in the 1990s. It is fortunate, therefore, that the majority of environmental experts are now accepting the sustainable development concept as a more effective tool for achieving environmental goals. The opportunities will become increasing clear as more and more implementation strategies are developed by companies, governments, and nonprofit agencies.

Two strategies are already emerging as successful implementations of sustainable development. Both green marketing programs and corporate greening programs are likely to become an established part of business planning in the 1990s. Governments are already studying participation in green marketing through the adoption of purchasing policies that give preference to environmentally helpful products and suppliers. Manufacturers and retailers of green products are frequently unable to keep up with the tremendous public demand. Companies that have successfully implemented greening programs, and announced the fact, are finding that their public image has been greatly enhanced.

From a business perspective the most important part of the new approach may be that those industry sectors that become leaders in implementing sustainable development and that can self-regulate in an effective way will avoid much of the "command and control" type of government directives that the public is currently demanding. Those that cannot may well find that their business activity is dictated more and more by government regulations.

Sustainable development is the one vision that is gaining widespread international support today. Every indication is that it is the Brundtland vision of a world that is more kind and more gentle to the environment that will be guiding the evolution of economies, East and West, North and South, in the early years of the 21st century.

REFERENCES

Berry, Jeffrey M. *The Interest Group Society*. Boston: Little, Brown & Company, 1984.

Canadian Study of Parliament Group. "Interest Groups and Parliament." (Ottawa, 12-13 April 1989; Quebec City: 1 June 1989).

Gibbins, Roger, and Neil Nevitte. "Canadian Political Ideology: A Comparative Analysis." *Canadian Journal of Political Science* 18 (March 1985), pp. 577-598.

Horowitz, Gad. "Conservatism, Liberalismm, and Socialism in Canada: An Interpretation." *Canadian Journal of Public Policy* 32 (May, 1966), pp. 143-171.

King, David C., and Jack L. Walker. "The Provision of Benefits by American Interest Groups." Paper presented at the Annual Meeting of the Midwest Political Science Association. Chicago, Illinois, 1989.

Leman, Christopher. *The Collapse of Welfare Reform: Political Institutions, Policy, and the Poor in Canada and the United States*. Cambridge, Massachusetts: MIT Press, 1980.

Lipset, Seymore M. "Canada and the United States: The Cultural Dimension." *Canada and the United States*. Eds. C. F. Doran and J. H. Sigler. Englewood Cliffs, New Jersey: Prentice Hall, 1985.

Milbrath, Lester W. *Environmentalists: Vanguard for a New Society*. Albany, New York: State University of New York Press, 1984.

Nelkin, Dorothy, ed. *Technological Decisions and Democracy: European Experiments in Public Participation*. Beverly Hills, California: Sage, 1979.

Presthus, Robert. *Elites in the Policy Process*. London: Cambridge University Press, 1974.

Pross, A. Paul. *Group Politics and Public Policy*. Toronto: Oxford University Press, 1986.

_____. "Pressure Groups: Adaptive Instruments of Political Communication." *Pressure Group Behavior in Canadian Politics*, Ed. A. P. Pross. Canada: McGraw-Hill Ryerson Limited, 1975.

White, Graham. *The Ontario Legislature: A Political Analysis*. Toronto: The University of Toronto Press, 1989.

World Commission on Environment and Development. *Our Common Future*. Oxford: Oxford University Press, 1987.

Chapter 9

Our Changing Climate: Challenges and Opportunities in a Changing Environment

Irving M. Mintzer

"The understanding of the greenhouse question is sufficiently developed that policymakers should now begin an active collaboration to explore the effectiveness of alternative policies and adjustments."

Concluding statement of the Villach Conference, sponsored by the World Meteorological Organization, the United Nations Environment Programme and the International Council of Scientific Unions, in Villach, Austria, October 1985

ENVIRONMENTAL PROTECTION: A STRATEGIC ISSUE FOR THE 1990s

Energy companies will face a new set of risks and opportunities during the 1990s. The emphasis of national energy policies is shifting from assuring adequate and reliable fuel supplies to controlling and minimizing environmental risks. The resulting policies are likely to constrain strategic planning decisions by energy companies in dramatic new ways.

During the energy crisis of the 1970s and early 1980s, the public assumed that modern industrial society's principal energy problem was too little fuel—especially oil—to meet future needs and sustain economic growth. The policy challenge was how to increase supplies to meet steadily growing future demands.

As we enter the 1990s, the energy problem has taken on a new cast. A string of unanticipated events and a growing scientific understanding of the costs of pollution have caused many citizens and politicians to question the integrity and even the fundamental competence of the companies that supply oil gas, coal, and electricity. Public attention has shifted to the risks of routine operations and occasional accidents, such as oil spills, toxic chemical releases, refinery fires, nuclear power plant accidents, and chronic air pollution. In this view, the principal risks facing society today are, in a sense, associated with too much energy. Traditional institutions seem incapable of addressing the problems of safely managing rapidly increasing (and sometimes inadequately supervised) energy supplies that must be delivered from ever more remote and fragile areas.

Policy responses to this growing public concern will shape the business climate of the 1990s. They may change the relative prices of fuels and alter the ability of companies to sell particular fuels in specific markets. Although policy responses to problems that have mainly local or regional impacts, such as accidents and the release of toxic substances, will raise corporate liability, the more strategically significant new challenges will arise from policy interventions in response to problems that have principally international or global impacts. Because attempts to solve the global problems are likely to become embedded in agreements between countries, they will be harder to change than those cast as local or regional legislation.

Efforts to explore alterative policy responses to the linked risks of chronic, energy-related air pollution have already begun in several countries. A number of national inquiries have recently been held to examine the relationships between energy policy, global warming, ozone depletion, local air pollution, and acid deposition. In the United States, for example, the Department of Energy, the Environmental Protection Agency, the National Academy of Sciences, the Congressional Office of Technology Assessment, and the Congressional Budget Office are all conducting major studies on issues related to energy policy and global warming. The EPA has issued a draft report, mandated by Congress in 1988, that evaluates a range of policy options to stabilize global climate.

As a result of increasing public concern, politicians have begun proposing a wide variety of unilateral and multilateral approaches to reduce the risks of environmental damage from energy use. These proposals range from energy taxes to new performance and pollution standards, from increases in energy R&D to alternative fuels programs, from new diplomatic initiatives to increased support for forestry and family planning.

For example, the U.S. Congress is considering more than 10 comprehensive bills and many single issue bills that have been introduced in the last two sessions to address these concerns.[1] The National Energy Policy Act, S.324 (Wirth, D-CO), seeks reductions in U.S. carbon dioxide emissions of 20 percent by 2000 and promotes international negotiations to reduce CO_2 by 20-50 percent by 2015. The same bill authorizes almost $1 billion of additional R&D funding for renewable energy systems and advanced nuclear reactors. The Global Environmental Protection Act, S.333 (Leahy, D-VT), would impose tighter standards for hydrocarbon and nitrogen oxide (NO_x) emissions from vehicles, utilities and appliances. This bill also limits the sulfur content, Reed Vapor Pressure and oxygen content of gasoline and other motor fuels.

The World Environmental Policy Act, S.201 (Gore, D-TN), would replace the President's Council on Environmental Quality with a new Council on World Environmental Policy. In addition, this bill would rapidly tighten the Corporate Average Fuel Economy (CAFE) standards, raise taxes on gas guzzlers, prohibit venting or flaring of gas from wells or refineries, and increase U.S. support for international family planning activities. The Global Pollution Control Act (Stafford R-VT, and Baucus, D-MT) aims to reduce CO_2 emissions by 35 percent by 2010 and establishes a national goal of delivering all U.S. energy from nonpolluting technologies by 2050. This bill imposes stiff performance standards on many important classes of equipment and requires significant reductions in the level of CO_2 emissions per unit of useful energy supplied.

The Global Climate Change Assessment Act, S.251 (Moynihan, D-NY), would establish a major new research program to identify the causes and effects of global environmental changes and to evaluate policies to mitigate those changes. The Global Warming Response Act (Boschwitz, R-MN) would create a new Office of Global Warming in the Department of State to coordinate policy evaluation, research and responses on global warming and to prepare a strategic plan for U.S. efforts in international negotiations. This bill requires negotiations on CO_2 with the objective of reaching an international agreement to reduce emissions by 20 percent by 2000. The Global Warming Prevention Act, H.R. 1078 (Schneider, R-RI), seeks international agreements to a 20 percent reduction of global CO_2 emissions by 2005 and a 30 percent reduction in global NO_x emissions by 1998. This bill authorizes an increase in the CAFE standard for cars to 45 mpg by 1999 and provides R&D funds to study the feasibility of converting fleets of gasoline powered vehicles to operate on natural gas.

In addition to these congressional bills, President Bush has proposed legislation to address the problems of chronic air pollutant emissions, the release of acid precursors and the introduction of alternative fuels. The President's proposals would promote market-oriented measures to limit future emissions of SO_2 and NO_x to minimize the risks of acid rain. They would also provide substantial stimulus for the development of alternative fuels, including methanol, ethanol and natural gas, for applications in the transportation sector. However, in November 1989, the Bush Administration appeared to deemphasize its interest in measures to curb acid rain, suggesting instead that there be more study of the issue.

Not only U.S. politicians are interested in the problems of air pollution and energy policies. International meetings and discussions on these subjects are occurring increasingly. In 1987, after 10 years of negotiation, 35 countries signed the Montreal Protocol on Substances that Deplete the Ozone Layer. In the spring of 1988, Prime Minister Brundtland of Norway and Prime Minister Mulroney of Canada proposed separately that negotiations begin on a new "Law of the Atmosphere" designed to control the production and emissions of dangerous air pollutants. In the fall of 1988, the President of the Maldives urged the United Nations General Assembly to coordinate actions that might prevent a catastrophic climate change (and the associated rise in sea level). His concern was only partly motivated by the fact that such a sea level rise could obliterate his island nation. His speech, along with others by Foreign Minister Shevardnadze of the Soviet Union and Senator Boschwitz of the United States, stimulated the General Assembly to pass a resolution initiating increased UN activity on these environmental issues. At about the same time, following extensive discussions under the auspices of the United Nations Economic Commission for Europe, 30 countries signed a historic protocol on NO_x reductions.[2]

In November 1988, a 40-nation body called the Intergovernmental Panel on Climate Change (IPCC) was organized by the United Nations Environment Programme and the World Meteorological Organization.[3] In January 1989, this panel began an 18-month assessment process to develop a basis for evaluating national policy responses and international approaches to reducing the risks of rapid global warming. The assessment process is not expected to lead directly to a new international agreement but will provide consensus documents on the scope of the problem, the strength of the science and the efficacy of various national strategies to limit the future risks.

During 1989, multilateral, ministerial-level discussions of international atmospheric problems were held at major meetings in the United Kingdom, the Netherlands, France, Kenya, and India. Additional discussions took place during the fall in Japan, Switzerland, the Netherlands, and the United States. In Paris during July 1989, environmental issues were the focus of a principal session of the G-7 summit meeting. More than one-third of the paragraphs of the final summit communique were devoted to environmental issues. For the first time on record, the leaders of the seven wealthiest nations actively considered exchanging emissions reductions for trade and economic concessions. In January 1990 in Moscow, President Gorbachev organized and addressed the Global Forum of Spiritual, Religious, Parliamentary, and Scientific Leaders on the Survival and Development of Humanity. Leaders of 80 countries met to discuss the impacts of global environmental problems and the options for their solutions. In February 1990, President Bush addressed the second full plenary session of IPCC when it met in Washington, D.C.

In these expanding discussions, international attention is focusing more and more on the problem of global warming due to the buildup of greenhouse gases. During the last two years, an unusual string of extreme weather events has aroused public concern about the stability of global climate. These events have included tropical hurricanes in Great Britain, droughts in the grain belt of the U.S. Midwest and the rice bowl of southeastern China floods in Bangladesh and the Sudan, and the "storm of the century" in the Caribbean Sea. Although none of these events can be proved to be the result of the greenhouse effect, they illustrate the sensitivity of modern societies in both developing and industrialized countries to comparatively small changes in the weather. These weather events, combined with the growing scientific understanding of the impacts of the buildup of greenhouse gases and the role of human activity in their accumulation, have moved the global climate issue onto the political agendas of many governments.

THE GREENHOUSE EFFECT: A NEW PHENOMENON?

"For generations we have assumed that the effects of mankind would leave the fundamental equilibrium of the world's system and atmosphere stable. But . . . we have unwittingly begun a massive experiment with the system of the planet itself"

Prime Minister Margaret Thatcher in a speech to the Royal Society, September 22, 1988

Although the recent spate of articles in the popular press would suggest that the greenhouse effect only began to have an important impact on our planet during the past several years, this is clearly not the case. The greenhouse effect is a fundamental geophysical process that has occurred for billions of years and has shaped the history of the earth. This effect, in an important way, contributed to the conditions that allowed life as we know it to evolve.

The physics of the greenhouse effect are quite simple. Energy, mostly in the form of visible sunlight, arrives continuously at the top of the earth's atmosphere. This energy is supplied at a rate of about 172,000 terawatt-years per year (TW-yr/yr), or about 17,000 times the rate of global commercial energy use.[4] About half the incoming solar energy is reflected back by clouds and by structures on the earth's surface. The rest, about 87,000 TW-yr/yr, is absorbed. To keep the earth from melting, an equal amount of energy must be released back into space. Continuously emitting energy, the planet acts like an object that physicists call a "black-body radiator." Because the earth's temperature is so much lower than the sun's, most of the energy is emitted into space as infrared radiation (i.e., heat).

For the last billion years, natural atmospheric concentrations of certain polyatomic gases that are transparent to incoming solar radiation have absorbed and reemitted the earth's infrared radiation. This process, called the greenhouse effect, has warmed the surface and thus allowed life to exist on our small planet. Today, however, the composition and behavior of that atmosphere is changing. During the last 30 years, the concentration of CO_2 in the atmosphere has increased at an average annual rate of about 0.4 percent. Recent observations suggest that the rate of increase in CO_2 concentration may have jumped dramatically in the past two or three years, approaching 0.7-0.8 percent during 1988.

Less precise estimates of the changing atmospheric CO_2 concentration over many centuries have been made by sampling the air trapped under glacial ice. The samples indicate unequivocally that the atmospheric concentration of CO_2 has increased by about 80 parts per million by volume (ppmv) or about 25 percent since the beginning of the Industrial Revolution.

The upward trend in greenhouse gas concentrations is largely due to human activities. For CO_2, the principal sources include combustion of fossil fuel, deforestation and changes in patterns of land use. Fossil fuel combustion causes emissions of about 5.5 billion metric tons of carbon per year as CO_2. Deforestation and land use changes emit a more uncertain amount, but most scientists believe that these biotic sources add an additional 0.5-2.5 billion tons of carbon to the atmosphere as CO_2.

If current trends in these activities continue and the atmosphere retains the same percentage of annual emissions (i.e., the same "airborne fraction") that it did prior to 1988, then the concentration of atmospheric CO_2 is expected to reach twice the preindustrial level by the beginning of the third quarter of the next century.

The natural greenhouse effect became the greenhouse "problem" during the last century as increasing concentrations of heat absorbing gases began to accumulate in the atmosphere and threatened to alter the global climate. For most of this last century, concerns about global warming due to the greenhouse effect have focused on the atmospheric buildup of CO_2. However, path-breaking work by V. Ramanathan and his colleagues at the National Center for Atmospheric Research in Boulder, Colorado has demonstrated that, at current rates of emission, other trace gases contribute about as much to global warming annually as does CO_2.

At the Villach Conference (noted above), the concluding statement warned that "the amounts of some trace gases in the atmosphere, notably carbon dioxide, nitrous oxide, methane and ozone, are increasing. . . . While other factors, such as aerosol concentrations, changes in solar energy input, and changes in vegetation may also influence climate, the increased amounts of greenhouse gases are likely to be the most important cause of climate change over the next century. . . . "

THE IMPACTS OF GLOBAL WARMING

"A growing scientific consensus exists that sometime in the next century, the surface of the earth will become warmer than it has been at any time in human history."

John Firor, Deputy Director, National Center for Atmospheric Research

"For 200 years we've been conquering Nature. Now we're beating it to death."

Tom McMillan, Former Canadian Minister of the Environment

Physical Impacts

Scientists everywhere now agree that if the atmospheric concentration of the heat-absorbing gases increases, the average temperature of the planet will rise. If current emission trends continue, the planet could experience a warming equivalent to doubling the preindustrial concentration level of CO_2 alone by about 2030. The doubling of CO_2 (or the equivalent effect from a combined buildup of trace gases) would result in an average global warming of 4-10°F (about 2.5-5.5°C). Such a warming is expected to be accompanied by a rise in average global sea levels of 1-4 feet (about 0.5-1.5 m), as small landed glaciers melt and the warmer ocean waters slowly expand.

Because the warming will not be equal the world over (but will be greatest in the polar regions), the traditional patterns of winds and ocean currents will shift. The timing and distribution of rainfall and snowfall will be altered, and the frequency of extreme weather events may increase substantially. The impacts of an uncontrolled global warming could alter historical patterns of regional climate with widespread and largely unpredictable costs, creating unprecedented challenges for modern societies.

Unfortunately, the stresses induced in human societies and natural ecosystems due to global warming will not occur in isolation. If current trends continue, these stresses will occur simultaneously with increases in population, tropospheric air pollution and stratospheric ozone depletion. In many cases, there may be important synergisms among these stressful factors.

For example, the combination of ozone depletion and global warming will increase the frequency and severity of urban smog by raising temperatures and increasing exposure to ozone-forming ultraviolet radiation in the lower atmosphere. Due to a buildup of the same chlorofluorocarbons (CFCs) that cause global warming and to increased ground-level exposure to ultraviolet light, stratospheric ozone depletion could reduce tree and crop yields at the same time that agricultural systems are being stressed by climate changes and acid deposition. Increased ultraviolet radiation may also damage oceanic plankton, the microorganisms responsible for removing significant quantities of CO_2 from the atmosphere.

Potential Economic Impacts

Changes of the magnitude that scientists estimate would accompany a 4-10° warming are likely to have important economic consequences for both industrialized and developing countries. For example, the rise in average global sea level could cause significant flooding and salt water intrusion into aquifers. In areas where residential and commercial development restricts landward movement of the shoreline, wetlands and beaches could be lost. A recent study by the EPA estimates that it would cost $50-$70 billion to protect the most vulnerable areas of the U.S. coastline from a three-foot rise in sea level.

In many developing countries, the costs of a sea level rise may prove unbearable. For many low lying deltaic regions at the mouths of the great river systems, there is no feasible way to build adequate earthwork defenses. Without such defenses, the cost of a sea level rise will be measured in the loss of some of the world's most fertile cropland.

In the Nile Delta, for example, a three-foot rise in sea level would flood about 15 percent of the country's best agricultural land and displace about 12 percent of the population. In Bangladesh a rise of this magnitude could force 20 million people from their homes. If these refugees migrated south to dry land in India, not only would their economic output be lost to Bangladesh, but their uninvited presence might significantly increase regional political tensions.

Changes in the timing and distribution of rainfall could prove equally costly. Results of experiments with several of the most advanced three-dimensional global climate models suggest that where greenhouse gas buildup has raised temperatures by 3-9°F, mid-continent, mid-latitude areas will experience decreased summer soil moisture. These areas are the heartlands of rain-fed agriculture in the United States, the Soviet Union, Australia, Central Europe, and China. A hotter, drier climate could cause sequential or simultaneous crop failures in some or all of them.

Changes in rainfall patterns can also affect energy supply and use. In California, for example, the availability of hydroelectric power declines during dry years by as much as a factor of three compared to wet years. In the U.S. Midwest during the summer of 1988, reduced stream flows threatened to close down production at nine nuclear power plants whose operating licenses required them to observe strict inlet water temperature constraints and rigid downstream recharge levels.

Expected alterations in the historical patterns of ocean currents may have unanticipated and disruptive effects. If, for example, as a result of global warming, the location of the Gulf Stream current shifted westward a few hundred kilometers and the strength of the current were reduced, the United Kingdom, Ireland and the west coast of Scandinavia might get cooler and wetter even as the rest of Europe got substantially hotter.

Changes in the frequency of extreme events could also have important impacts. Hot spells during sensitive periods of plant and tree growth can reduce yields or destroy crops. Preliminary research suggests that a rise in temperature of 8-10°F would cause a decline of 90 percent in the fertility of the world's rice crops. In addition, extreme temperatures often place added stress on human health and affect the most vulnerable—the very old and the very young.

Economic dislocations resulting from rapid climate change would require costly adjustments by human societies to ensure provision of adequate supplies of food, water and energy. For natural and unmanaged ecosystems, whole species might disappear if they could not migrate as rapidly as their habitats moved poleward. Commercially important tree species, for example, might be pushed out of their natural range, replaced by less valued or slower growing species. For instance, the combined effects of stresses due to acid deposition and global warming could substantially reduce the range and yields of Canada's sugar maple trees.

While no one questions the basic physics of the greenhouse effect or the global consequences of a rapid greenhouse gas buildup, 20-50 years of intense research will be required before scientists can predict the regional distribution of impacts from global warming. Not all local effects will be negative. However, no country now can be sure that on balance it will be a winner.

For example, Canada will enjoy a longer growing season on the Canadian prairie. However, unless rain comes reliably, the weak podzolic soils of the Canadian shield will be unable to support much of the corn crop that is likely to be displaced northward from Iowa and Kansas in a warmer world. Furthermore, if shifts in the Gulf Stream caused by the warming trends combined with losses of plankton due to ozone depletion, traditionally rich Canadian fish catches on the Grand Banks of the Atlantic could be substantially reduced. Would the net effect be positive for Canada? Most scientists argue that it is impossible to be sure.

THE DETERMINANTS OF GLOBAL WARMING

Recent research suggests that significant future global warming is inevitable. However, the rate of future emissions and the resulting global warming are hard to estimate. They depend on a complex interplay of policy decisions, development strategies and investment choices. If the world chooses an energy strategy designed to increase coal use rapidly, if the production and use of the most dangerous CFCs continue to increase, if tropical deforestation continues to accelerate, and if little attention is paid to increasing energy efficiency, the planet will be committed to a warming of 3-9°F by 2010 and to a warming of about 14-25°F by 2075.

On the other hand, if national governments and corporate leaders choose to emphasize sustainable economic growth while increasing the efficiency of energy use, eliminating production of the most harmful CFCs, reversing the pattern of deforestation, and shifting the fuel mix from coal toward natural gas, nuclear and renewable sources of energy, then a warming of 3-9°F can be postponed beyond 2075.

The stakes are high—potentially the very survival of modern civilization. In a matter of decades, a warming of little more than 10°F could take the planet beyond the range of any change experienced in the past million years. However, by making policy choices that slow the rate of greenhouse gas emissions, the world can buy time to develop successful adaptive responses to those climate changes that are now unavoidable.

Slowing the rate of greenhouse gas emissions represents a kind of global insurance policy. For the most part, the "premiums" can be paid through measures that are technically feasible and economically attractive today. Moreover, such measures have the potential for multiple benefits independent of the goal of forestalling a climate catastrophe.

NEW OPPORTUNITIES IN A WARMING WORLD

Public and political responses to the linked problems of global warming, ozone depletion and acid deposition will change the business environment during this decade. International controls on the production and use of CFCs already have affected the chemical industry. Political responses to the risks of chronic pollution are also likely to be directed toward the energy industry in the form of measures such as taxes, fees and performance standards. These measures will alter the relative prices of fuels and the attractiveness of certain technological options. Emphasis is likely to increase on R&D activities to provide alternatives to traditional energy technologies.

The impacts of these policy responses will provide many new business opportunities and shape strategic decisions in the 1990s. On the supply side, concern about atmospheric emissions will tend to encourage cleaner-burning and high efficiency technologies. In the United States, a number of current proposals to alter the relative price of fuels and shift the fuel mix may be implemented even before their full effects are completely understood. On the demand side, policy responses will seek to stimulate more rapid turnover of capital stock and its replacement with more energy-efficient equipment.

In the electricity sector, burning natural gas is likely to be favored relative to increased combustion of coal. New, advanced gas turbines and combined-cycle machines can supply electricity at efficiencies 50 percent higher than conventional gas or steam turbines, with very low emission rates for criteria air pollutants. Because burning natural gas, even in a conventional turbine, releases only half as much carbon dioxide per unit of energy supplied as does coal combustion, gas-fired technologies may face little or no penalty if a carbon-based fuel tax is implemented. Increased demand for natural gas is likely both in urban areas where ambient pollution standards are currently unattainable and in areas where the economic alternatives are limited to increased imports of oil, construction of new nuclear plants or increased combustion of coal.

Because nuclear and renewable energy technologies produce even lower levels of harmful atmospheric pollutants, accelerating their deployment is likely to gain support. Substantial increases in R&D funding at the national level are likely in several countries. Tax credits and other incentives for renewables may be reintroduced in the United States. Rather than generate additional kilowatt-hours from their own plants, utilities will be encouraged to make concessions on standard contract offers to independent power producers where the new, small facilities can supply power at economically attractive (or even marginally attractive) rates and significantly reduce emissions.

Building new supply is most attractive when the rate of demand growth is small. When it is rapid, all technically feasible options must be pursued aggressively, often leading to inefficiency, duplication and wasted efforts. However, when demand growth is moderate, it is possible to match technological options to local conditions and thereby enhance investment returns. Thus, to maximize the value of cleaner-burning or smokeless technologies, national energy policies are likely to encourage the increased efficiency of energy use. In the 1970s, the emphasis on efficiency was motivated principally by moral and security concerns. In the 1990s, it will be motivated by increasing concern for the environment and the sustainability of economic growth.

In the United States, such policies may be expressed directly in terms of energy efficiency standards (the Schneider bill approach). Or they may be expressed indirectly in terms of tax incentives or pollution reduction requirements per unit of useful energy supplied (the Leahy bill approach). Energy supply companies that can join forces with hardware manufacturers to produce fuel equipment combinations that are more efficient and less polluting will be well positioned to take advantage of these different regulatory approaches.

Substantial opportunities now exist to market cost-effective investments in efficiency-improving technologies. For electric utilities, the challenge will be to make the marketing of energy services (and energy efficiency) as profitable as the traditional marketing of increased energy supply. High efficiency lights, motors, system controllers, and appliances are especially attractive to individuals and firms who are concerned about the consequences of excessive combustion. By establishing unregulated subsidiaries that operate outside their historic service territories, utilities can sell energy services to these new clients—either through shared savings in efficiency improvements or through direct sale of advanced end-use devices—and capture the emerging benefits in this changing environment. By developing cooperative partnerships and joint venture agreements, the unregulated subsidiaries of well managed utilities in one area may be able to build and profitably operate cogeneration and independent power facilities in other service territories that reduce emissions and increase overall system efficiency.

Nonetheless, the cooperation of regulatory authorities will be necessary. Environmental costs must begin to be included in the price of electricity. At the same time, the profitability of integrated service companies must be insured. New planning and rate-making approaches will be needed so that utilities profit as much from selling fewer kilowatt-hours as they do from selling more.

For oil and gas companies, the challenges will be somewhat more complex. A variety of regulatory approaches will be proposed that will seem to constrain business decisions and to advantage some new players. Increased gasoline consumption taxes combined with taxes for gas guzzling vehicles are likely to be popular measures for reducing emissions and raising federal revenues during the next five years. The taxes may reduce the quantities of gasoline sold, while not necessarily reducing gross margins or net income.

Proposals like the President's Clean Air package will encourage and perhaps subsidize the introduction of alcohol fuels and compressed natural gas into the transportation sector. Reformulated, cleaner-burning gasoline may be able to compete in this new environment if it can be shown to reduce ozone formation.

Furthermore, the high efficiency and low emission levels that are achievable with the emerging generation of combustion turbines and compressed natural gas vehicles may expand old markets and open new ones for forward looking firms. The downside risk for gas companies lies in concerns about methane leakage during the extraction, transportation and distribution of natural gas. Because each methane molecule has 20-30 times the warming potential of a molecule of CO_2, regulators are likely to pressure companies to monitor and ultimately to reduce methane leakage, lest the global warming advantage of clean-burning natural gas be negated.

One of the most important issues facing oil and gas companies in the 1990s is the public perception of their role in society. In practically every Western country, recent opinion surveys con firm the public's emphasis on the value of environmental protection. If the public perceives oil and gas companies to be doggedly resisting efforts to protect the environment, then when accidents inevitably occur, they will not be seen as isolated incidents or individual failures. Rather, they will be seen as reflections of the companies' obsessions with squeezing the last dollar out of every dangerous enterprise, of their fundamental incompetence and of their determined resistance to meeting the needs of the larger community.

Thus energy companies in general and oil companies in particular must strive to demonstrate their commitment to making reasonable profits through safe operations. Management must demonstrate with dollars and deeds that its commitment to sustainable economic development and environmental quality stretches beyond the horizon of next quarter's income statement. This may mean forgoing profitable opportunities to expand the coal side of the business in favor of exploration and production activities on the gas side. It may mean untraditional joint ventures to develop advanced fuel-engine combinations and new projects to develop low emission technologies. It could also mean expanding support for research on the environmental and health effects of alternative fuels.

As stockholders with an obvious self-interest, but with a desire for acceptance as credible players in the debate on national and regional energy policies, energy companies must demonstrate their willingness to provide complete and honest information, to share the burden of developing safe alternatives to traditional technologies, and to admit past errors.

By carefully evaluating the strategic choices of today, prudent energy companies on both sides of the border can help to reduce the risks of rapid climate change and, at the same time, take advantage of the opportunities to develop profitable new products and penetrate new and expanding markets.

NOTES

1. Among the most significant of the comprehensive bills that have been introduced are the Wirth bill, the Chaffee bill, the Stafford-Baucus bill of the 100th Congress, the Baucus bill of the 101st Congress, the Boschwitz bill, the Leahy bill, the Gore bill, the Schneider bill, the Bonker bill, and the AuCoin bill. In addition, the proposed amendments to the Clean Air Act will have a major impact on U.S. energy and environmental policy.

2. The UN ECE membership includes the United States, Canada, the countries of Western Europe and Eastern Europe, and the Soviet Union.

3. The IPCC is chaired by Dr. Bert Bolin of Sweden. The secretariat comprises representatives of 13 countries. The Scientific Working Group is chaired by the United Kingdom; the Climatic Effects Working Group, by the Soviet Union; and the Policy Response Working Group, by the United States. Cochairs of the Policy Response Working Group include Canada, Malta, the Netherlands, and the People's Republic of China. The Energy and Industry subgroup of the Policy Response Working Group is cochaired by Canada and Japan.

4. One terawatt is equal to 10^{12} watts. One terawatt-year per year is equal to about 30 quads per year. Annual global commercial energy is approximately 300 quads per year or about 7,400 million tons of oil equivalent (MTOE).

Chapter 10

Environmental Pollution and Energy Production: A Framework for Policy

Richard L. Stroup

"It is lack of information that is the heart of the matter."

J. H. Dales, 1968, *Pollution, Property & Prices*[1]

The production and use of energy almost inevitably lead to the production of byproducts—pollutants. Energy producers thus may impose aesthetic, ecologic, and human health costs on others. What policies should be adopted to deal with such costs or risks? The main point of this chapter is that designing and evaluating policy options is trickier and more difficult than it might seem. The unintended effects of policies to protect us can easily harm us.

Imposing costs on others in the course of producing goods is not an automatic recipe for trouble, especially if the costs are voluntarily accepted by those who bear them. With adequate compensation, workers willingly allow their working days to be "ruined" for all other purposes; suppliers of materials, if they are properly compensated, willingly give up goods that have many other valuable uses. But in the quote above, University of Toronto energy economist J. H. Dales recognizes the heart of the pollution problem: lack of information. If all costs imposed by polluters were clearly known, then polluters would have to compensate fully all those affected, just as any motorist must compensate the owner of a car negligently damaged by the motorist. Under such an obligation, the quantity of pollution would be optimized. When information is lacking, however, the rights of those polluted cannot be easily defended against chemical invasion by the polluter.

When information is missing, as when we cannot be sure about the effects of an air pollutant on downwind people and their property, a case can be made for substituting direct government regulation for court-enforced protection against invading pollutants. One alternative is to have government forbid the polluting behavior or at least to regulate it closely. Unfortunately, turning to regulation does not produce the information needed to determine a rational or fair risk-reduction policy. If we cannot even estimate who is doing what to whom, then fairly allocating the costs is likely to be impossible.

This chapter discusses the information problems bedeviling environmental policymaking and suggests that the property-rights regime can serve two purposes. First, it can handle directly a great many pollution problems and has done so more than most of us recognize. It can also serve as an analytical framework for considering the likely outcome of various regulatory policy alternatives. Consideration of the information problem along with other factors in the framework of property rights has important implications for environmental policy decisions facing the United States and Canada today.

In the following section we will see why there cannot be a "no regrets" policy and why it is dangerous to seek one. The section after discusses the importance of due process and evidentiary rules in efforts to improve the safety of any community or nation. The next section lays out the property-rights paradigm, which has often worked to hold polluters and potential polluters accountable for their actions. The final section discusses the need for accountability in the absence of full knowledge and in the presence of national boundaries.

WHY THERE IS NO SUCH THING AS A
"NO REGRETS" POLICY

Today, the press is filled with claims that in the presence of great uncertainty, policymakers should follow a "no regrets" policy; that is, they should anticipate the possibility of large harms and take actions to avoid them so that society does not later regret inaction. But the unfortunate fact is that government controls aimed at reducing risk (from pollution and other sources) to zero can actually make society less safe.[2] The safety measures themselves may later be regretted.

A conservative policy stance, by distorting the true picture of alternative risks, can actually increase danger. Berkeley political scientist Aaron Wildavsky, in his important book *Searching for Safety*, tells how.[3] For example, he points out that additional safety devices on nuclear reactors can be hazardous due to the increased complexity they impose and the added difficulties of maintenance.[4] Keeping new pesticides off the market increases the dangers from the pests they would control and from greater use of older, more dangerous pesticides. Keeping new drugs off the market for years until exhaustive tests can "prove" that they are safe, does, of course, reduce the risk of unexpected side effects from the drugs, but it also keeps potentially helpful drugs from patients who might benefit from them, including those who are desperately ill and dying. Research indicates that on balance, this "risk reduction" measure harms the nation's health.[5] Researchers Albert Nichols and Richard Zeckhauser of Harvard's Kennedy School argue the EPA risk assessments so overestimate the risks of some things that they lead to replacements that may actually be less safe.[6]

There are better ways to increase health and safety in society. Wildavsky observes that resilience and agility in response to threats are often a more effective strategy for safety than is anticipation. Unlike the turtle, which anticipates blows to its body by growing a shell to hide under, the human body reacts quickly to danger and repairs injuries. Less protected than the turtle in an anticipatory sense, humans are more agile and resilient. Wildavsky illustrates the point by noting that a person who exercises by running initially may be at higher risk of suffering a heart attack from the running itself than a person who does not run. The runner, however, by continuing to run, builds resilience to ward off future health threats.[7]

Similarly, a resilient society often is safer than an anticipatory one that attempts to protect itself from specific expected threats. Of course there are costs. If our society is to reap the benefits of technological change, we must also accept some personal risk from innovative products and technological missteps. But refusal to accept the need for individual adjustments and dangers leads to a society that does not advance. In such societies, life tends to be nasty, brutish, and short.

Wildavsky surveys existing literature that shows that people in rich societies, whatever their income level, live longer, healthier lives than do those in societies with simpler life-styles. This is true even though they face risks from advanced technological development. He notes that an earthquake in California in 1971 caused 62 deaths. The next year a slightly less powerful earthquake in Nicaragua killed tens of thousands. Why the difference? The wealthier country had better-built houses, better means of transportation and communication, and better health facilities.

Even within a given society, more income increases health and safety. Evidence from the literature suggests, for example, that for a 45-year-old man working in the manufacturing sector, a 15 percent increase in income has about the same risk-reducing value as eliminating all hazards from the workplace.[8] If the choice is between reducing his job hazards by half or allowing him a 15 percent increase in pay, the latter appears to be not only more rewarding in all other respects but also better from a narrow health safety point of view.

Under its current policies aimed at zero risk, the United States is retreating under a shell to avoid risk, thereby stifling technological development and reducing the rate of income growth. A better strategy for society is to recognize the potential danger of pollutants and to develop policies to handle the risks without further harming people by hampering technological and economic advancement.

DUE PROCESS AND THE WITCH HUNTS

In determining the appropriate environmental policy, it is important to recognize the dangers of being overzealous in the seeking of safety. Ecologist William C. Clark, in an insightful essay, "Witches, Floods, and Wonder Drugs," compares today's pursuit of zero risk to the European witch hunts of the 16th and 17th centuries.[9] Clark, admittedly an amateur historian, learned that the witch hunts stemmed from a response by the ecclesiastical authorities of the day to fears of mysterious and troubling occurrences such as wheat rotting in the fields and sheep dying of unknown causes. The focus on witches emerged especially strongly after a polemic against witches, *The Hammer of the Witch*, was published in 1486.

The Inquisition, a church agency, undertook the job of investigating witchcraft, and over the next two hundred years tens of thousands of witches were condemned to death (by both Catholic and Protestant authorities). What Clark finds applicable to environmental risk was the problem of proving one's innocence. By and large, there was no way for an accused witch to prove she was innocent. If a witch did not at first admit her guilt, she could be tortured a little more and she might. Or a little more. "Acquittal was arbitrary, dependent on the flagging zeal of the prosecutor," says Clark. "It was always reversible if new evidence appeared."[10]

Clark believes that today we cope with environmental risks in a similar way. Ever since the publication of *Silent Spring* (one might call it the *Hammer of the Witch* of the 20th century), a growing number of experts have been trying to stamp out risk. Regulators attempt to determine if a pollutant is a risk and, if it is, to eliminate that risk. But there is no way to prove that a substance is not a risk. A chemical that does not harm rats at moderate levels may harm them at higher levels. "In neither case [the witch hunts or risk assessment] is there any conceivable empirical observation which could logically force an answer 'No!'" says Clark, In both cases, "the only stopping rule is discovery of the sought-for-effect, or exhaustion of the investigator (or his funds)."[11]

Clark points out that few people have spoken out against today's shrill alarmists; anyone who criticizes the goal or process is "accused at least of callousness" (as were the few who spoke out against witch hunting). In the same way that the Inquisition became a growth industry of its day, identifying potential risks has become a good source of career advancement today. And in the United States, with the passage in 1980 of Superfund, a federal program to clean up abandoned waste sites, the confiscated property of oil and chemical companies has paid for much of the effort, just as the confiscated property of convicted witches helped to finance the Inquisition.

The problem is that government regulatory systems are run by a political process that has no standards of evidence or due process. Indeed, Robert Hahn, a former senior economist with the President's Council of Economic Advisers, says that "in drafting legislation, politicians are free to ignore scientific facts and economic forces."[12] In the United States, the Clean Air Act, which has been amended twice since its 1970 creation, illustrates how factional political interests override the public interest. As Bruce Ackerman and William Hassler showed in 1981 and Robert Crandall showed more recently, politicians used the Clean Air Act to serve regional economic interests rather than Americans' desire for cleaner air.[13]

Ackerman and Hassler point out that the Clean Air Act amendments mandated that electric utilities reduce sulfur dioxide emissions by installing expensive scrubbing devices even though emissions could have been reduced merely by using cheaper low-sulfur coal. But Eastern coal interests, the companies and unions that produce high-sulfur coal, did not want competition from low-sulfur coal. They froze out competition by insisting on scrubbers, which will not even work when used with low-sulfur coal. Furthermore, says Crandall, mandatory scrubbing led to higher electricity prices in the West and Southwest, stifling growth in the Sun Belt, and concentrated power production in old, sulfur-emitting factories in the East and Midwest, making the air there dirtier that it would have been.[14] When revised in 1990, the Clean Air Act allowed a little more use of low-sulfur coal, but still included regulatory incentives to force the use of expensive scrubbers.

Hysteria about chemical pollutants coupled with the self-interest of politicians and a growing cadre of bureaucrats has escalated the harm that the government can do in the environmental area. For example, in early 1983, newspaper headlines screamed about the contamination of Times Beach, Missouri. Ten years earlier, the town's streets had been spread with oil contaminated by the chemical dioxin. No actual damage to health or property had even been alleged, but in pursuit of zero risk and bureaucratic reputation, the EPA decided to spend $33 million to buy up the town's homes and businesses. Needlessly, Times Beach has become a ghost town.

More widespread in its impact is the harm caused by the proliferation of laws that are aimed at zero risk. Superfund started out as a $1.6 billion fund, composed of taxes on chemical and petroleum companies. Expanded by $8.5 billion in 1986, it is now widely recognized as a political pork barrel. (The Clean Water Act, too, whatever its initial intention, is now primarily a way for politicians to reward construction companies by funding sewage treatment plants.)

The juggernaut of zero risk pursuit goes on. In 1988, the people of California passed a sweeping chemical regulatory law. Proposition 65 bans the discharge into drinking water of chemicals "known" to cause cancer or reproductive harm and requires warnings to individuals exposed to these chemicals. Public employees are required to notify the news media when they discover violations and are subject to criminal penalties if they do not disclose the violations they discover. A bounty-hunter provision allows private citizens to collect 25 percent of the fines imposed if they initiate successful suits against violators.

The pursuit of zero risk, in spite of its ultimately enormous costs, is not carried out by people acting in bad faith. (By and large, the inquisitors were probably acting out of duty as well.) Many of today's environmentalists and regulators are drawn to their work precisely because they believe in the "anti-pollution" mission. But even selfless individuals, as decisionmakers, are inherently limited to a narrow view. Each person lacks the knowledge (and many lack the inclination as well) to understand and to weigh the effects that a decision has on others.

For example, both the chief executive officer of Exxon, seeking larger oil industry profits, and Mother Teresa, seeking succor for the destitute and ill in Calcutta, can be expected to have a narrow focus when making decisions. Each is likely to see his or her own goals as so important that careful consideration of other goals, preservation of a wilderness or a species, say, will be accorded secondary importance at most.

Constructing a refinery complex or hospital may, without institutions to protect people and property from damage, cause considerable environmental harm; but both the CEO and Mother Teresa will be loath to reduce their operations or to divert limited funds from their primary goals to eliminate unintended harm to the goals of others. The broader effects of a resource decision will be seriously considered only to the degree that institutional forces provide information about a decision's effect on others and the incentive for the decisionmaker to act upon that information.

Moving the decision to the government arena does not change the human tendency to pursue narrow goals: the dedicated manager of a government agency, whose mission might be to preserve wilderness, or instead to flood land while building a dam, will have a strong desire to further the specific mission and only scant understanding and concern for the other values sacrificed in doing so. It is important that institutions be in place to control such narrow vision.

PROPERTY RIGHTS AND ACCOUNTABILITY

Imperfect though they are, private property rights can often provide a better way to control pollution than does government regulation. Traditionally in the United States, much of the economy, including the protection of citizens against harm due to the pollution of others, has been controlled through the exercise of private property rights. The system has not been perfect because full information is seldom available and thus in some cases private property rights cannot be established or cannot be enforced. Such failures (sometimes called "market failures") have been one force leading to the governmental intervention that has failed to correct the problem. Along with the zealous pursuit of "zero risk," it has landed us in the situation we experience today.

The key to whether a system of human relationships is working well is accountability. Economists view decisionmakers as accountable if they face incentives that reward or penalize them according to the gains and losses that their decisions impose on society. A company that produces waste in the course of its business and makes outsiders bear some of its costs—imposing significant health risks or obnoxious odors, for example—is not accountable. In contrast, if that company takes care of its waste without endangering outsiders or forcing them to bear significant costs, the system is operating in a socially desirable way.

Most people will agree that the system of property rights works most of the time to keep people accountable in dealing with objects such as cars or tracts of land. That is because property rights to these things exist and are efficiently configured in three dimensions: they are "3-D property rights."

Property rights must be *defined* clearly so as to reside with a specific person or entity; *defended* easily against nonowners who might wish to use or "steal" the asset; and *divestible*, or transferable, by the owner to others on whatever terms are mutually satisfactory to buyer and seller.

When property has these characteristics and when trades can be transacted easily, the owner of any asset, whether land, house, factory, or some other commodity, has both the incentive and the authority to use that asset in such a way as to maximize its value to society.[15]

What do we mean by maximizing its value to society? The owner has an incentive to use property in the manner most valued by members of the society. An owner of property considering whether to use it to store chemical wastes must consider both the reduction in value imposed by the storage and the resulting limits placed on subsequent uses for the land, and the benefits gained by (and revenue received from) those who want chemical storage. If the asset is used in a way that reduces services available from it, its value falls and the owner loses commensurate wealth. But if it is not used at all (that is, if the desires of others who want to pay for its use are ignored), the owner reaps no immediate income. Of course, one key feature of a private property rights regime is liability. If the owner misuses the land in a way that damages others, by chemical leaks, for example, he or she is liable for damages.

Property rights also provide long-term incentives for maximizing the value of property, even for owners whose personal outlook is short-term. If I use my land as a toxic waste dump and impair its future productivity or its groundwater, the reduction in the land's value reduces my wealth. That is because land's current worth reflects the value of its future services: the revenue from production or the aesthetic pleasure I receive from the land minus the costs (including liabilities) that may arise from the presence of wastes.

Of course this market force is not automatic. Polluters may seek to conceal the results of their actions, as in the case of "midnight dumping," in order to push the costs off onto others and avoid the loss of their own wealth. But buyers have a strong incentive to investigate potential problems of this sort, indeed, a much stronger incentive than does a bureaucrat who is charged with enforcing a law but who lacks direct financial exposure. Disclosure laws associated with real estate transactions and the services of title insurance firms and specialists in estimating liability risks are intended to relieve this problem.

An important advantage of private ownership of a resource, in the absence of successful fraud or deception, is that fewer services from the resource or greater costs associated with it in the future mean lower value now. In fact, the day an appraiser or potential buyer first can see future problems, my wealth declines by the amount of the reduction in potential buyers' willingness to pay for the resource. Not only does using land to store hazardous waste reduce future options for the land's productivity; the value also may be reduced by increasing my future liability from lawsuits due to leakage and resulting damage to other people or property. The key fact here is that any reduction in *future* services and *future* net value due to potential liability is visited on me now as they directly affect the present capitalized value of my asset.

In effect, the value of the property right, which gives the asset owner the privilege as well as the responsibility of control, serves as a hostage to the owner's socially responsive stewardship of the asset. Any decision resulting in less value produced, either now or in the future, reduces the property's value now. The reverse is also true: Any new and better way employed to produce more value now or in the future is capitalized into the asset's present value. Even a short-sighted owner has the incentive to be alert to new possibilities and new dangers and to act as if he or she cares about the future usefulness of the land.[16]

This is true even if the owner of the land is a corporation, and the corporate officers, rather than the owner-stockholders, are in control. Corporate officers may be concerned mainly about the short term, not expecting to be present when future problems arise. Contrary to much popular opinion, property rights hold such decisionmakers accountable, too. If current actions are known to cause future problems or if current expenditures are seen to promise future benefits, corresponding changes in the stock price captures the reduction or increase in future net benefits. Current profits do not look to the future, but buyers and sellers of the corporation's stock do. Even though the average owner of stock is not a pollution expert, stock analysts look at liabilities and are tuned in to all phases of the industry they cover. Watchdog environmental groups also spread the work about suspected problems. It is in the stockholder's interest to keep an ear to the ground because a correct guess as to how the market will react can allow the discerning investor to buy before good news is fully captured in the stock price or to sell before bad news is fully capitalized by a falling stock price.

For better and for worse, even the rumor of future benefits or expenses can strongly influence today's stock price.[17] It is not clear whether analysts, commentators, and interest groups publicizing future problems overreact or underreact to problems as they occur. But in either case, even short-sighted decisionmakers are visited by the fruits of their actions immediately, even though the bottom line of the profit-and-loss statement may not reflect the results of bad decisions and good investments for a long time to come.

In addition to their implications for stewardship and conservation, three-dimensional property rights also play an important role in stimulating creative and anticipatory investments. A creative investment might result in new technology to clean up hazardous waste—bacteria that eat waste, for example—more efficiently than isolating and capping it with clay, thus freeing the land of the hazardous-waste encumbrance. Since the property value would immediately rise if no wastes remain, the long-term benefits accrue immediately to the landowner. For this reason, the landowner becomes an eager customer for improved techniques. Without ready customers who can gain by adopting new technology, innovation becomes more difficult to finance.

In summary, a property rights regime encourages good stewardship, responsiveness to the wishes of others, and care in preventing damages to others. Does the property rights paradigm apply in the real world? Consider the case of hazardous waste management at Love Canal. Its history, as reported by Eric Zuesse in *Reason* in 1981, and highlighted by and investigative report by ABC's "Nightline," is revealing.[18]

Although few people realize it even now, it apparently was government, not Hooker Chemical, that caused the escape of chemicals from Love Canal. Hooker (then known as the Hooker Electrochemical Company) began dumping chemical waste into abandoned Love Canal in 1942, but only after seeing that the canal was lined with impermeable clay. The clay prevented the escape of chemicals so as to avoid future damages to others and liability for Hooker. After the canal was filled, a clay cap was installed over the top, sealing the chemicals so that rainwater could not penetrate and wash the chemicals out. In fact, the chief of EPA's office of Hazardous Waste Implementation was quoted in June 1980 as saying that Hooker's disposal of the wastes at Love Canal would meet even the stringent 1980 Resource Conservation and Recovery Act regulations.[19] To this point, the property rights system was working well, and no danger was apparent. Soon after the canal dumpsite was sealed, however, the situation changed.

The local Niagara Falls school board, searching for a site for a new school, inquired about the Love Canal site, under which the sealed wastes lay. Hooker warned them of the chemicals below and provided for their representatives a tour of the site, where they took some test borings into the ground to demonstrate that chemicals were indeed present and where they were. Despite warnings of liability from its own attorney, the school board was eager to get the site and prepared for eminent domain proceedings. Under these conditions, Hooker donated the site in 1952 to the school board in return for $1. Hooker insisted on writing into the transfer papers the presence and potential danger from the chemicals sealed below. The school board now had the land, but they, as decisionmakers, were not personally liable. No stockholders, waiting vigilantly for the opportunity to gain by buying or to avoid losses by bailing out of their stock position early, were looking over their shoulders ready to hold them accountable via stock-price changes. The discipline of private property rights had not, for them personally, followed control of the property into their hands.

The school board subsequently built the school and scraped away part of the clay cap to provide "fill dirt" for other school sites. Some of the construction plans had to be changed to avoid the partially exposed chemicals. Now, however, rain could get into the dump. Then, over the strong public objections of Hooker (noted at the time in the local press), the board tried in 1957 to sell the remaining land. Hooker won that fight, though, and the land was retained temporarily.

At about the same time, however, apparently without the knowledge of Hooker, the city was constructing a sewer line, surrounded by permeable gravel, that punctured both the clay walls and the cover of the canal dumpsite. A storm sewer was placed through one wall of the canal in 1960, again in a bed of gravel. These and later punctures in 1968, when the state built an expressway through the end of the site where Hooker had done most of its dumping, meant that incoming rainwater and the stored chemicals inside could escape and could flow freely through nearby neighborhoods along the gravel beds of the sewer pipes. Escape they did.

The Love Canal area, sparsely populated when Hooker was using the dumpsite, had become a suburb. The south end of the site itself, where the chemical wastes were concentrated, was sold by the school board (after the first sewers were constructed through the canal walls) and had become a residential development. The escaped waste began to invade the neighborhoods, and the disaster hit the national press. Little attention was paid to the history of the property rights, however, or the fact that when Hooker had the land it had acted responsibly. The fact that the avenues of chemical waste escape were punched into the walls of the canal by units of government after strong and repeated warnings against such practices by Hooker was overlooked. Hooker was judged guilty by the press and the public, and private rights were assumed insufficient. Superfund was born.

Our system of individual responsibility under the common law has successfully screened us from the worst of the possible risks. This protection is weakest when units of government have control, since government decisionmakers lack individual financial responsibility.

When property owners, backed by an effective liability system, have a stake in protecting their property, they will find new ways to do so, even in difficult circumstances. If whales and commercially valuable fisheries in the oceans were owned, it seems likely that ocean dumpers would avoid harming them. If such ownership seems far-fetched, consider England and Scotland, where sports and commercial fishing rights are privately owned and transferable. Long before Earth Day and before the environmental movement took hold, fishing rights owners successfully sued polluters of streams for damages and obtained injunctions against polluting activities. It worked, and now they seldom have to go to court. Polluters generally leave those waters (and thus the fish) alone. When resources are owned, political wars are no longer necessary to protect them. Owners do the job on a self-interested and cost-effective basis.

When incentives are provided by property rights and liability, new technologies constantly develop both to protect against damages (and thus costly lawsuits) and to assess (and thus collect) damages when they occur. When grazing lands in the American West became private property, owners looked for new ways to build fences to prevent trespassing. Materials were not available to make ordinary wood or stone fences. First they found that human "fences"—cowboys on patrol—could do the job; then barbed wire came along and greatly reduced the cost.

The means to enforce property rights, like everything else of value, are not freely available. But when the means of enforcement become more valuable (because the property rights become more valuable), people invest more effort in finding and marketing them. In our own day, forensic methods to trace the origins of oil spills in order to establish liability are being developed. Methods of "fingerprinting" chemicals to establish their origin can serve both plaintiffs and potential sources of chemicals. Producers who are careful want to be able to establish that theirs is not the material that became fugitive and caused harm.

ACCOUNTABILITY IN THE PRESENCE OF UNCERTAINTY

Environmental policy should make people accountable through a private property rights regime backed by liability law. Where the government must intervene, the emphasis should be on local, not federal, control. With states, provinces, and municipalities trying a variety of approaches, differing policies would be tested. Citizens are in no mood to allow overly lax pollution control, yet jurisdictions choosing more-rigorous control would find whether their citizens wanted to pay the price. Regulation that is too loose allows risks without sufficient compensating benefits to the community. Regulation that is too tight brings on economic costs without compensating safety or other benefits to the community. This time-honored variety of approaches among the states is an important part of American life and is also part of the genius of the federal system. Experiments are small rather than national in scope, and more of them are tried. Some, of course, are found to be failures, at least in some locations.

An interesting and important analogy can be seen here between the multiple approaches taken by various units of government when they are free to choose and the mutations within a natural species. When unexpected conditions arise, the natural mutations can sometimes allow survival. "Mistakes" can turn out to be the way the species adapts to the new circumstances. Similarly, among human institutions, as scientific knowledge increases and circumstances change in unpredictable ways, a rich variety of working technical and institutional models can be extremely valuable. In a world of uncertainty, it simply is not possible to avoid error or to find quickly the best answer for a given circumstance. Even when survival is not at stake, the information produced by widely varying local and state arrangements is useful nationally and internationally.

The federal role in pollution control, where one is politically demanded, can logically take the form of strengthening the workings of the property rights system which protects individuals against invasion by pollution. For example, technical forensic assistance in tracing, or even finding ways to brand, pollutants as they are emitted can help to enhance responsibility among actual and potential polluters. Those who do pollute would more often be made to pay when harm is done, and innocent parties would less often be forced to pay in error. A careful oil company, for example, would want to be able to show that its stored wastes, having been branded, did not show up where damage occurred.

For their part, states may seek to strengthen the common law through statute. Restoring the right of contract in the voluntary transfer of risk, for example, would help to revitalize the insurance industry which historically has help to "regulate" in cost-effective ways the businesses they insure. Requirements for the posting of bonds would also strengthen the liability approach, for example, by ensuring the solvency of a firm producing, processing, or storing hazardous wastes. These measures would provide added citizen confidence and put the onus for care squarely where it belongs—on the potential polluter. Greatly lengthening the statute of limitations period for the recovery of damages in pollution cases where long expected delays occur before health problems show up might be another important measure. Better ways to brand chemicals that might escape into the water or air could also be a real help to the liability approach. Many other innovations will presumably be tried at the state level without the need for national consensus or a national commitment.

There are, of course, pollution problems that cross national boundaries, too. Acid rain has been a big political issue between Canada and the United States because sulfur dioxide emissions caused by U.S. energy production cross the border and may, over time, have affected Canadian lakes.[20] Despite the current scientific dispute over the facts of this case, the important question remains: How can accountability be established for such pollutants? Properly, legal liability should apply here as well; Canadians ought to be able to take American companies to court for damage they cause. Proving actual damage may be difficult, but if the damage is real and serious, such proof should be available. U.S. civil courts require a "preponderance of the evidence," or a 51 percent probability, in the court's judgement, that the allegations are true.

In place of such proof, political action has been taken instead. The 1990 Clean Air Act, with its acid rain provisions, quieted Canadian political complaints against the United States by requiring hefty controls on sulfur dioxide emissions from utilities. Unfortunately, the expensive requirements will not have much noticeable effect on lakes in Canada or the American Northeast that have already become acidic over many decades. Damages, had they been sought and granted, could have gone toward remediation—for example, liming of important lakes.

Political agreements between nations are likely to be costly and relatively unproductive, just as regional politics interfere with correcting local problems. However, the difficulties of writing agreements between the United States and Canada are not as formidable as those involved in obtaining international agreements among many countries. Yet such agreements have been recommended to solve international problems such as the risk of depletion of the ozone layer and the risk of global warming. Optimism that such agreements will be worth more than their cost does not seem warranted.

Negotiations over the past decade to establish a Law of the Sea Treaty illustrate the problem. Nations could not agree on how to develop seabed minerals; Third World governments demanded that an international authority be formed to collect fees that would be distributed to Third World nations. The United States opposed this demand and refused to sign the treaty. Similar conflicts have developed in the negotiation of the Montreal Protocol, an international effort to control the production of chlorofluorocarbons.

The challenge in environmental policy is to develop better institutions—ones that will preserve environmental quality where it is most important and minimize the constraints that would keep us from increasing wealth and prosperity. Only with more of the latter can our society better serve all our needs, including demands for safety and amenity values.

We need to recognize that there is no widespread environmental crisis requiring action so urgent that the need for scientific knowledge should be bypassed or emergency actions undertaken. Secondly, despite colorful rhetoric to the contrary, the risks due to rapid technological change, which we have faced for several decades, have thus far proved to be well worth it. We are far wealthier, and thus our society is far healthier and more resilient in the face of challenges, than we would be had the technological changes not been allowed to occur. If we can encourage accountability through property rights, liability law, and local action, we will go a long way toward solving our environmental problems while increasing our health and safety.

NOTES

1. J. H. Dales, *Pollution, Property & Prices* (Toronto: University of Toronto Press, 1968), p. 40.

2. This section is adapted from Richard L. Stroup, "Hazardous Waste Policy: A Property Rights Perspective," *Environment Reporter* 20:21 (September 22, 1989), p. 869.

3. Aaron Wildavsky, *Searching for Safety* (New Brunswick: Transaction Books, 1988).

4. See Wildavsky, especially ch. 6.

5. See Sam Peltzman, *Regulation of Pharmaceutical Innovation* (Washington, D.C.: American Enterprise Institute, 1974) and citations therein.

6. See Albert L. Nichols and Richard J. Zeckhauser, "The Periods of Prudence: How Conservative Risk Assessments Distort Regulation," (November/December 1986), pp. 13-23, and the more technical article by the same authors cited in it.

7. Wildavsky, p. 14.

8. See Peter Huber, "The Market for Risk," *Regulation* (March/April 1984), p. 37, for the basis of this calculation.

9. In Richard C. Schwing and Walter A. Albers, Jr., eds., *Societal Risk Assessment: How Safe is Safe Enough?* (New York-London: Plenum Press, 1980).

10. Clark, p. 291.

11. Ibid.

12. Robert Hahn, "The Politics and Religion of Clean Air," *Regulation* (Winter 1990), p. 30.

13. See Bruce A. Ackerman and William T. Hassler, *Clean Coal/Dirty Air or How the Clean Air Act Became a Multibillion Bail-Out for High-Sulfur Coal Producers and What Should Be Done About It* (New Haven: Yale University Press, 1981), and Robert W. Crandall, "Economic Rents as a Barrier to Deregulation," *The Cato Journal* 6:1 (Spring/Summer 1986), pp. 186-189.

14. Crandall, pp. 186-189.

15. The incentive is to maximize value as expressed by buyers and sellers in markets. Markets aggregate the values of individuals, self-centered and altruistic, as does the political "marketplace." In both cases, values without substantial resources behind them will typically be ignored.

16. For example, had the Kesterson Wildlife Refuge in California, which received irrigation drainage waters that damaged the refuge's waterfowl, been privately owned, it seems likely that the owner (unlike the U.S. Fish and Wildlife Service) would have investigated the possible consequences and discovered the potential disaster brought on by the drainage waters. In fact it was a neighboring landowner who "blew the

whistle" on the problem, causing it to become a public concern. Certainly a private owner has more wealth at stake, and a greater personal incentive to do so, than does a bureaucratic manager.

17. A significant and growing portion of the economics literature concerns "event studies," which quantify the link between an event, such as a plane crash for an airline or the announcement of a new marketing strategy for a retailer, or a product development strategy for a manufacturer, and the stock market's evaluation of that event with respect to future profits. The rise or fall in the stock price captures the market's evaluation of the future impacts of the event.

18. See Eric Zuesse, "The Truth Seeps Out," *Reason* 12:10 (February 1981), pp. 16-23.

19. He was, however, saying this in the context of arguing for even tighter RCRA rules.

20. The damage done by acid precipitation and whether it has actually caused the depletion of game fisheries in Nova Scotia, and the acidification of lakes in the northeastern United States and in Canada are scientific questions in serious dispute. See for example Edward Krug, "Fish Story: The Great Acid Rain Flimflam," *Policy Review* 52 (spring 1990), p. 44, and J. Laurence Kulp, "Acid Rain: Causes, Effects, and Control," *Regulation* 13:1 (Winter 1990), pp. 41-50. Krug is a soil scientist with the Illinois State Water Survey, and Kulp was a professor of geochemistry at Columbia University and director of research of the National Acid Precipitation Assessment Program.

Selected Bibliography

Ackerman, Bruce A., and William T. Hassler. *Clean Coal/Dirty Air or How the Clean Air Act Became a Multibillion Bail-Out for High-Sulfur Coal Producers and What Should Be Done About It*. New Haven: Yale University Press, 1981.

Asimov, I. "Water, water everywhere, but. . . ." *National Wildlife* 8, no. 12 (1978).

Borst, Kenneth E. "Assessing the effects of acid precipitation on natural freshwater." Talk presented at the Association for Canadian Studies in the U.S. meeting, San Francisco, November 18, 1989.

Bourassa, Robert. *Power from the North* (Scarborough, Ontario: Prentice Hall, 1985); portion reprinted In *Canada-U.S. Outlook: The Energy-Environment Tradeoff*. Jonathan Lemco, ed. 1, nos. 3/4. Washington, D.C.: National Planning Association, May 1990.

Caldwell, Lynton D., ed. *Perspective on Ecosystem Management for the Great Lakes*. Albany, New York: State of New York University Press, 1988.

_____."Garrison Diversion: Constraints on Conflict Resolution." *Natural Resources Journal* 24 (1984): 839-63.

Carmichael, Edward A. "Energy and the Canada-U.S. Free Trade Agreement." *Trade Monitor* (C. D. Howe Institute, May 1988): 1-15.

_____."In Pursuit of Power." *The Economist* (October 28, 1989): 25-26.

Carroll, John, E. *Environmental Diplomacy: An Examination and a Prospective of Canadian- U.S. Transboundary Environmental Relations*. Ann Arbor, Michigan: University of Michigan Press,

1983.

_____. *Environmental Diplomacy*. Chapter 8, "Wilderness and Development: Alaska-Yukon Issues": 168-171.

_____. *Environmental Diplomacy*. Chapter 8, "Wilderness and Development: Cabin Creek": 163-168.

_____. *Environmental Diplomacy*. Chapter 12, "Formalizing Environmental Relations": 277-309.

Ciacca, Charles M. P. "Balance of Bankruptcy for the Environment." *Policy Options* (September 1988): 35.

Cohen, Maxwell. "Transboundary Environmental Attitudes and Policy—Some Canadian Perspectives." Paper prepared for Harvard Center for International Affairs, September 1980.

Cook, James. "Power play." *Forbes*. August 11, 1988.

Crandall, Robert W. "Economic Rents as a Barrier to Deregulation." *The Cato Journal* 6, no. 1 (Spring/Summer 1986): 186-189.

Dales, J. H. *Pollution, Property & Prices*. Toronto: University of Toronto Press, 1968, p.40.

Daly, John. "The Real Value of A Treasure." *Maclean's*, June 27, 1988.

Dearden, Richard G., and John C. Richard. commentators. The *Canada-U.S. Free Trade Agreement: Final Text and Analysis*. Don Mills, Ontario: CCH Canadian Ltd. 1988.

Dinwoode, D. H. "The Politics of International Pollution Control: The Trail Smelter Case," *International Journal* 27 (Spring 1972): 219-350.

Dixon, J. A. and R. B. Norgaard. "Pluralistic Project Design: An Argument for Combining Economic and Coevolutionary Methodologies," *Policy Sciences* 19, no. 3 (1986): 297-317.

Doemel, Nancy J. *The Garrison Diversion Unit: Science, Technology, Politics, and Values*. Bloomington: Indiana University, Advanced Studies in Science, Technology Policy, p. 198.

Doran, Charles. "Twenty Years After: Change and Continuity in United States-Canada Relations." In *Canada and The United States: Enduring Friendship, Persistent Stress*, ed. John Sigler and Charles Doran. Englewood Cliffs: Prentice-Hall, 1985, pp. 231-247.

Eberlee, John. "The Problem is Blowing in the Wind," *Canada and the World* (December 1988): 20-23.

"Eight Arctic Countries Agree to Ministerial Meeting on Environment." *Canadian Secretary of State for External Affairs* Press Release, April 23, 1990.

Fifth Biennial Report on Great Lakes Quality—Part I. Washington, D.C.

and Ottawa: International Joint Commission, February 1990.

The Global 2000 Report to the President:Entering the Twenty-first Century. Vol.1: The Technical Report. Washington D.C.: Government Printing Office, 1980.

Goldberg, Charlotte K. "The Garrison Diversion Project: New Solutions for Transbournday Dispute." *Manitoba Law Journal* 11, no. 2 (1981): 177-89.

Hahn, Robert. "The Politics and Religion of Clean Air." *Regulation* (Winter 1990): 30.

Halle, Eric. "Undermining a Mountain." *Sierra 75*, no. 4 (July-August 1990): 55-56.

Kirn, Jackie Krolopp, and Marion E. Marts. "The Skagit-High Ross Controversy: Negotiation and Settlement." *Natural Resources Journal U.S.-Canada Transboundary Resource Issues.* (Spring 1986): 261-289.

Kirton, John, Kim Richard Nossal, and Robert Spencer, eds. *The International Joint Commission—Seventy Years On.* Toronto: University of Toronto, Centre for International Studies, 1981.

Krug, Edward. "Fish Story: The Great Acid Rain Flimflam." *Policy Review* 52 (Spring 1990); 44.

Krutilla, John V. *The Columbia River Treaty: The Economics of International River Basin Development.* Baltimore: Johns Hopkins University Press, 1967.

Kulp, Laurence. "Acid Rain: Causes, Effects, and Control." *Regulation* 13, no. 1 (Winter 1990): 41-50.

_____."The Columbia River Treaty." *International Rivers: The Politics of Cooperation*, Chapter 4. Vancouver: The University of British Columbia, Westwater Research Centre 1977: 53-78:

Levy, Yvonne. "Pricing Federal Irrigation Water." *Economic Review*, Federal Reserve Bank of San Francisco (Spring 1987).

Macrae, Robert N. "Canadian Energy Development." *Current History* (March 1988).

McInnes, Craig. "Environmental Conference Told of Energy-Related Woes." *The Globe and Mail*, September 19, 1989.

McNulty, Peter. "Get Ready for Power Brownouts." *Fortune*, June 5, 1989.

Moll, Kendall, and Ned Rosenbrook. "Will Free Trade Release a Flood of Canadian Water?" In *Canada-U.S. Outlook: The Energy-Environment Tradeoff.* Jonathan Lemco, ed. 1, nos. 3/4. Washington, D.C.: National Planning Association, May 1990.

"NAWAPA: A Continental Water System—Symposium." *Bulletin of the*

Atomic Scientists 23 (September 1967): 8-27.

Nichols, Albert L., and Richard J. Zeckhauser. "The Perils of Prudence: How Conservative Risk Assessments   Distort Regulation." *Regulation* (November/December 1986): 13-23.

Nicholson, Max. *The Environmental Revolution.* London: Hodder & Stoughton and New York: McGraw-Hill.

Paquet, G. "A Social Learning Framework for a Wicked Problem: The Case of Energy." *Energy Studies Review* 1, no. 1 (1989).

"Paradiplomacy Between the U.S. States and Canadian Provinces: The Case of Acid Rain Memoranda of Understanding." *Journal of Borderland Studies* 3, no. 1 (Spring 1988): 13-38.

Park, Chris C. *Acid Rain: Rhetoric and Reality.* London: Methuen, 1987.

Pearce, D., A. Markandya, and E. B. Babier. *Blueprint for a Green Economy.* London: Earthscan Publications Ltd. 1989.

Peltzman, Sam. *Regulation of Pharmaceutical Innovation.* Washington, D.C.: American Enterprise Institute, 1974.

Perrings, C. *Economy and Environment.* Cambridge: Cambridge University Press, 1987.

Quinn, Hal. "Trans-Border Pollution." *Maclean's*, July 3, 1989, pp. 44-45.

Rao, P. K. "Planning and Financing Water Resource Development in the United States." *American Journal of Economics and Sociology* 47, no. 1 (January 1988).

Regens, J. L., and R. W. Rycroft. "Funding for Environmental Protection: Comparing Congressional and Executive Influences." *The Social Science Journal* 26, no. 3 (1989).

Rittle, H. W., and M. M. Webber. "Dilemmas in the General Theory of Planning." *Policy Sciences* 4 (1973).

Roots, F. "The Brundtland Challenge: Background and Objectives." In *The Brundtland Challenge and the Cost of Inaction.* A. Davidson and M. Dence eds., Halifax: The Institute for Research on Public Policy, 1989.

Rosenbaum, W. A. *Environmental Politics and Policy.* Washington, D. C.: Congressional Quarterly Press, 1985.

Schwartz, J. "The Rights of Nature and the Death of God." *The Public Interest* 97 (Spring, 1989).

Schwing, Richard C., and Walter A. Albers, Jr. eds. *Societal Risk Assessement: How Safe is Safe Enough?* New York-London: Plenum Press, 1980.

Shoji, Kobe. "Drip Irrigation." *Scientific American* (November 1977).

Smith, Nancy Paige. "Transboundary Relations and Acid Rain: New York's Memorandum of Understanding with Quebec and Ontario." *Journal of Borderlands Studies* 5, no. 1 (Spring 1990): 111-133.

Solow, R. M. "The Economist's Approach to Pollution Control." *Science* 173 (1971): 489- 503.

Stobaugh, R., and D. Yergin, eds., *Energy Future*. 3d ed. New York: Vintage, 1983.

Stroup, R. "Hazardous Waste Policy: A Property Rights Perspective." *Environment Reporter* 20, no.21 (September 22, 1989): 869.

Stroup, R. L. and J. S. Shaw. "The Free Market and The Environment." *The Public Interest* 97 (Fall, 1989).

Swainson, Neil A. *Conflict Over the Columbia: The Canadian Background to an Historic Treaty*. Montreal: McGill-Queen's University Press, 1979.

Uslaner, E. M. "Energy Politics in the USA and Canada." *Energy Policy* 15, no.5 (October, 1987).

Vertinsky, I. "An Ecological Model of Resilient Decision-Making: An Application to the Study of Public and Private Decision Making in Japan." *Ecological Modelling* 38 (1987) pp.141-158.

Water Resources of the St. Croix River Basin: Maine-New Brunswick. Report on Preliminary Investigations to the International Joint Commission (Under the Reference of 10 June 1955 by the St. Croix River Engineering Board)—Supplementary Report on Pollution Survey, 1959, and subsequent progress reports to the IJC.

Watkins, G. C. "Living Under a Shadow: U.S. Oil Policies and Canadian Oil Pricing." In *Energy: Markets and Regulation*. R. L. Gordon, H. D. Jacoby, and M. B. Zimmermann, eds. Cambridge: MIT Press, 1987.

Weller, Geoffrey R. "Canadian Water Exports: A Controversy In The Making" *American Review of Canadian Studies* 16, no. 4 (1986).

Western States Water Council. "A Review of Inter-Regional and International Water Transfer Proposals." Salt Lake City, 1969.

Wheelock, Angela. "Of Trees and Trash." *Canada and the World* (December 1988): 15.

Wildavsky, Aaron. *Searching for Safety*. New Brunswick: Transaction Books, 1988.

Wilensky, H. L. *Organization Intelligence*, New York: Basic Books, 1967.

Index

About the Contributors

LYNTON K. CALDWELL is the Arthur F. Bentley Professor Emeritus of Political Science and Professor of Public and Environmental Affairs at Indiana University.

JOHN E. CARROLL is a Professor of Environmental Conservation at The University of New Hampshire.

COLIN F. W. ISAACS was formerly Director of Pollution Probe and is currently a consultant on energy and environmental issues.

NICHOLAS P. LOVRICH, JR. is Professor of Political Science and Director of the Division of Governmental Studies and Services at Washington State University.

IRVING M. MINTZER is a Professor at the Center for Global Change of The University of Maryland.

GILLES PAQUET is a Professor of Economics and Management at The Faculty of Administration of The University of Ottawa.

JOHN C. PIERCE is Professor of Political Science and Dean of Humanities and Social Sciences at Washington State University.

RODNEY D. SCHMIDT is a Senior Economist with The Petroleum Finance Co.

BRENT S. STEEL is an Assistant Professor of Political Science at Oregon State University.

MARY ANN E. STEGER is Associate Professor of Political Science and Interim Director of the Social Science Research Laboratory at Northern Arizona University.

RICHARD L. STROUP is a Professor of Economics at Montana State University and a Senior Associate of The Political Economy Research Center.

ERIC M. USLANER is a Professor in the Department of Government and Politics at The University of Maryland—College Park.

About the Editor

JONATHAN LEMCO is a Senior Fellow at the National Planning Association and adjunct professor of Canadian Politics at the Paul Nitze School of Advanced International Studies of The Johns Hopkins University. His books include *Canada and the Crisis in Central America, Political Stability in Federal Governments*, and *State and Development* (co-edited).